Analytical Grammar:
a systematic approach to language mastery

Student Workbook

Created by R. Robin Finley

Analytical Grammar: Student Workbook
©1996 R. Robin Finley
Published and distributed by Demme Learning

All rights reserved. No part of this book may be reproduced, stored in a retrieval system, or transmitted in any form by any means—electronic, mechanical, photocopying, recording, or otherwise—without prior written permission from Demme Learning.

analyticalgrammar.com

1-888-854-6284 or +1 717-283-1448 | demmelearning.com
Lancaster, Pennsylvania USA

Revision Code 0196-C

Printed in the United States of America by The P.A. Hutchison Company
3 4 5 6 7 8 9 10

For information regarding CPSIA on this printed material call: 1-888-854-6284 and provide reference #0196-08132020

Grammar Notebook Instructions

Analytical Grammar is not only a great way to master your grammar, punctuation, and usage, it becomes a reference book for you to use long after you've completed the final unit. The creation of the Grammar Notebook is important. We don't expect you to remember every little thing we've taught you. Instead, we want to give you a way to look up what you need to at a later date.

If you follow these instructions, you will be "building" your own Grammar Notebook along the way. The student workbook pages are perforated. You can pull them out of the book as you go (or wait until you've completed the program ... your choice.) What we recommend is that you pull the Notes pages out, hole punch them, and put them in a small three-ring binder. You can even use the title page as a cover to slip in a clearview binder. Voila! A grammar reference book!

You will notice that the pages of Notes are numbered in the upper corner. Those numbers correspond to the Table of Contents and to the Index at the back of this book. Include all these pages.

You will find your Grammar Notebook to be extremely useful throughout high school and college. With this as a reference resource, you will have no problem in future writing assignments. It is also a real help in preparing for standardized tests.

Be sure to take care of your notebook. Believe me! In the future you will be very glad you have it!

ANALYTICAL GRAMMAR

TABLE OF CONTENTS

Unit #1: NOUNS, ARTICLES & ADJECTIVES	1
Unit #2: PRONOUNS	3
Unit #3: PREPOSITIONAL PHRASES	5
Unit #4: SUBJECT & VERB	7
Unit #5: ADVERBS	9
Unit #6: PATTERNS 1 & 2	11
Unit #7: PATTERN 3	13
Unit #8: PATTERNS 4 & 5	15
Unit #9: HELPING VERBS	17
Unit #10: CONJUNCTIONS	19
Unit #11: PARTICIPIAL PHRASES	23
Unit #12: GERUND PHRASES	25
Unit #13: INFINITIVE PHRASES	27
Unit #14: APPOSITIVE PHRASES	29
Unit #15: ADJECTIVE CLAUSES	31
Unit #16: ADVERB CLAUSES	33
Unit #17: NOUN CLAUSES	35
COMMA SPLICES	37
Unit #18: COMMA RULES 1, 2, & 3	39
Unit #19: COMMA RULE 4	41
Unit #20: COMMA RULE 5	43
Unit #21: COMMA RULES 6, 7, & 8	45
Unit #22: COMMA RULES 9, 10, & 11	47
Unit #23: PUNCTUATING QUOTATIONS	49
Unit #24: PUNCTUATING DIALOGUE	51
Unit #25: PUNCTUATING TITLES	53
Unit #26: SEMICOLONS & COLONS	55
Unit #27: FORMING THE POSSESSIVE	57
Unit #28: CAPITALIZATION	59
Unit #29: USAGE: PRONOUN-ANTECEDENT AGREEMENT	63
Unit #30: USAGE: SUBJECT-VERB AGREEMENT	65
Unit #31: USAGE: WHICH PRONOUN?	67
Unit #32: WHO AND WHOM	69
Unit #33: ADJECTIVE OR ADVERB	71
Unit #34: ASSORTED ERRORS	73
Unit #35: ACTIVE & PASSIVE VOICE	75
INDEX	i

Photocopying this product is strictly prohibited by copyright law.

ANALYTICAL GRAMMAR

TABLE OF CONTENTS

Unit #1: NOUNS, ARTICLES & ADJECTIVES ... 1
Unit #2: PRONOUNS. ... 13
Unit #3: PREPOSITIONAL PHRASES ... 25
Unit #4: SUBJECT & VERB ... 37
Unit #5: ADVERBS. ... 51
Unit #6: PATTERNS 1 & 2 ... 63
Unit #7: PATTERN 3 ... 75
Unit #8: PATTERNS 4 & 5 ... 87
Unit #9: HELPING VERBS ... 99
Unit #10: CONJUNCTIONS. ... 111
Unit #11: PARTICIPIAL PHRASES ... 127
Unit #12: GERUND PHRASES ... 137
Unit #13: INFINITIVE PHRASES ... 147
Unit #14: APPOSITIVE PHRASES ... 157
Unit #15: ADJECTIVE CLAUSES ... 167
Unit #16: ADVERB CLAUSES ... 179
Unit #17: NOUN CLAUSES ... 189
COMMA SPLICES ... 199
Unit #18: COMMA RULES 1, 2, & 3 ... 201
Unit #19: COMMA RULE 4 ... 213
Unit #20: COMMA RULE 5 ... 225
Unit #21: COMMA RULES 6, 7, & 8 ... 237
Unit #22: COMMA RULES 9, 10, & 11 ... 251
Unit #23: PUNCTUATING QUOTATIONS ... 263
Unit #24: PUNCTUATING DIALOGUE ... 273
Unit #25: PUNCTUATING TITLES ... 279
Unit #26: SEMICOLONS & COLONS ... 289
Unit #27: FORMING THE POSSESSIVE ... 301
Unit #28: CAPITALIZATION ... 313
PUNCTUATION REVIEW ... 325
Unit #29: USAGE: PRONOUN-ANTECEDENT AGREEMENT ... 337
Unit #30: USAGE: SUBJECT-VERB AGREEMENT ... 343
Unit #31: USAGE: WHICH PRONOUN? ... 349
Unit #32: WHO AND WHOM ... 359
Unit #33: ADJECTIVE OR ADVERB ... 365
Unit #34: ASSORTED ERRORS ... 371
Unit #35: ACTIVE & PASSIVE VOICE ... 381
INDEX. ... 393

Use this Table of Contents when you're going through the units.
The Table of Contents on the other side of this sheet will work for your Analytical Grammar Handbook
when you're finished with the course.

Season One

ANALYTICAL GRAMMAR (UNIT #1)   NOTES-PAGE 1

NOUNS, ARTICLES, & ADJECTIVES

THE NOUN is a word that names a person, place, thing, or idea.

A COMMON NOUN is a word that names a person, place, thing, or idea. These nouns are NEVER CAPITALIZED and always consist of ONE WORD ONLY. Examples:

PERSONS: teacher, man, girl
PLACES: school, yard, city
THINGS: bridge, carrot, building, day
IDEAS: anger, democracy, inspiration* (these are often called ABSTRACT nouns)
(*watch for the "ion" ending - that's a strong clue that the word is a noun)

A PROPER NOUN is the NAME of a person, place, etc. These words are CAPITALIZED and MAY CONSIST OF MORE THAN ONE WORD; however, no matter how many words are in a proper noun, it still equals only one noun. Examples:

PERSONS: Mr. Jones, Mary, Thomas John Matthews
PLACES: Cranford High School,   Anchorage, Alaska,   Russia
THINGS: The Golden Gate Bridge, Thursday, The Empire State Building, April 1, 1492
IDEAS: The Theory of Relativity, the Industrial Revolution

THE ARTICLE: There are only three articles; they are A, AN, and THE. They always come in front of the noun they modify. The article *A* is used in front of nouns which begin with consonants (a tree); the article *AN* is used in front of nouns which begin with vowels or vowel sounds (an apple).

THE ADJECTIVE: Adjectives describe or MODIFY NOUNS and PRONOUNS. They usually come in front of the noun they modify. Examples are TALL, SILLY, BEAUTIFUL, SEVERAL. For now, all the adjectives you will be studying will be next to the noun they modify. Watch out for PROPER ADJECTIVES, which are adjectives made out of proper nouns (England = English); they always begin with capital letters. Since a proper noun can consist of more than one word (Tim Smith), a proper adjective can also consist of more than one word (Tim Smith's house). If this is the case, then you would mark such an adjective "adj" and use "wings." (See "Elvis Presley's" below.)

We've just learned the NAMES of three words: noun, article, and adjective. Words also do certain JOBS: the job done by articles and adjectives is called MODIFIER. Nouns have five different jobs that they do; we'll learn about those jobs soon.

STEPS TO TAKE:

1. Find all the nouns in each sentence. Write N over the common nouns and PN over the proper nouns. If a proper noun consists of more than one word, write PN over the middle and draw lines ("wings") over all the words in the noun (see example).
                        n   *n*   ——— *pn* ———
   EXAMPLE: The teenagers loved Elvis Presley's famous song, "Blue Suede Shoes."

2. Go back to EACH noun you found and ask "Which?" Any word located next to that noun that answers this question is either an article or an adjective. Write ART over the articles and ADJ over the adjectives.

   Which teenagers? <u>the</u> teenagers. *the* is an article
   Which song? <u>Elvis Presley's famous</u> song. *Elvis Presley* is an adjective (with wings); *famous* is an adjective.
   Which "Blue Suede Shoes"? It doesn't say.

                    art   *n*   ——— *adj* ——— *adj*   *n*   ——— *pn* ———
   EXAMPLE: The teenagers loved Elvis Presley's famous song, "Blue Suede Shoes."

Photocopying this product is strictly prohibited by copyright law.

ANALYTICAL GRAMMAR (UNIT #1)   EXERCISE #1

NOUNS, ARTICLES, & ADJECTIVES: EXERCISE #1

NAME:_____DATE:_____

DIRECTIONS: *Write **n** over the common nouns, **pn** over the proper nouns (put "wings" [——pn——] over proper nouns that consist of more than one word), **art** over the articles, and **adj** over the adjectives.*

1. Every morning at Madison Middle School we salute our nation's flag.

2. The students stand at their desks and put their hands over their hearts.

3. Some students do not choose to say the Pledge of Allegiance, but it is the custom for those students to stand quietly to show respect for the beliefs of the students who do.

4. In twelve years of school, each boy and girl will say the Pledge of Allegiance on approximately 2,160 occasions.

5. The constant repetition of the pledge often means that students ignore the meaning of this daily ritual.

DIRECTIONS: *Mark the nouns, articles, and adjectives as you were instructed above.*

1. The young boy was a recent immigrant from the war-torn Central American country of El Salvador.

2. On his first day at his new school in America, he noticed that the students stood every morning, faced the flag, and said words he didn't understand.

3. By the second week he was able to say the first few words by imitating his fellow students.

4. The boy's family were happy to live in a prosperous country where the people could work at their jobs and raise their children in peace and safety.

5. By the end of his first month of school, Juan stood every morning and proudly pledged allegiance to the flag of his adopted country.

(over)

Photocopying this product is strictly prohibited by copyright law.

ANALYTICAL GRAMMAR (UNIT #1) — EXERCISE #1 - PAGE 2

WRITE THE DEFINITION OF A NOUN IN A COMPLETE SENTENCE.
(You will be tested on these definitions.)

WHICH TYPE OF NOUN BEGINS WITH A CAPITAL LETTER AND MAY CONSIST OF MORE THAN ONE WORD?

ANALYTICAL GRAMMAR (UNIT #1)   EXERCISE #2

NOUNS, ARTICLES, & ADJECTIVES: EXERCISE #2

NAME:_____ DATE:_____

DIRECTIONS: *Write **n** over the common nouns, **pn** over the proper nouns (with "wings" [——pn——] if necessary), **art** over the articles, and **adj** over the adjectives.*

1. The American flag was officially adopted by the Continental Congress in Philadelphia on June 14, 1777. (Hint: the date in this sentence is a proper noun with wings.)

2. The first flag had seven red stripes and six white stripes to symbolize the original thirteen colonies.

3. In the upper left-hand corner, known as the canton, was a blue field with thirteen white stars.

4. After Vermont and Kentucky joined the union in 1795, the canton held fifteen stars and there were now fifteen red-and-white stripes.

5. In 1818 the decision was made to keep thirteen red-and-white stripes and add new stars to the canton to show the current number of states in the union.

6. Many people believe that our American flag was made by the legendary Betsy Ross.

7. This story is probably not an accurate version of how our nation's symbol was made.

8. According to the popular story, the young seamstress known as Betsy Ross sewed and helped design our nation's first flag under the direction of George Washington.

9. Historical records show that Betsy Ross was a real flagmaker, but there is no evidence that she made the first Stars and Stripes.

10. This delightful legend about Betsy Ross gained popularity with the American public at the time of the national centennial in 1876.
   WRITE THE DEFINITION OF THE ADJECTIVE IN A COMPLETE SENTENCE.

Photocopying this product is strictly prohibited by copyright law.

ANALYTICAL GRAMMAR (UNIT #1)   EXERCISE #3

NOUNS, ARTICLES, & ADJECTIVES: EXERCISE #3

NAME:_____DATE:_____

DIRECTIONS: *Write **n** over the common nouns, **pn** over the proper nouns (with "wings" [——pn——] if necessary), **art** over the articles, and **adj** over the adjectives.*

1. It is the tradition throughout the entire world to have rules and regulations about the proper method of displaying any country's flag.

2. During the twentieth century flag etiquette received particular attention because flags have become a prime focus of patriotism.

3. In the United States the anniversary of the flag's adoption by the Continental Congress in 1777 has been celebrated as Flag Day.

4. In 1942 the United States Congress adopted a Flag Code listing uniform rules for displaying the American flag in a respectful manner.

5. Many legal battles have been waged over the so-called desecration of the flag.

6. Political protesters, such as the anti-Vietnam War marchers of the 1960s, may try to dramatize their particular causes by burning the flag.

7. The highest courts in the land usually decide that, since the American flag is a powerful symbol of freedom, citizens should be free to treat it as they choose, even if this treatment causes outrage in others.

8. In one American city, an artist was criticized for displaying the Stars and Stripes in a disrespectful manner as a means of symbolizing his freedom of speech.

9. Other citizens chose to exercise their own First Amendment rights by removing flags displayed in this manner.

10. Flags symbolize deep-felt emotions, and they have become an important means of political communication on our planet.

LIST THE THREE ARTICLES IN OUR LANGUAGE.

WHERE WILL THE ARTICLE BE LOCATED, IN RELATIONSHIP TO THE NOUN?

Photocopying this product is strictly prohibited by copyright law.

ANALYTICAL GRAMMAR (UNIT #1)   SKILLS SUPPORT

SKILLS SUPPORT

PARAPHRASING: On these Skills Support exercises, you will be asked to "paraphrase" something. Paraphrasing is a skill you will use in these tests, in writing book reports, and in writing essays and reports all through school. When you paraphrase, you take what someone else has written and you write it in your own words. Here's an example from a famous poem called "Casey at the Bat."

It looked extremely rocky for the Mudville nine that day;
The score stood two to four, with but one inning left to play.
So, when Cooney died at second and Burrows did the same,
A pallor wreathed the features of the patrons of the game.

My paraphrase:
Things didn't look good for the Mudville baseball team that day.
It was two to four in the bottom of the ninth.
So when Cooney was tagged out at second base and the same thing had happened to Burrows,
The fans' faces became deathly pale.

The next example is from Mark Twain's great classic **Tom Sawyer**:

"Hello, old chap, you got to work, hey?"
Tom wheeled suddenly and said:
"Why it's you, Ben, I warn't noticing."
"Say - I'm going in a'swimming, I am. Don't you wish you could? But of course you'd druther work - wouldn't you? Course you would!"
Tom contemplated the boy a bit, and said:
"What do you call work?"
"Why, ain't *that* work?"
Tom resumed his whitewashing, and answered carelessly: "Well, maybe it is, and maybe it ain't. All I know is, it suits Tom Sawyer."
"Oh, come now, you don't mean to let on that you like it?"
The brush continued to move.
"Like it? Well, I don't see why I oughtn't to like it. Does a boy get a chance to whitewash a fence every day?"
That put the thing in a new light. Ben stopped nibbling his apple. Tom swept his brush daintily back and forth - stepped back to note the effect - added a touch here and there - criticized the effect again - Ben watching every move and getting more and more interested, more and more absorbed. Presently he said:
" Say, Tom, let *me* whitewash a little."

My paraphrase:
"Hiya, pal, got chores to do, huh?"
Tom turned around quickly and said:
"Oh! It's you, Ben! Sorry, I wasn't paying attention."
"Hey, I'm goin' for a dip! Bet you wish you could go too. But I see you're really having a great time! SURE you are!"
Tom stared at Ben for a moment.
"Why shouldn't I be having a great time?"
"Are you trying to tell me that's fun?" Tom went back to his painting and remarked off-handedly:
"Maybe. Maybe not. All I can tell you is I enjoy it."
"Oh, please, Tom, don't tell me you're having fun!"
The paintbrush moved slowly back and forth.
"Why not? It's not every day a guy gets to whitewash a fence!"
This was a new slant on the situation. Ben stopped chewing his apple. Tom took a swipe with the brush - stood back to get the full effect - moved forward to dab again - moved back to look again - Ben watching like a hawk, becoming increasingly fascinated, increasing hooked. After a few moments he said:
"Tom? Can I try it a little?"

Photocopying this product is strictly prohibited by copyright law.

DIRECTIONS : *Mark all the common and proper nouns, articles, and adjectives in the Pledge of Allegiance. Then, as neatly as you can, write a paraphrase of it. You will probably have to look some words up in the dictionary.*

I pledge allegiance to the flag of the United States of America and to the republic for which it stands, one nation under God, indivisible, with liberty and justice for all.

ANALYTICAL GRAMMAR (UNIT #1)   TEST

NOUNS, ARTICLES, & ADJECTIVES: TEST

NAME:_____ DATE:_____

(RAW SCORE:_____/117____GRADE:_____CLASS POINTS:____/20____)

DIRECTIONS: Write **n** over the common nouns, **pn** over the proper nouns (with "wings" [—pn—] if necessary), **art** over the articles, and **adj** over the adjectives.

1. In the course of an average day, people rarely stop and think about their own country and its flag.

2. As we lead our busy lives, the citizens of this country often overlook their hard-won personal freedom.

3. In school our teachers work to teach about the events of our early history, which help us understand the burning issues which led to the American Revolution.

4. Since 1775 many men and a growing number of women have made the ultimate sacrifice for the freedom which we enjoy now.

5. The Revolutionary War and the Civil War were fought on our own American soil to preserve freedom at home.

6. Other wars were fought to preserve the freedom of people in other countries.

7. Every single day in America, lawyers, law officers, and judges struggle to protect the freedom won in many desperate battles.

8. Our much-criticized politicians spend their entire working lives seeing that this huge, complicated country runs smoothly and that our freedom is preserved.

ANALYTICAL GRAMMAR (UNIT #1) — TEST - PAGE 2

9. Many students have family members who have served their time in the military protecting and preserving America's precious freedom.

10. Perhaps when we say the Pledge of Allegiance, it is our way of thanking the many dedicated people who have struggled for the freedom we enjoy.

11. *Define **NOUN**:*

12. *Define **ADJECTIVE**:*

13. *Which kind of noun always begins with a lower-case letter and can consist of only one word?*

14. *List the **ARTICLES** in our language.*

PRONOUNS

DEFINITION: A word that takes the place of one or more nouns. A pronoun can do anything a noun can do. Pronouns are even occasionally modified by adjectives! The only way to learn pronouns, unfortunately, is to MEMORIZE THEM. There are four main categories of pronouns in our language:

PERSONAL PRONOUNS: These pronouns occur in four "cases."

Subjective	Objective	Possessive	Reflexive
I	me	mine	myself
you	you	yours	yourself/yourselves
he	him	his*	himself
she	her*	hers	herself
it	it	its	itself
we	us	ours	ourselves
they	them	theirs	themselves

(Just memorize all these pronouns; you won't have to worry about which are objective and which are subjective for now.)

DEMONSTRATIVE PRONOUNS: this*, that*, these*, those*

INTERROGATIVE PRONOUNS: These also often come in "cases."

Subjective	Objective	Possessive	No Case
who	whom	whose	which, what
whoever	whomever	whosever	whichever, whatever

INDEFINITE PRONOUNS:

each*	anybody	many*
either*	anyone	more*
neither*	anything	much*
one*	everybody	most*
some*	everyone	both*
any*	everything	few*
other*	somebody	several*
another*	someone	all*
none	something	two*, three* etc.
	nobody	
	no one	
	nothing	

Pronouns do the same jobs that nouns do; we'll learn about those jobs later.

(over)

ANALYTICAL GRAMMAR (UNIT #2) NOTES - PAGE 4

*NOTE: In the lists of pronouns on the first page, there were some that had asterisks next to them. Those pronouns with asterisks can also be used as adjectives sometimes. If the word in question is an adjective, you would already know it by now because it would have answered the question "Which?" Look at the examples below:

```
   pn           adj  n
Jack loaned me his book.         (Note that HIS is being used as an adjective in this sentence)
   pn     art  n    pro
Jack said the book was his.      (Note that HIS is a pronoun in this sentence)
```

Many words that you might think of as pronouns (such as MY, YOUR, OUR) can only be used as adjectives. That's why they are not listed with the personal pronouns on the first page. Some grammar books call these words "possessive pronouns." In this program, however, we call them adjectives if they are doing an adjective's job and pronouns if they are doing a pronoun's job.

ANTECEDENTS: An antecedent is the noun or nouns that the pronoun stands for. You usually concern yourself with antecedents when you are using the personal pronouns. Here's an example:

```
   pn     pro
Jane said she was tired.    (The word JANE is the antecedent for SHE.)
```

ANALYTICAL GRAMMAR (UNIT #2)　　　　　　　　　　　　　　　　EXERCISE #1

PRONOUNS: EXERCISE #1

NAME: _____ DATE: _____

DIRECTIONS: The purpose of this exercise is to give you practice with personal pronouns. Write **n** over the nouns, **pn** over the proper nouns, **art** over the articles, **adj** over the adjectives, and **pro** over the pronouns. In the space below each sentence, write the pronoun and its antecedent for each personal pronoun that you find.

```
              pn       art adj   n    pro           pro
```
1. EXAMPLE: Ted fired at the distant target, but he just couldn't hit it.

　　　　　　　　　he = Ted　　　it = target

2. "I know the reason you missed the target, but do you know what it is, Ted?" asked Jody.

3. Ted looked at Jody, but he had no idea what she meant.

4. Bill and Tom, both friends of Ted, were puzzled by her question themselves.

5. Ted muttered to himself, "Seems to me the problem must be this old rifle."

6. When Jody heard his response, she chuckled to herself about it.

7. She said to Ted, "If you think you can hit the target, you will hit it."

8. She knew that just thinking a positive thought could have a large impact on whether he hit the target or missed it.

9. Ted realized she was right and wished he had thought of the idea himself!

10. As if the situation were a self-fulfilling prophecy, Ted raised his rifle, thought about the bullseye, and placed a shot in the center of it.

DEFINITION: A pronoun is a word which takes the place of a _____.

　　　　　　　　The noun the pronoun takes the place of is called the _____.

Photocopying this product is strictly prohibited by copyright law.

ANALYTICAL GRAMMAR (UNIT #2)　　　　　　　　　　　　　　EXERCISE #2

PRONOUNS: EXERCISE #2

NAME: _____ DATE: _____

DIRECTIONS: *This exercise is designed to give you extra practice in the demonstrative and interrogative pronouns, although it also contains personal pronouns. Write **n** over the nouns, **pn** over the proper nouns, **art** over the articles, **adj** over the adjectives, and **pro** over the pronouns. Since demonstrative and interrogative pronouns usually don't have antecedents, it won't be possible to write them down. As long as you know what an antecedent is, you're in fine shape!*

1. Once, Johnny Carson made a joke on his television show, but this caused some trouble for him.

2. What he claimed was that there was a shortage of paper towels in this country.

3. He went on to describe what the consequences of this shortage might be, which alarmed many people who listened to him.

4. The implication of this joke was that people had better stock up on paper towels quickly or face the consequences.

5. This was a humorous skit to those who knew a shortage of paper towels did not exist.

6. Within days, however, a real shortage developed which surprised everyone.

7. Those who did not realize there was not a real shortage went out and bought up all of the paper towels they could find.

8. This disrupted the normal paper towel distribution, which created shortages for whoever really needed paper towels.

9. Whoever believed the shortage to be true acted on it and, by his action, caused the belief to become true.

10. This is another example of a self-fulfilling prophecy which came about because of what people thought.

DEFINITIONS: A pronoun is a word which_____ of a noun.

　　　　　　　　A noun is the name of _____

　　　　　　　　An adjective _____

　　　　　　　　An antecedent is _____

Photocopying this product is strictly prohibited by copyright law.

ANALYTICAL GRAMMAR (UNIT #2)   EXERCISE #3

PRONOUNS: EXERCISE #3

NAME:_____ DATE:_____

DIRECTIONS: This exercise is designed to give you practice in the indefinite pronouns, but all the other types of pronouns are here too. Write **n** over the nouns, **pn** over the proper nouns, **art** over the articles, **adj** over the adjectives, and **pro** over the pronouns.

1. Many who are successful at what they do in life have a positive mental attitude.

2. Everyone knows that students in our school have positive and creative attitudes.

3. All of us believe our school is the best and, because we think it is the best, we act in ways that make it the best.

4. Everyone who visits our school is impressed by the friendly and helpful students and faculty.

5. All of us work to keep our halls and cafeteria clean so everyone can enjoy them as much as we do.

6. When we see someone who is careless about our school, we remain positive and do whatever we can to correct the problem.

7. Hundreds of people watch our sports teams, but no one has ever accused us of poor sportsmanship.

8. Anyone who has a question or problem can always get help from a teacher, a counselor, or a principal.

(over)

ANALYTICAL GRAMMAR (UNIT #2)   EXERCISE #3 - PAGE 2

9. We cannot manage everything at one time, so we manage one thing at a time.

10. Often if someone believes he or she can do something, he or she will do it!

DEFINITIONS: A pronoun_____.

   The three articles are _____.

ANALYTICAL GRAMMAR (UNIT #2) — SKILLS SUPPORT

SKILLS SUPPORT: PRONOUNS

DIRECTIONS: *Mark all the nouns, proper nouns, articles, adjectives, and pronouns in the paragraph below. Then write a paraphrase of this paragraph. Remember: you must change as many words as you can, but try to leave the sentence structure as it was originally written. A good paraphrase should contain all the ideas that are in the original paragraph.*

Epictetus, an ancient philosopher, once said, "What concerns is not the way things are, but rather the way people think things are." He was aware that the world of thought overlaps the world of action. He knew that if a person believes something to be true which may or may not be so, and acts on that belief, often his actions can cause the belief to become true.

ANALYTICAL GRAMMAR (UNIT #2)   TEST

PRONOUNS: TEST

NAME: _____ DATE: _____

(RAW SCORE: _____ /105 LETTER GRADE: _____ CLASS POINTS: __/20__)

DIRECTIONS: Write **n** over the nouns, **pn** over the proper nouns, **art** over the articles, **adj** over the adjectives, and **pro** over the pronouns.

1. Ted once said to me, "Bob, if you think something is true even if it isn't true, you can make it become true."

2. Once a teacher was told that she had a class of gifted children, but later it was found that she had average students.

3. Because she thought her students were gifted, she went out of her way to develop lessons that were challenging for them.

4. The class itself had no idea that she thought it was a gifted class.

5. This is an example of what can happen to many of us if we believe something to be true.

6. Whatever you may think about it, the class responded to the challenge and few, if any, did poorly on the lessons.

7. Everyone responded in a positive way, and they did quite well on the tests which were given to them.

8. It was discovered that, because they were treated as gifted students, many had performed as gifted students and most were very pleased with themselves.

ANALYTICAL GRAMMAR (UNIT #2)   TEST - PAGE 2

9. All of this happened because someone thought something was true even though it was not true.

10. Whatever one may think, few can deny that an unusual, difficult-to-explain event took place in this classroom.

DEFINITIONS: *Complete the sentences below.*

1. A noun is _____.

2. A proper noun always begins with _____

3. A _____ noun can only consist of one word, but a _____ can be more than one word.

4. The articles are _____

5. An adjective _____

6. A pronoun _____

7. An antecedent is _____.

PREPOSITIONAL PHRASES

DEFINITION: A preposition is a word used to show the relationship between two nouns.

EXAMPLES: The package <u>under</u> the tree is mine. (<u>under</u> is the preposition)
The package <u>in</u> the tree is mine. (<u>in</u> is the preposition)
The package <u>near</u> the tree is mine. (<u>near</u> is the preposition)

NOTICE HOW THE RELATIONSHIP BETWEEN THE PACKAGE AND THE TREE CHANGES WHEN THE PREPOSITION CHANGES.

HOW TO FIND A PREPOSITION:

Almost all prepositions will fit into the following little sentence (it's very handy; memorize it!).

"THE MOUSE GOES _____ THE BOX (OR BOXES)."

Try it out with the prepositions underlined in the three sentences used for examples. They fit, don't they?

PREPOSITIONS ARE LABELED "PP."

There are, however, some prepositions that won't fit into the "mouse-box" sentence. There are nine very common ones, which may seem like a lot to remember. Here's a little memory aid: you may not be able to remember them, BUT AL DOES!

B = but (but me)   **A** = as (as a wink)   **D** = during (during recess)
U = until (until lunch)   **L** = like (like a dog)   **O** = of (of the homework)
T = than (than the others)   **E** = except (except Bob)
                                                           S = since (since breakfast)

A word may fit into the "mouse-box" sentence and look like a preposition, but IT ISN'T A PREPOSITION UNLESS IT'S IN A PREPOSITIONAL PHRASE. To find a prepositional phrase, you say the preposition and ask, "What?" The answer you are looking for is a noun or pronoun that answers that question. That noun or pronoun is called the OBJECT OF THE PREPOSITION. Each prepositional phrase will -

begin with a preposition, and
end with a noun or pronoun.
If there are any words between the preposition and its object, they are modifiers for the object.

In the three sentences above, the prepositional phrases are "under the tree," "in the tree," and "near the tree" and "tree" is the object of the preposition in all three phrases.

PREPOSITIONAL PHRASES HAVE A JOB TO DO; THEY ARE ALWAYS **MODIFIERS**.

Look at the following three sentences:

I ate my lunch before recess.   (the prepositional phrase is "before recess")
I ate my lunch before.   ("before" isn't a preposition because there's no object.)
I ate my lunch before I saw you. ("before" isn't a preposition because if you ask, "before what?",
                                  the answer would be "before I saw you." That's not a prepositional
                                  phrase because you won't have a verb in a prepositional phrase.)

(over)

ANALYTICAL GRAMMAR (UNIT #3) — NOTES - PAGE 6

DIAGRAMING: Sentence diagraming is a tool we use much like drawing a picture. We use diagrams to make it easier to understand concepts which might be hard to understand. Diagrams consist of three types of lines: horizontal (——), vertical (|), and diagonal (\ ).

The basic diagram of a prepositional phrase looks like this:

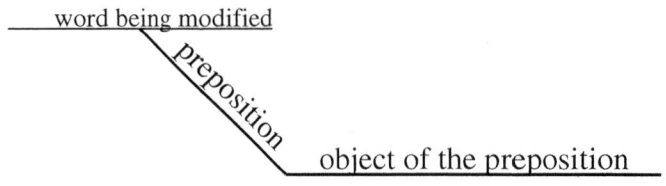

```
      word being modified
         \
          \preposition
           \
            \____object of the preposition____
```

EXAMPLE:

art n   prep adj adj n
the class (after my lunch hour)

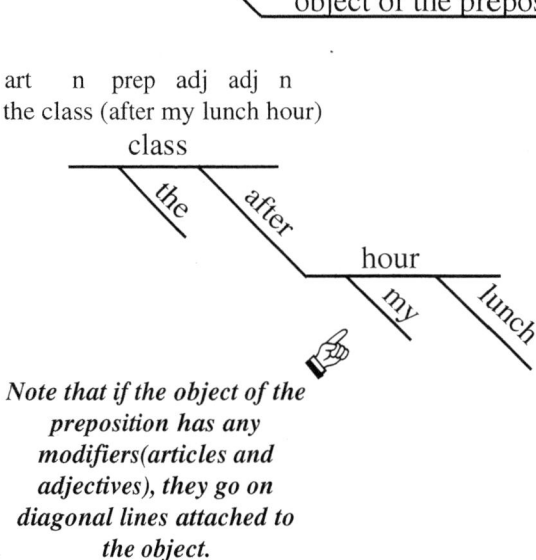

```
        class
       /    \
      /the   \after
               \
                hour
               /    \
              /my    \lunch
```

☞ *Note that if the object of the preposition has any modifiers (articles and adjectives), they go on diagonal lines attached to the object.*

NOTE: A few prepositions consist of more than one word. They are *because of, on account of, in spite of, according to, instead of, contrary to* and *out of*. If you find one of these prepositions, label it "pp" with "wings" (as you do with proper nouns of more than one word).

ANALYTICAL GRAMMAR (UNIT #3)   EXERCISE #1

PREPOSITIONAL PHRASES: EXERCISE #1

NAME:_____ DATE:_____

DIRECTIONS: *Mark all the nouns, proper nouns, articles, adjectives, pronouns, and prepositions in the sentences below. Put parentheses around the prepositional phrases. Then, on a separate sheet of paper (and as neatly as you can), diagram the prepositional phrases in each sentence. Sentence #1 has been done for you as an example. Notice that some of the words below are underlined. That will be explained to you on the other side of this page.*

     pp adj   n pro   art adj   n   pp   n

1. (In math class) we use a certain method (of thinking).

(For now, we're not going to worry about what word goes on this line. Just diagram the prepositional phrases and leave that line blank.)

2. A person with a <u>mind</u> for <u>math</u> has the advantage over other <u>people</u>.

3. Such people learn concepts about mathematical <u>principles</u> easily.

4. They solve problems in <u>math</u> quickly.

5. Emotional blocks in your <u>mind</u> prevent success in <u>math</u>.

6. A belief in your <u>ability</u> as a <u>mathematician</u> gives you a better chance at <u>success</u>.

7. The "gift" of mathematical <u>ability</u> exists in all <u>people</u>.

(over)

27

8. A lack of <u>success</u> with certain <u>problems</u> seldom indicates a lack of <u>ability</u>.

9. In <u>school</u> we look for the <u>key</u> to <u>success</u> in <u>mathematics</u>.

10. Instead of "special" <u>brains</u> with <u>ability</u> in <u>math,</u> we need more hard work!

All the underlined words in this exercise are doing the same job. Look at your notes and write what that job is.

_____

ANALYTICAL GRAMMAR (UNIT #3) EXERCISE #2

PREPOSITIONAL PHRASES: EXERCISE #2

NAME:_____ DATE:_____

DIRECTIONS: Mark all the nouns, proper nouns, articles, adjectives, pronouns, and prepositions in the sentences below. Put parentheses around the prepositional phrases. Then, on a separate sheet of paper, diagram the prepositional phrases in each sentence. Look on the back of this paper for additional work having to do with the underlined words below.

1. Johnny counts on his fingers in math <u>class</u>!

2. Counting on his fingers helps him with some <u>math</u> problems.

3. Early in many students' educations, teachers prohibit counting on fingers.

4. Counting on their fingers in <u>public</u> embarrasses some people.

5. Do your math in your head!

6. In an emergency, finger-count under the table!

7. In <u>many</u> cases, finger counting indicates an understanding of arithmetic.

(over)

ANALYTICAL GRAMMAR (UNIT #3)   EXERCISE #2 - PAGE 2

8. In ancient China, they used a sophisticated finger-counting machine called an abacus.

9. The Chinese still use the abacus in their everyday <u>lives</u>.

10. Clever, imaginative <u>finger-counting</u> schemes work effectively for many people.

DIRECTIONS: *The underlined words in these sentences are doing one of two jobs. Choosing your answer from the jobs below, write what job each underlined word is doing.*

	MODIFIER	OBJECT OF THE PREPOSITION
SENTENCE #	WORD	JOB
1	class	_____
2	math	_____
4	public	_____
7	many	_____
9	lives	_____
10	finger-counting	_____

ANALYTICAL GRAMMAR (UNIT #3)   EXERCISE #3

PREPOSITIONAL PHRASES: EXERCISE #3

NAME:_____ DATE:_____

DIRECTIONS: *Mark all the nouns, proper nouns, articles, adjectives, pronouns, and prepositions in the sentences below. Put parentheses around the prepositional phrases. Then, on a separate sheet of paper, diagram the prepositional phrases in each sentence. The underlined words have to do with additional work on the other side of this page.*

1. Contrary to popular belief, you use your imagination in math class.

2. Early in the history of mathematics, the imagination of <u>mathematicians</u> led to the discovery of each new mathematical theorem.

3. The act of mathematical creation involves the use of all <u>one's</u> abilities.

4. In most cases, the gift of logic plays only a part in the mathematical process.

5. In your classes at school, success in mathematics requires an <u>intuitive</u> sense of the <u>rightness</u> of things.

6. You often give the solution to the problem an "educated" guess.

7. Sometimes you find the answer without conscious awareness of the creative process.

8. In your mind you instinctively know the answer to the problem.

(over)

9. Creativity exists in all aspects of math.

10. The <u>logical</u> part of your mind is not the only intellectual tool in use.

DIRECTIONS: Write what job the underlined words are doing. Choose your answer from among the following:

OBJECT OF THE PREPOSITION   MODIFIER

SENTENCE #	WORD	JOB
2	mathematicians	
3	one's	
5	intuitive	
5	rightness	
10	logical	

SKILLS SUPPORT

DIRECTIONS: *Mark all the words in the passage below that you know. Put parentheses around the prepositional phrases. Diagram the prepositional phrases. Then paraphrase the entire paragraph.*

Research has failed to show any difference between the sexes in mathematical ability. The perception of math as a masculine domain stems from other myths about the subject. Math is seen as the epitome of cool, impersonal logic - nonintuitive and abstract.

ANALYTICAL GRAMMAR (UNIT #3)   TEST

PREPOSITIONAL PHRASES: TEST

NAME:_____DATE:_____

(RAW SCORE:_____/279 GRADE:_____ POINTS:_____/20_____)

DIRECTIONS: *Mark all the nouns, proper nouns, articles, adjectives, pronouns, and prepositions in the sentences below and put parentheses around the prepositional phrases. Then, on a separate sheet of paper, diagram the prepositional phrases.*

1. Men really have no advantage over women in mathematical <u>ability</u>.

2. The perception of math as a masculine domain stems from other myths about the <u>subject</u>.

3. Ability in math is seen as the triumph of <u>cool</u>, impersonal logic.

4. This perhaps fits with the stereotypical image of <u>men</u>.

5. In <u>many</u> cases men will not readily admit to difficulty with math.

6. Women, early in their schooling, will often admit too readily to personal <u>inadequacy</u> as a reason for failure.

7. Both sexes may be expressing the same fears about math in <u>different</u> ways.

8. Do <u>female</u> experts in mathematics have the same degree of femininity as women in other fields?

(over)

Photocopying this product is strictly prohibited by copyright law.   35

ANALYTICAL GRAMMAR (UNIT #3)   TEST - PAGE 2

9. According to studies at U.C.L.A., women in math-related professions actually exhibit more <u>feminine</u> characteristics than non-mathematics majors.

10. In light of these studies, both sexes can give themselves high marks in natural math <u>ability</u>.

DEFINITIONS:

1. The noun or pronoun at the end of the prepositional phrase is called the _____.

2. Pronouns are words that_____.

3. A proper noun begins with a _____.

4. A common noun ( ) can ( ) cannot consist of more than one word.

DIRECTIONS: *Write what job the underlined words are doing. Choose your answers from among the following:*

OBJECT OF THE PREPOSITION   MODIFIER

SENTENCE #	WORD	JOB
1	ability	
2	subject	
3	cool	
4	men	
5	many	
6	inadequacy	
7	different	
8	female	
9	feminine	
10	ability	

SUBJECT & VERB

The first thing we must discuss in this unit is the verb. In our language we have two kinds of verbs: action verbs and linking verb. This unit will be about action verbs; we will learn about linking verbs in Unit #8.

DEFINITION: An action verb is a word that expresses mental or physical action.

    EXAMPLES: (physical action) jump, search, carry, run, examine
                          (mental action) worry, think, believe, consider

A verb has a SUBJECT. The subject is the noun or pronoun that is DOING THE ACTION OF THE VERB.

                      art   n   pp art n   av   pp   art adj   n
    EXAMPLE: The horse (in the lead) raced (across the finish line).

The verb is raced. Who or what "raced"? The horse, right? So horse is the subject of raced.
HANDY HINT: The subject will NEVER be inside a prepositional phrase.

NOTE: If you find a word that looks like a verb but doesn't have a subject, you call it a "verbal." We'll learn all about verbals later on in Units #11, 12, and 13. For now, if you find a verbal just mark it "v." If it does have a subject, then it's a real verb, so for now mark it "av."

                      pn   av —v— art pn pp adj   n
    EXAMPLE: Joe hopes to get an A (on this test).

"To get" looks like a verb, but if you asked, "Who or what to get?" there is no stated answer in the sentence. A subject and verb always GO TOGETHER and sound right when spoken together. So "to get" in this sentence is a verbal. NOTE: Many verbals end in "ing" and any verb with "to" in front of it (to see, to throw) is always a verbal.

SIMPLE SUBJECT AND SIMPLE PREDICATE: These are terms that many language teachers and textbooks use, but they will not be used in this course. Just for your information, a "simple subject" is the noun or pronoun that is doing the action of the verb, without any of its modifiers. A "simple predicate" is just the verb by itself, without any modifiers. (We'll learn about those verb modifiers in the next unit.)

On the next page is the beginning of a "flow chart" which will be called THE PROCESS. It represents the mental steps you must take in order to figure out what the words in a sentence are doing, specifically the verbs.

I. DIAGRAMING THE SUBJECT & VERB:
    A diagram shows the structure of a sentence by making a "picture" of it. Every diagram starts with a BASE LINE which contains the subject and the verb.

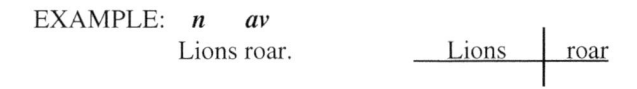

    EXAMPLE: *n   av*
                         Lions roar.   <u>Lions</u> | <u>roar</u>

Notice that the base line is a horizontal line and that the subject and verb are separated by a vertical line which goes ALL THE WAY THROUGH the horizontal line. In a diagram, you capitalize the first word of the sentence, but you don't include punctuation.

II. TO FIND THE SUBJECT AND VERB: After marking n, art, adj, pp, and putting parentheses around the prepositional phrases, mark any word that looks like a verb "v." Then ask "Who or what (say the verb)?" The answer, a noun or a pronoun, will be the subject of that verb.

    EXAMPLE: *adj   n   av   adj   n   adj   n*
                          My   uncle runs five miles every morning.

        1. The verb is "runs."   <u>uncle</u> | <u>runs</u>
        2. "Who or what runs?" Answer: uncle

III. HOW TO DIAGRAM ARTICLES AND ADJECTIVES.
  A. Adjectives and articles are diagramed on diagonal lines attached to the noun or pronoun they modify. They should be diagramed in the order in which they come in the sentence.

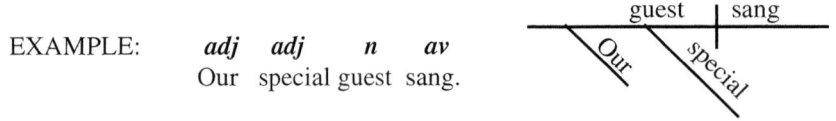

  EXAMPLE:
  adj   adj   n   av
  Our   special guest sang.

  B. Two or more adjectives joined by a conjunction ("and," "but," or "or") are diagramed like this:

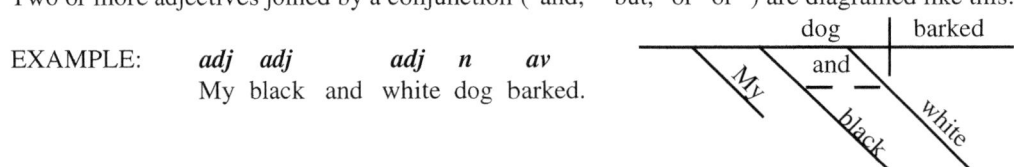

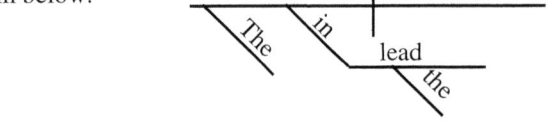

  EXAMPLE:
  adj   adj   adj   n   av
  My   black and white dog barked.

IV. HOW TO DIAGRAM A PREPOSITIONAL PHRASE:
From now on, if a prepositional phrase modifies the subject, you must diagram it. Remember, if it modifies a noun, it will tell you "Which?" about that noun. In the sentence on the other side of this page about the horse, the phrase "in the lead" tells you which horse. Look at the diagram below.

V. HOW TO DIAGRAM A COMMAND:
It is a bit tricky to diagram a command or request, because it may appear that there is no subject.

  EXAMPLE:
  av   adj   n
  Brush your teeth.

The verb is "brush," but if you ask "Who or what brush?" - it doesn't say. In the case of commands or requests, the subject is an understood "you." The diagram will look like this:

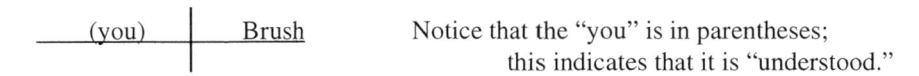

  (you) | Brush   Notice that the "you" is in parentheses; this indicates that it is "understood."

VI. HOW TO DIAGRAM AN "INVERTED" SENTENCE.
"Inverted" sentences are sentences which begin with "here" and "there." We use these sentences all the time in our language, but they may be a bit tricky to diagram. Once you find the verb and ask, "Who or what comes?" in the sentence below, you'll see that the subject is *principal*. It's tricky because you're used to seeing the subject in front of the verb - and these sentences are "in-verted"!

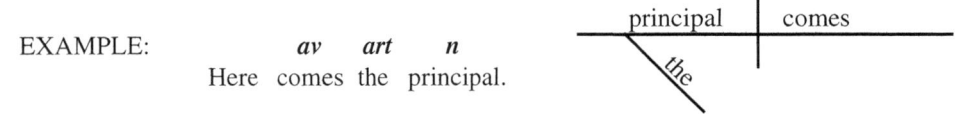

  EXAMPLE:
  av   art   n
  Here comes the principal.

The chart on the next page, which we call "The Process," represents the mental steps you must go through to analyze a sentence grammatically. We will be adding steps to this chart, but at this point, as long as you understand what you see now, you're in fine shape!

THE PROCESS

Step 1. Find and mark *n* all the nouns in the sentence. (*pn* over proper nouns)

Step 2. Find all the articles and adjectives (Ask, "Which (say the noun)?")

Step 3. Find all the pronouns.

Step 4. Find all the prepositions and put parentheses ( ) around the prepositional phrases.

Step 5. Find all words that look like verbs and mark them "v."

Step 6. Ask, "Who or what (say the verb)?"

No answer? It's a verbal. Leave it marked "v" and go on.

Answer? It's an action verb. Draw a baseline and fill in the subject and verb.

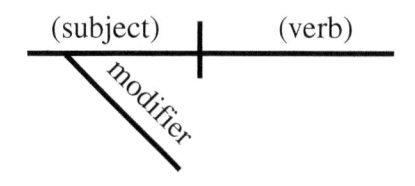

(subject) | (verb)
modifier

Complete your diagram with the modifiers that go with the subject.

ANALYTICAL GRAMMAR (UNIT #4) EXERCISE #1

SUBJECT AND VERB: EXERCISE #1

NAME:_____ DATE:_____

DIRECTIONS: *Mark all the parts of speech that you know in the sentences below. Put parentheses around the prepositional phrases. In the space provided or on a separate piece of paper, diagram the subject and its modifiers (including prepositional phrases) and the verb. Since you don't know how to diagram anything else at this point, don't try.*

1. People from Mexico settled in Texas in the seventeenth and eighteenth centuries. (See Notes III-B)

2. These people came to Texas before the settlement of the Europeans.

3. They established farms and ranches there.

4. These early settlers plowed the land.

5. Their crops grew in the harsh Texas climate.

6. These Texans bestowed Spanish names on their towns.

7. They called one of these towns San Antonio.

8. Mexican culture spread from Texas throughout the southwestern United States.

(over)

Photocopying this product is strictly prohibited by copyright law.

41

ANALYTICAL GRAMMAR (UNIT #4)   EXERCISE #1 - PAGE 2

9. There went these early Texas pioneers. (See Notes VI)

10. The names of these states <u>resulted</u> from the influence of these Spanish-speaking settlers. (See Notes IV.)

DEFINITIONS:

1. A verb is not a "real" verb unless it has a _____.
2. The articles in our language are _____, _____, and _____.

DIRECTIONS: Write what jobs the underlined words are doing. Choose your answers from among the following:

SUBJECT   OBJECT OF THE PREPOSITION   VERB   MODIFIER

SENTENCE #	WORD	JOB
1	People	_____
1	Mexico	_____
4	These	_____
6	towns	_____
8	southwestern	_____
10	resulted	_____

ANALYTICAL GRAMMAR (UNIT #4)　　　　　　　　　　　　　EXERCISE #2

SUBJECT & VERB: EXERCISE #2

NAME: _____ DATE: _____

DIRECTIONS: *Mark all the parts of speech that you know in the sentences below. Put parentheses around the prepositional phrases. Then, in the space provided or on a separate sheet of paper, diagram the subject and its modifiers and the verb. Do not try to diagram anything else at this point. WATCH OUT FOR VERBALS!!*

1. Roberto Felix Salazar wrote a poem about the early Mexican settlers of Texas.

2. These people settled the land known as Texas.

3. This Mexican-American poet wanted to tell the story of the contributions of these Texas pioneers.

4. This joyful and passionate poem describes these hard-working farmers and ranchers. (See Notes III-B)

5. They built their thick-walled adobe houses from the dry Texas earth.

6. Devout Catholic people struggled mightily to build their churches.

7. Their strong but gentle Mexican wives willingly sacrificed to make homes for their families. (See Notes III-B)

(over)

ANALYTICAL GRAMMAR (UNIT #4) — EXERCISE #2 - PAGE 2

8. <u>Read</u> this poem at your first opportunity. (See Notes V)

9. These brave Mexican settlers left a rich legacy.

10. The soft Spanish names of their <u>towns</u> survive to this day. (See Notes IV)

DEFINITIONS:

1. If there are any words between a preposition and its object, they are _____.

2. Only a _____ noun can consist of more than one word.

3. If a word looks like a verb but doesn't have a subject, it's a _____.

DIRECTIONS: Write what job the underlined word is doing. Choose your answers from among the following:

SUBJECT   OBJECT OF THE PREPOSITION   MODIFIER   VERB

SENTENCE #	WORD	JOB
1	Roberto Felix Salazar	
3	poet	
4	describes	
5	adobe	
6	struggled	
7	families	
8	Read	
10	towns	

ANALYTICAL GRAMMAR (UNIT #4) EXERCISE #3

SUBJECT & VERB: EXERCISE #3

NAME: _____ DATE: _____

DIRECTIONS: *Mark all the parts of speech that you know in the sentences below. Put parentheses around the prepositional phrases. Then, in the space provided or on a separate sheet of paper, diagram the subject and its modifiers and the verb. Do not try to diagram anything else at this point.*

1. Today we study the contributions of all <u>sorts</u> of people to American culture.

2. Roberto Felix Salazar obviously <u>took</u> pride in his ancestors.

3. "The Other Pioneers" by Roberto Felix Salazar celebrates the accomplishments of <u>these</u> Texas pioneers.

4. Mexican-Americans in the southwestern United States identify with these rugged <u>people</u>.

5. <u>Mexican</u> and Anglo settlers left their mark on the Texas landscape.

6. American students try to learn about all the different contributions to their culture.

7. Here on the land were the marks of these early settlers. (See Notes VI)

Photocopying this product is strictly prohibited by copyright law.

ANALYTICAL GRAMMAR (UNIT #4)   EXERCISE #3 - PAGE 2

8. Anglo and Mexican culture really <u>shapes</u> the life of the American Southwest.

9. Poems like this one help us to understand more about our country.

10. Please read these stories and poems about your <u>antecedents</u>.

DEFINITIONS:

1. In a diagram, a _____ goes on a diagonal line attached to another word.

2. Pronouns are words that _____.

3. Adjectives are words that _____.

DIRECTIONS: *Write what job the underlined word is doing. Choose your answers from among the following:*

    SUBJECT   OBJECT OF THE PREPOSITION   VERB   MODIFIER

SENTENCE #	WORD	JOB
1	sorts	_____
2	took	_____
3	these	_____
4	people	_____
5	Mexican	_____
8	shapes	_____
10	antecedents	_____

SKILLS SUPPORT

DIRECTIONS: *Below is a stanza from "The Other Pioneers" by Roberto Felix Salazar. Mark all the parts of speech that you know. Paraphrase this stanza.*

They saw the Texas sun rise golden-red with promised wealth

And saw the Texas sun sink golden yet, with wealth unspent.

"Here," they said. "Here to live and here to love."

"Here is the land for our sons and the sons of our sons."

And they sang the songs of ancient Spain

And they made new songs to fit new needs.

They cleared the brush and planted the corn

And saw green stalks turn black from lack of rain.

They roamed the plains behind the herds.

And stood the Indians's cruel attacks.

There was dust and there was sweat.

And there were tears and the women prayed.

ANALYTICAL GRAMMAR (UNIT #4)   TEST

SUBJECT & VERB: TEST

NAME: _____ DATE:_____

(RAW SCORE: _____ /206 GRADE: _____ CLASS POINTS:_____/20____)

DIRECTIONS: *Mark all the nouns, proper nouns, pronouns, articles, adjectives, prepositions, and action verbs in the sentences below. Put parentheses around the prepositional phrases. Then, on a separate sheet of paper, diagram the subject and verb of each sentence. Add to your diagram the modifiers for the subject, including articles, adjectives, and prepositional phrases.*

1. Study this beautiful poem about Texas' early settlers.

2. Students of American culture read the literature of all our poets.

3. They want information about America's early settlers.

4. Students in this school read examples of this type of literature.

5. They want more information about their roots.

6. An understanding of our roots helps us to understand ourselves.

7. All patriotic Americans appreciate the many contributions of America's different cultural groups.

8. The best writers in America created a great body of work on this subject.

(over)

Photocopying this product is strictly prohibited by copyright law.   49

ANALYTICAL GRAMMAR (UNIT #4)

TEST - PAGE 2

9. Great literature about our early ancestors <u>gives</u> us pride in ourselves.

10. Here comes that positive <u>self-esteem</u> about our ancestors!

DEFINITIONS:

1. A verb is a "real" verb when it has a _____.

2. The articles in our language are _____, _____, and _____.

3. Which kind of noun begins with a capital letter? _____.

4. Which kind of noun consists of only one word? _____.

5. A pronoun is a word that _____.

6. Adjectives are words that _____.

7. If a word looks like a verb but doesn't have a subject, it's a _____.

DIRECTIONS: Write what job the underlined words are doing. Choose your answers from among the following:

SUBJECT   MODIFIER   VERB   OBJECT OF THE PREPOSITION

SENTENCE #	WORD	JOB
1	Study	
2	American	
3	settlers	
4	Students	
5	more	
6	understanding	
7	groups	
8	work	
9	gives	
10	self-esteem	

ADVERBS

DEFINITION: An adverb is an "all-purpose" **MODIFIER**. It can modify a **verb**, an **adjective**, or another **adverb**.

As is stated above, adverbs modify three different things. We will discuss these things in order.

1. When an adverb modifies a VERB, it tells you IN ONE WORD "How?" "When?" "Where?" or "Why?" about that verb.

                       art   n   av   adv   adv
   EXAMPLE: The students arrived promptly today.

   What does "promptly" tell you? Yes, it tells you HOW the students ARRIVED. It's an adverb, so it's marked "adv."

   What does "today" tell you? Right, it tells you WHEN the students ARRIVED. It's also an adverb. Here's how you diagram this sentence:

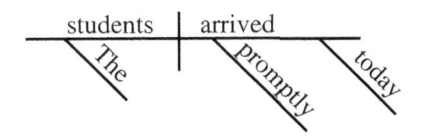

ADVERBS THAT MODIFY VERBS ARE MOVEABLE.

This is extremely important and that's why it's in such big type! This concept will be tremendously helpful to you when it comes to figuring out what an adverb modifies. Words in our language usually have to be in a certain place in a sentence (articles must come before nouns, helping verbs must come before verbs, subjects usually precede verbs, etc.), but that's not true of ADVERBS WHICH MODIFY VERBS. You can usually move such adverbs to two or three different places in the sentence without it sounding odd or changing the meaning in any way. Let's try it out with the sentence above. Can "promptly" be moved around? How about "today"?

Today the students arrived promptly.
        The students promptly arrived today.
                The students arrived today promptly.

All three of these variations make complete sense, don't they? So if you see a word in a sentence that can be moved without changing the sentence's meaning, that tells you two things: 1.) it's an adverb, and 2.) it modifies the verb! If it's an adverb and it <u>cannot</u> be moved, then <u>it modifies the word that it must stay next to.</u>

2. Adverbs that modify adjectives tell you "How?" or "To what extent?" about adjectives.

                     art   adv   adj   n   av pp art   adj   n
   EXAMPLE: The extremely nervous patient sat (in the dentist's chair).

   What does "extremely" tell you? Yes, it tell you HOW NERVOUS. It's an adverb. Notice also that "extremely" is NOT moveable. It must stay next to the word "nervous," because it modifies an adjective, not a verb. Here's how you diagram it.

We call this nifty little construction a "dog's hind leg"!

(over)

ANALYTICAL GRAMMAR (UNIT #5)   NOTES - PAGE 10

3. Adverbs that modify other adverbs also tell you "How?" or "To what extent?" about adverbs.

                         adj   n   av adv   adv
EXAMPLE: Our guest left quite abruptly.

What does *quite* tell you? Yes, it tells you HOW ABRUPTLY. It's an adverb. Notice, also, that it cannot be moved away from the word *abruptly*. Here's how to diagram it:

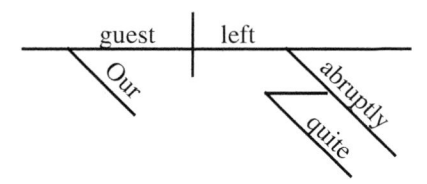

You use a "dog's hind leg" every time you have a modifier that modifies another modifier.

4. Prepositional phrases can modify verbs and other modifiers too. When they do, they answer the same "How?" "When?", etc. questions as adverbs do Here are a few examples of how to diagram them.

                        pro av   n   pp art   n
EXAMPLE: We ate lunch (in the park).   (*in the park* tells you WHERE we ATE)

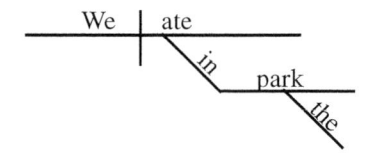

                pro av pro adv   pp art n
EXAMPLE: I saw him later (in the day).   (*in the day* tells you LATER TO WHAT EXTENT)

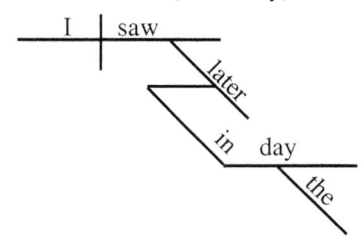

If you're having a little trouble understanding that *in the day* modifies *later*, remember that, if it modified the verb, it would be <u>moveable</u>. Since it can't be moved away from *later*, it must modify it.

In the sentence above this one, you can move *in the park* to the front of the sentence without changing its meaning. That tells you that it modifies the verb. When prepositional phrases come at the beginning of a sentence, they almost always modify the verb.

SOME HANDY LITTLE NOTES:
Many adverbs end in "ly." In our language you can change many adjectives (such as beautiful) into adverbs by adding the suffix "ly" (beautifully). Not all adverbs end in "ly," and not all words that end in "ly" are adverbs. Only adjectives with the "ly" suffix are adverbs.

The words *how, when, where*, and *why* are frequently adverbs. For now, mark them that way.

The words *not, never, really,* and *very* are very commonly used adverbs.

If you just can't figure out what a word is, it's probably an adverb!

<u>When your having a hard time figuring out where a modifier (adverb or prepositional phrase) goes,</u> try saying the modifier together with the word you think it modifies. For instance, in the last sentence above "saw in the day" doesn't sound right, but "later in the day" does! That tells you that "in the day" goes with "later"! This, along with the "moveability" trick and using the questions (how, when, where or why) will almost always show you what an adverb or prepositional phrase modifies.

Photocopying this product is strictly prohibited by copyright law.

ANALYTICAL GRAMMAR (UNIT #5)   EXERCISE #1

ADVERBS: EXERCISE #1

NAME: _____ DATE: _____

DIRECTIONS: Mark all the nouns, articles, adjectives, prepositions, action verbs, and adverbs in the sentences below. Then diagram the subject and verb and their modifiers. Don't attempt to diagram anything else.

1. We recognize Dr. Martin Luther King, Jr. as a truly great black <u>American</u>.

2. Dr. King <u>certainly</u> had a brilliant, well-disciplined mind.

3. At a very young <u>age</u>, Martin sadly experienced prejudice.

4. The black and white children <u>always</u> played separately.

5. <u>This</u> bothered Martin deeply.

6. He always wondered about the unequal <u>treatment</u> of his people.

7. At fifteen, Martin proudly <u>enrolled</u> at Morehouse College in Atlanta.

8. Martin worked diligently for his future in life.

9. He <u>finally</u> chose the ministry as his profession.

10. Young Dr. King always inspired his congregation with his <u>fiery</u> sermons against injustice.

DEFINITIONS:

1. A pronoun is a word that _____

2. An antecedent is _____

3. Adverbs are words that modify _____, _____,

   and _____.

4. An adverb which can be moved modfies _____.

5. If an adverb cannot be moved, it modifies _____
   _____.

(over)

Photocopying this product is strictly prohibited by copyright law.

ANALYTICAL GRAMMAR (UNIT #5)   EXERCISE #1 - PAGE 2

DIRECTIONS: *Write what jobs the words below are doing. Choose your answer among the following:*

OBJECT OF THE PREPOSITION   MODIFIER   VERB   SUBJECT

SENTENCE #	WORD	JOB
1	American	_____
2	certainly	_____
3	age	_____
4	always	_____
5	This	_____
6	treatment	_____
7	enrolled	_____
9	finally	_____
10	fiery	_____

ANALYTICAL GRAMMAR (UNIT #5)   EXERCISE #2

ADVERBS: EXERCISE #2

NAME: _____ DATE: _____

DIRECTIONS: *Mark all the nouns, articles, adjectives, prepositions, action verbs, and adverbs in the sentences below. Put parentheses around the prepositional phrases. Then diagram the subject and verb and their modifiers. There may be words you can't yet diagram; if so, just leave them alone for now.*

1. Martin Luther King, Jr. ultimately graduated from Morehouse College.

2. He then received a scholarship to Crozer Theological Seminary.

3. The teachings of Mahatma Gandhi totally fascinated Martin.

4. With non-violent methods, Gandhi successfully freed his people from British domination.

5. Martin sincerely believed in the success of this method.

6. He studied hard for his doctoral degree at Boston University.

7. Upon his graduation, Dr. King started his adult life as the very young pastor of a church in Alabama.

8. At that time in our history, the law mandated the separation of the races.

9. In his Sunday sermons, Dr. King bravely denounced these unjust laws.

10. *Because of Martin's words, the black leaders in the community also favored the use of Gandhi's methods.   *(See Notes: Unit #3, pg. 6)

(over)

ANALYTICAL GRAMMAR (UNIT #5)   EXERCISE #2 - PAGE 2

DEFINITIONS:

1. Which kind of noun begins with a lower case letter and consists of only one word?
   _____.

2. If a word looks like a verb but it doesn't have a subject, it's called a
   _____.

3. If you find a verb and ask, "Who or what (and say the verb)?"- what are you looking for?
   _____

DIRECTIONS: *Write what jobs the words below are doing. Choose your answers from among the following:*

   SUBJECT   MODIFIER   VERB

   OBJECT OF THE PREPOSITION

SENTENCE #	WORD	JOB
1	Martin Luther King, Jr.	_____
2	received	_____
3	totally	_____
4	methods	_____
5	success	_____
6	He	_____
7	pastor	_____
8	history	_____
9	bravely	_____
10	black	_____

ADVERBS: EXERCISE #3

NAME: _____ DATE: _____

DIRECTIONS: *Parse (mark all the parts of speech in) the sentences below. Then diagram the subject and verb and their modifiers.*

1. Dr. King's <u>message</u> about non-violent resistence to segregation laws certainly struck a chord in the hearts of many Americans.

2. <u>Mrs. Rosa Parks</u>, with a simple act of bravery, provided an opportunity for the implementation of Dr. King's plan of action.

3. Against the laws of her city, Mrs. Parks simply sat in a "Whites Only" <u>section</u> of a city bus.

4. The city police <u>quickly</u> arrested her for her "crime."

5. Dr. King promptly <u>organized</u> the Blacks of that city in a bus boycott.

6. The Selma Bus Company soon <u>suffered</u> the daily loss of money.

7. Now Dr. King <u>led</u> non-violent marches in protest against these completely unjust laws.

8. Finally, on <u>November 12, 1956</u>, the United States Supreme Court issued a decision in support of these civil rights crusaders.

9. In Washington, D. C., in 1963, Dr. King delivered a very beautiful and <u>now</u> famous speech about his dream of racial equality for America.

10. Tragically in 1968, a white <u>ex-convict</u> ended the career of this truly great American hero.

(over)

ANALYTICAL GRAMMAR (UNIT #5) — EXERCISE #3 - PAGE 2

DEFINITIONS:

1. The three articles are _____, _____, and _____.

2. A proper noun begins with a _____

    and may consist of _____.

3. An action verb expresses _____

    and must have a _____.

4. If a word looks like a verb but doesn't have a subject, it's a _____.

DIRECTIONS: What jobs are the words below doing. Choose your answers from among the following:

MODIFIER   VERB   SUBJECT   OBJECT OF THE PREPOSITION

SENTENCE #	WORD	JOB
1	message	
2	Mrs. Rosa Parks	
3	section	
4	quickly	
5	organized	
6	suffered	
7	led	
8	November, 12, 1956	
9	now	
10	ex-convict	

ANALYTICAL GRAMMAR (UNIT #5) — SKILLS SUPPORT

SKILLS SUPPORT

DIRECTIONS: *The following is an exerpt from Dr. Martin Luther King, Jr.'s historic "I Have a Dream" speech, given on the steps of the Lincoln Memorial in 1963. Parse the words in the passage below. Then paraphrase it.*

"We refuse to believe the bank of justice is bankrupt....Now is the time to make justice a reality for all of God's children...I have a dream today."

ANALYTICAL GRAMMAR (UNIT #5)   TEST

ADVERBS: TEST

NAME: _____ DATE: _____

(RAW SCORE: _____ /251 GRADE: _____ POINTS: _____ /20)

DIRECTIONS: Mark all the nouns, articles, adjectives, pronouns, prepositions, action verbs, and adverbs in the sentences below and put parentheses around the prepositional phrases. Then, on a separate sheet of paper, neatly diagram the subject and verb and their modifiers.

1. The crowds at the Lincoln Memorial joyfully received Martin Luther King, Jr.

2. All Americans take tremendous pride in this often repeated speech.

3. Many Americans in that generation instantly hailed him as a hero.

4. Today his courage inspires Americans of all colors.

5. Dr. King emphasized discipline as a very important aspect of the struggle against injustice.

6. Dr. King reminded Americans of the guarantee of equality for all people in our Constitution.

7. Constitutionally, the Founding Fathers formed this country as a home for all God's children.

8. People from all corners of the world come to this sweet land of liberty.

9. Tragically, James Earl Ray robbed America of the life of this truly great man.

10. Today Americans of all colors remember the courage of this man of peace.

(over)

Photocopying this product is strictly prohibited by copyright law.

ANALYTICAL GRAMMAR (UNIT #5) TEST - PAGE 2

DEFINITIONS:

1. A noun is the name of _____.

2. A _____ noun begins with a lower-case letter.

3. A _____ noun begins with a capital letter.

4. A _____ noun can consist of only one word.

5. An adjective is a word that _____.

6. The articles in our language are _____, _____, and _____.

7. A pronoun is a word that _____.

8. An antecedent is _____.

9. A word may look like a preposition, but it's not unless it has a(n) _____.

10. Adverbs modify _____, _____, and _____.

DIRECTIONS: Write what jobs the words below are doing. Choose your answers from among the following:

   SUBJECT   VERB   MODIFIER   OBJECT OF THE PREPOSITION

SENTENCE #	WORD	JOB
1	crowds	_____
2	speech	_____
3	hailed	_____
4	Today	_____
5	aspect	_____
6	Dr. King	_____
7	home	_____
8	People	_____
9	robbed	_____
10	colors	_____

ANALYTICAL GRAMMAR (UNIT #6)   NOTES-PAGE 11

PATTERNS 1 & 2

Now that you know the basics of diagraming, it is necessary for you to know the FIVE SENTENCE PATTERNS. No matter how different sentences may look, they all fall into one of five basic patterns. This unit deals with PATTERNS 1 & 2. These two patterns contain ACTION VERBS ONLY.

PATTERN 1: N - V

The N-V pattern contains only two items on the baseline: a subject (N) and an action verb (V). The subject and verb may have modifiers, and there may be prepositional phrases in the sentence, but THERE WILL BE NO OTHER NOUNS OR VERBS.

EXAMPLE: *art   n   av   prep art adj   n*
          The boy stood (on the boat's deck).

As you already know, this sentence should be diagramed like this:

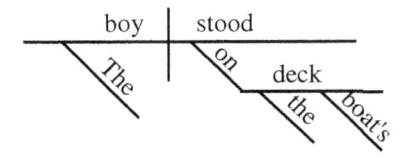

(EXERCISE #1 features the N-V pattern; do it now)

PATTERN 2: N - V - N

To learn about Pattern 2, you must become familiar with a new "job" called the DIRECT OBJECT. The N-V-N pattern contains three main parts: a subject (N), an action verb (V), and a DIRECT OBJECT (N). All three parts may have modifiers, and there may be prepositional phrases in the sentence, but THERE ARE NO OTHER NOUNS OR VERBS.

To find the DIRECT OBJECT, you first find the subject and the verb. Then you simply SAY THE SUBJECT, SAY THE VERB, AND ASK "WHAT?" The answer will be a noun or a pronoun and is called the DIRECT OBJECT.

EXAMPLE: *adj adj   n   av   art   adj   n*
          My best friend had   a birthday party.

The subject is FRIEND; the verb is HAD. Now say, "friend had WHAT?" The answer is PARTY - which is your DIRECT OBJECT. The diagram for this Pattern 2 sentence is like this:

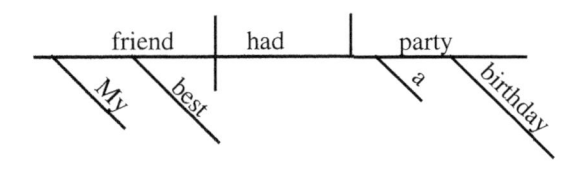

(Exercise #2 features these N-V-N patterns; Exercise #3 contains sentences which are both Pattern 1 and Pattern 2; do them now)

THE PROCESS:
On the back of this page is an expanded version to the flow chart that was introduced in Unit #4. We will be adding new mental steps, but for now - as long as you understand what you see - you're doing fine!

(over)

THE PROCESS

Step 1. Find and mark *n* all the nouns in the sentence. (*pn* over proper nouns)

Step 2. Find and mark all the articles and adjectives (Ask, "Which [say the noun]?")

Step 3. Find and mark all the pronouns.

Step 4. Find all the prepositions and put parentheses around the prepositional phrases.

Step 5. Find any word that looks like a verb and mark it "v."

Step 6. Ask, "Who or what (say the verb)?"

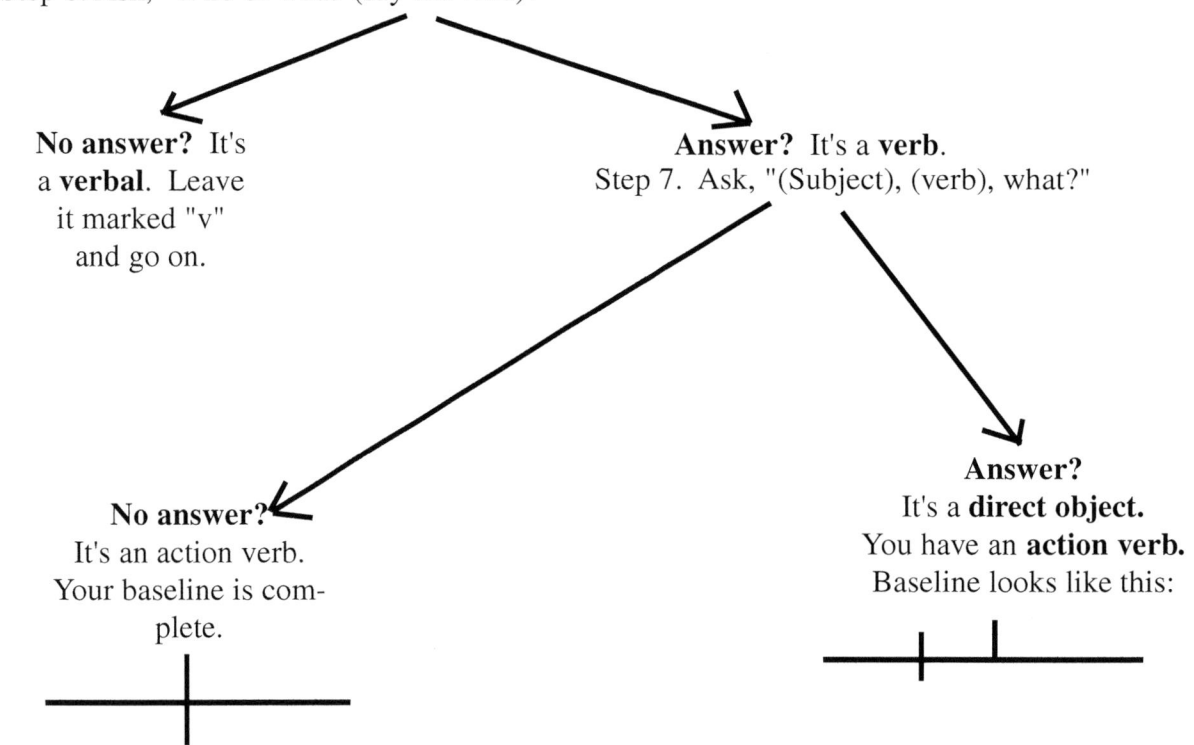

No answer? It's a **verbal**. Leave it marked "v" and go on.

Answer? It's a **verb**.
Step 7. Ask, "(Subject), (verb), what?"

No answer?
It's an action verb.
Your baseline is complete.

Answer?
It's a **direct object.**
You have an **action verb.**
Baseline looks like this:

ANALYTICAL GRAMMAR (UNIT #6)   EXERCISE #1

PATTERNS 1 & 2: EXERCISE #1

NAME:_____ DATE:_____

DIRECTIONS: *All the sentences below are Pattern 1. Parse them and put parentheses around the prepositional phrases. Diagram the subject and verb and their modifiers including the prepositional phrases.*

1. Many Americans' <u>grandparents</u> live in other states.

2. Many of us <u>go</u> to our grandparents' houses very rarely.

3. People in former generations seldom moved to other <u>places</u> with the frequency of today's families.

4. Most American children <u>lived</u> in the same town as their grandparents.

5. They visited often in <u>their</u> grandparents' homes.

6. During these long and frequent visits, they learned about the lives of the <u>grandparents</u>.

7. Children in America today <u>visit</u> with their grandparents during short vacations.

8. Families from all economic <u>levels</u> move frequently from place to place.

(over)

Photocopying this product is strictly prohibited by copyright law.

ANALYTICAL GRAMMAR (UNIT #6) EXERCISE #1 - PAGE 2

9. A lucky <u>few</u> visit with their grandparents for a long time.

10. Before the <u>end</u> of your grandparents' lives, speak to them of your gratitude for all their love. (See Notes: Unit #4: p. 8, V)

DEFINITIONS:

1. Pronouns are words that _____.

2. To look for the direct object you say the _____, say the _____ and ask _____.

3. A verb must have a _____ to be a "real" verb.

DIRECTIONS: *Write what job the underlined words are doing. Choose your answers from among the following:*

    SUBJECT   OBJECT OF THE PREPOSITION   VERB   MODIFIER

SENTENCE #	WORD	JOB
1	grandparents	
2	go	
3	places	
4	lived	
5	their	
6	grandparents	
7	visit	
8	levels	
9	few	
10	end	

ANALYTICAL GRAMMAR (UNIT #6)　　　　　　　　　　　　　EXERCISE #2

PATTERNS 1 & 2: EXERCISE #2

NAME:_____DATE:_____

DIRECTIONS: *All the sentences below are Pattern 2. Parse them and put parentheses around the prepositional phrases. Diagram the entire sentence. Remember to use your Process chart.*

1. In today's youth-oriented society we seldom appreciate the wisdom of our elders.

2. The past gives many valuable lessons for our modern lives.

3. Young people today rarely show their appreciation for the lessons of the past.

4. Older people sometimes lack patience with younger people.

5. These conflicts occasionally cause misunderstandings between younger and older people.

6. An enjoyable hour with an older person opens doors from the past for you.

7. These doors from the past shed light on things in our often confusing world.

8. Some older people in nursing homes never get visits from younger people.

(over)

Photocopying this product is strictly prohibited by copyright law.

ANALYTICAL GRAMMAR (UNIT #6)   EXERCISE #2 - PAGE 2

9. A visit like this benefits <u>both</u> of you!

10. <u>Take</u> time out of your busy life for a visit with an older person. (See Notes: Unit #3, p.6)

DIRECTIONS: *Write what job the underlined words are doing. Choose your answers from among the following:*

SUBJECT   DIRECT OBJECT   OBJECT OF THE PREPOSITION   VERB   MODIFIER

SENTENCE #	WORD	JOB
1	wisdom	
2	past	
3	appreciation	
4	Older	
5	misunderstandings	
6	person	
7	light	
8	nursing	
9	both	
10	Take	

ANALYTICAL GRAMMAR (UNIT #6)   EXERCISE #3

PATTERNS 1 & 2: EXERCISE #3

NAME:_____DATE:_____

DIRECTIONS: *The sentences below are either Pattern 1 or Pattern 2. Parse them and put parentheses around the prepositional phrases. Diagram the entire sentence. Remember to use your Process chart.*

1. Rudolfo A. Anaya wrote a <u>story</u> about his grandfather.

2. This old <u>farmer</u> <u>lived</u> in a valley on the Pecos River in New Mexico.

3. Rudolfo's culture teaches respect for <u>elders</u>.

4. He lived on his <u>grandfather's</u> farm during the summer.

5. His uncles also lived in that valley beside the grandfather's farm.

6. Rudolfo's grandfather used few words for advice.

7. "<u>Pray</u> for rain."

8. Beside his grandfather in the wagon, Rudolfo <u>drove</u> into town for supplies.

(over)

Photocopying this product is strictly prohibited by copyright law.

ANALYTICAL GRAMMAR (UNIT #6)   EXERCISE #3 - PAGE 2

9. The beloved <u>grandfather</u> of his childhood died after a long and <u>useful</u> life.

10. Rudolfo gained a great <u>deal</u> of wisdom from his close association with his grandfather.

DIRECTIONS: *Write what job the underlined words are doing. Choose your answers from among the following:*

SUBJECT   DIRECT OBJECT   OBJECT OF THE PREPOSITION   VERB   MODIFIER

SENTENCE #	WORD	JOB
1	story	
2	farmer	
2	lived	
3	elders	
4	grandfather's	
7	Pray	
8	drove	
9	grandfather	
9	useful	
10	deal	

SKILLS SUPPORT

The following is an exerpt from a poem. Mark the nouns, articles, adjectives, pronouns, prepositions, verbs, and adverbs in the lines below. Put parentheses around the prepositional phrases. Then paraphrase these two stanzas.

LEGACY II

Leroy V. Quintana

NOW I LOOK BACK

ONLY TWO GENERATIONS REMOVED

REALIZE I AM NOTHING BUT* A POOR FOOL

WHO WENT TO COLLEGE

TRYING TO FIND MY WAY BACK

TO THE CENTER OF THE WORLD

WHERE GRANDFATHER STOOD

THAT DAY.

(* See Notes: Unit 3: "BUT AL DOES")

ANALYTICAL GRAMMAR (UNIT #6)   TEST

PATTERNS 1 & 2: TEST

NAME:_____DATE:_____

(RAW SCORE:_____/254 GRADE:_____ POINTS: ___/20___)

DIRECTIONS: *Parse the sentences below and put parentheses around the prepositional phrases. Then, on a separate sheet of paper, diagram the entire sentence.*

1. An old man sat quietly on a <u>bench</u> in the park.

2. <u>Some</u> boys from the neighborhood <u>played</u> a game of baseball in a nearby vacant lot.

3. Paul hit the <u>ball</u> over the fence onto the old man's bench.

4. "The baseball from our game fell on your bench."

5. "Your stupid ball nearly hit <u>me</u> on the head!

6. Please take <u>it</u> away immediately!"

7. Paul studied the old man on the bench for a moment.

8. In a polite tone, he <u>apologized</u> to the old man.

(over)

ANALYTICAL GRAMMAR (UNIT #6)   TEST - PAGE 2

9. The old man on the bench smiled at Paul in <u>surprise</u>.

10. "You certainly have very nice manners!"

11. A real <u>friendship</u> between the two grew from this chance <u>encounter</u> in the park.

DIRECTIONS: Write what job the underlined words are doing. Choose your answers from among the following:

SUBJECT   DIRECT OBJECT   OBJECT OF THE PREPOSITION   VERB   MODIFIER

SENTENCE #	WORD	JOB
1	bench	_____
2	Some	_____
2	played	_____
3	ball	_____
5	me	_____
6	it	_____
8	apologized	_____
9	surprise	_____
11	friendship	_____
11	encounter	_____

ANALYTICAL GRAMMAR (UNIT #7)   NOTES-PAGE 13

PATTERN #3

To learn about Pattern 3, you must learn a new concept called the INDIRECT OBJECT.

PATTERN 3:   N-V-N-N

It consists of four main parts IN THIS ORDER: the subject (N), an action verb (V), an indirect object (N), and a direct object (N). All four parts may have modifiers, and there may be prepositional phrases in the sentence, but THERE WILL BE NO OTHER NOUNS OR VERBS.

IMPORTANT: A SENTENCE CANNOT HAVE AN INDIRECT OBJECT UNLESS IT HAS A DIRECT OBJECT.

EXAMPLE: *pn   av   pro   art   n   pp   n*
Mom gave   me   a   dollar   (for   candy).

If you "strip down" this sentence (take out all the modifiers and prepositional phrases), what would be left?

Mom   gave   me   dollar

When you "strip down" a sentence as you did above, count the number of nouns (or pronouns) left over. If you have one noun left over, you have a Pattern 1 (N-V) sentence. If you have two nouns left over, you have a Pattern 2 (N-V-N) sentence. If you have three nouns left over, you have Pattern 3 (N-V-N-N); the first noun will be the subject, the second will be the indirect object, and the third will be the direct obect.

The diagram of your complete Pattern 3 sentence would look like this:

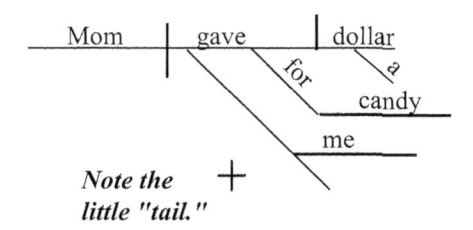

```
   Mom  |  gave  |  dollar
              \    \a
              for   candy
                \
                 me
```
Note the little "tail."

VERY IMPORTANT: The INDIRECT OBJECT will always be located <u>between</u> the VERB and the DIRECT OBJECT in the sentence. The words will ALWAYS come in this order:

SUBJECT - VERB - INDIRECT OBJECT - DIRECT OBJECT.

These sentences will only contain ACTION VERBS.

The easiest way to determine which sentence pattern you have is to "strip the sentence down." That means to take out all the modifiers and only focus on the NOUNS and VERB in the sentence. If you have three nouns, then you have a pattern #3 sentence and the middle noun is the indirect object.

ANALYTICAL GRAMMAR (UNIT #7)   EXERCISE #1

PATTERN 3: EXERCISE #1

NAME:_____DATE:_____

DIRECTIONS: *All the sentences below are Pattern 3. Parse them and put prepositional phrases in parentheses. Then, in the space provided or on a separate sheet of paper, diagram the entire sentence.*

1. African-Americans gave <u>America</u> many great Congressmen.

2. <u>Blanche Kelso Bruce</u> gave Missouri its first school for Blacks in 1864.

3. In 1874 the Mississippi legislature made Mr. Bruce that state's first black Senator.

4. In 1888 Henry Plummer Cheatham gave North Carolina its first black <u>Congressman</u>.

5. After his defeat in 1892, Cheatham gave North Carolina an orphanage for two hundred students.

6. Wood High School in Charleston, South Carolina, gave <u>Robert Carlos DeLarge</u> his early education.

7. In 1870 the South Carolina legislature appointed <u>him</u> land <u>commissioner</u> in charge of that state's public lands.

(over)

Photocopying this product is strictly prohibited by copyright law.

ANALYTICAL GRAMMAR (UNIT #7)   EXERCISE #1 - PAGE 2

8. The same state legislature gave him the nomination for representative of the Second Congressional District.

9. In 1966 Massachusetts gave the United States its first <u>black</u> Senator from a popular election.

10. Senator Edward William Brooke III gave the people of Massachusetts twelve years of dedicated <u>service</u> in the Senate.

DIRECTIONS: *Write what job the underlined words are doing. Choose your answers from among the following:*

SUBJECT   DIRECT OBJECT   INDIRECT OBJECT
OBJECT OF THE PREPOSITION   MODIFIER   VERB

SENTENCE #	WORD	JOB
1	America	
2	Blanche Kelso Bruce	
4	Congressman	
6	Robert Carlos DeLarge	
7	him	
7	commissioner	
9	black	
10	service	

ANALYTICAL GRAMMAR (UNIT #7) EXERCISE #2

PATTERN 3: EXERCISE #2

NAME:_____DATE:_____

DIRECTIONS: *The sentences below are either Pattern 2 (N-V-N) or Pattern 3 (N-V-N-N). Parse the sentences and then, in the space provided or on a separate sheet of paper, diagram the entire sentence.*

1. Black Americans represent <u>America</u> in all aspects of our culture.

2. Mary McLeod Bethune gave the southeastern <u>United States</u> one of its finest teacher-training institutions.

3. The Brooklyn Dodgers named Roy Campanella <u>"Most Valuable Player"</u> in three different years.

4. Wilt Chamberlain broke almost <u>every</u> scoring record in professional basketball.

5. In 1839 <u>Joseph Cinque</u> led a successful revolt against the captain of a slave ship.

6. Harriet Tubman <u>gave</u> many slaves their freedom through the famous <u>Underground</u> <u>Railroad</u>.

7. After his own escape to freedom in 1835, Frederick Douglas denounced <u>slavery</u> in his fiery speeches.

(over)

ANALYTICAL GRAMMAR (UNIT #7) — EXERCISE #2 - PAGE 2

8. W. E. B. Dubois founded the National Association for the Advancement of Colored People.

9. James Baldwin gave the world such <u>magnificent</u> essays as "The Fire Next Time."

10. Lorraine Hansberry won the New York Drama Critics Circle Award for her *A Raisin in the Sun*.

DIRECTIONS: Write what job the underlined words are doing. Choose your answers from among the following:

SUBJECT   DIRECT OBJECT   INDIRECT OBJECT
OBJECT OF THE PREPOSITION   MODIFIER   VERB

SENTENCE #	WORD	JOB
1	America	
2	United States	
3	"Most Valuable Player"	
4	every	
5	Joseph Cinque	
6	gave	
6	Underground Railroad	
7	slavery	
9	magnificent	

PATTERN 3: EXERCISE #3

NAME:_____ DATE:_____

DIRECTIONS: *The sentences below are either Pattern 1(N-V), Pattern 2 (N-V-N), or Pattern 3 (N-V-N-N). Parse the sentences and then, in the space provided or on a separate sheet of paper, diagram the entire sentence.*

1. Langston Hughes achieved <u>fame</u> from his magnificent poems about the black experience in America.

2. Langston Hughes <u>made</u> his entrance into the world in Joplin, Missouri, on February 1, 1902.

3. His father left the family for Mexico in a fit of <u>rage</u> over discrimination.

4. His mother gave her <u>son</u> the best home within her power.

5. His classmates in grammar school elected him class <u>poet</u>.

6. On that same day <u>Langston</u> wrote sixteen verses in praise of them.

7. At his father's request Langston moved to Mexico in his junior year in high school.

8. He published his first <u>poem</u> during his senior year.

(over)

ANALYTICAL GRAMMAR (UNIT #7)   EXERCISE #3 - PAGE 2

9. Langston put himself through Lincoln College in Pennsylvania.

10. Throughout his long career Langston Hughes gave <u>America</u> the priceless <u>legacy</u> of his <u>poetry</u>.

DIRECTIONS: *Write what job the underlined words are doing. Choose your answers from among the following:*

SUBJECT	DIRECT OBJECT	INDIRECT OBJECT	OBJECT OF THE PREPOSITION
VERB		MODIFIER	

SENTENCE #	WORD	JOB
1	fame	
2	made	
3	rage	
4	son	
5	poet	
6	Langston	
8	poem	
10	America	
10	legacy	
10	poetry	

PATTERN 3: SKILLS SUPPORT

Parse and diagram the first line of this poem. Then paraphrase the poem.

I, TOO, SING AMERICA

by Langston Hughes

I, too, sing America.

I am the darker brother.

They send me to eat in the kitchen

When company comes,

But I laugh,

And eat well,

And grow strong.

Tomorrow,

I'll be at the table

When company comes.

Nobody'll dare

Say to me,

"Eat in the kitchen,"

Then.

Besides,

They'll see how beautiful I am

And be ashamed —

I, too, sing America.

ANALYTICAL GRAMMAR (UNIT #7) TEST

PATTERN #3: TEST

NAME:_____ DATE:_____

(RAW SCORE: _____ /255 GRADE: _____ POINTS:_____ /20____)

DIRECTIONS: *Parse the sentences below and put prepositional phrases in parentheses. Then, in the space provided or on a separate sheet of paper, diagram the entire sentence.*

1. African-Americans give the <u>United States</u> their gifts in all areas of American culture.

2. Black <u>writers</u> touch our hearts with their <u>stories</u>.

3. Black soldiers come to <u>America's</u> aid in time of war.

4. Show business in this country benefits from the talents of African-American entertainers.

5. Black poets write <u>us</u> <u>poems</u> of great beauty.

6. The <u>talents</u> of great black athletes enrich the sports scene in America.

7. <u>American</u> history <u>contains</u> the names of many black patriots.

8. The ranks of America's Blacks give <u>us</u> countless dedicated <u>educators</u>.

(over)

Photocopying this product is strictly prohibited by copyright law.

85

ANALYTICAL GRAMMAR (UNIT #7)   TEST - PAGE 2

9. Citizens of color contribute <u>greatly</u> to all walks of American life.

10. America <u>prospers</u> from the contributions of all her cultural <u>groups</u>.

DIRECTIONS: *Write what job the underlined words are doing. Choose your answers from among the following:*

SUBJECT   DIRECT OBJECT   INDIRECT OBJECT

OBJECT OF THE PREPOSITION   VERB   MODIFIER

SENTENCE #	WORD	JOB
1	United States	
2	writers	
2	stories	
3	America's	
5	us	
5	poems	
6	talents	
7	American	
7	contains	
8	us	
8	educators	
9	greatly	
10	prospers	
10	groups	

ANALYTICAL GRAMMAR (UNIT #8)   NOTES-PAGE 15

LINKING VERBS AND PATTERNS 4 & 5

DEFINITION: A linking verb is a word that links its subject with a noun (or pronoun) or an adjective in the predicate. (The predicate is everything except the subject and its modifiers)

THE SUBJECT OF AN ACTION VERB IS <u>DOING</u> SOMETHING.

THE SUBJECT OF A LINKING VERB IS <u>BEING</u> SOMETHING.

There are only a small group of verbs that can be linking verbs. For the most part, they are -

BE (is, are, am, was, were, being, been)	SMELL	STAY
SEEM	TASTE	APPEAR
BECOME	LOOK	REMAIN
	FEEL	GROW

Some of these verbs are always linking verbs (such as *seem* and *become*), but most of them can be action verbs too. In order to be sure it's a linking verb, you have to determine if it's in a LINKING VERB SENTENCE PATTERN.

PATTERN 4 - N-LV-N: This is the first linking verb sentence pattern. We call it "noun - linking verb - noun." The first noun (or pronoun) is the SUBJECT, next comes the LINKING VERB, and then comes the second noun which is called the PREDICATE NOMINATIVE. The most important thing to remember is that the **subject and the predicate nominative are always the same person or thing.**

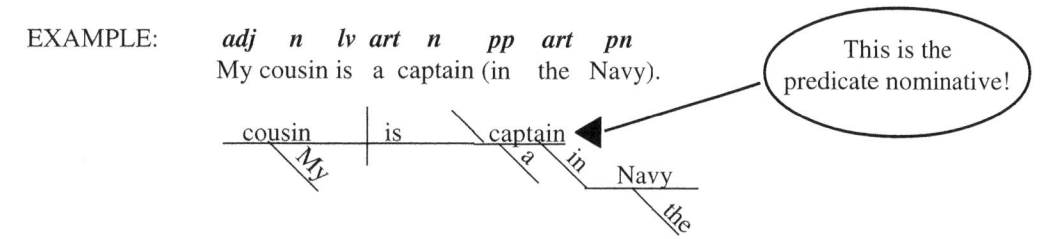

EXAMPLE:
```
adj  n   lv art  n   pp  art  pn
My cousin is  a captain (in  the Navy).
```

(This is the predicate nominative!)

Notice how *cousin* and *captain* are the same person in this sentence? If the sentence said, "My cousin married a captain in the Navy," that wouldn't be the case, would it? Notice how the base line differs from a Pattern 2 sentence: the line which separates the action verb from its direct object is **vertical**, whereas the line which separates a linking verb from its predicate nominative is **diagonal** and slants upward to the left. The **predicate nominative** is the noun or pronoun that completes the linking verb pattern.

PATTERN 5 - N-LV-ADJ: This is the second linking verb pattern. We call it "noun - linking verb - adjective." The noun is the SUBJECT, then comes the LINKING VERB, and then comes an adjective called the PREDICATE ADJECTIVE. **The predicate adjective always describes the subject.**

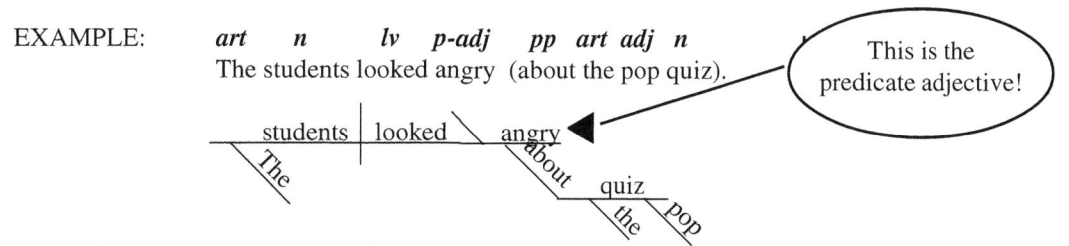

EXAMPLE:
```
art   n    lv  p-adj   pp  art adj  n
The students looked angry (about the pop quiz).
```

(This is the predicate adjective!)

REMEMBER: If you have an action verb in your sentence, then you have either Pattern 1, Pattern 2, or Pattern 3. If, however, you have a linking verb, then you have either Pattern 4 or Pattern 5. In a Pattern 4 sentence the linking verb LINKS the subject with another noun or pronoun in the predicate. In a Pattern 5 sentence the linking verb LINKS the subject to an adjective in the predicate. On the back of this page is the completed Process chart. Use it as you do these exercises. If you understand the Process chart, it will be your "best friend" in mastering this material.

(over)

Photocopying this product is strictly prohibited by copyright law.   87

ANALYTICAL GRAMMAR (UNIT #8) NOTES-PAGE 16

THE PROCESS

Step 1. Find & mark "n" all the nouns in the sentence.

Step 2. Find & mark all the articles and adjectives (Ask, "Which [say the noun]?")

Step 3. Find & mark all the pronouns.

Step 4. Find & mark all the prepositions and put parentheses around the prepositional phrases.

Step 5. Find all words that look like verbs and mark them "v."

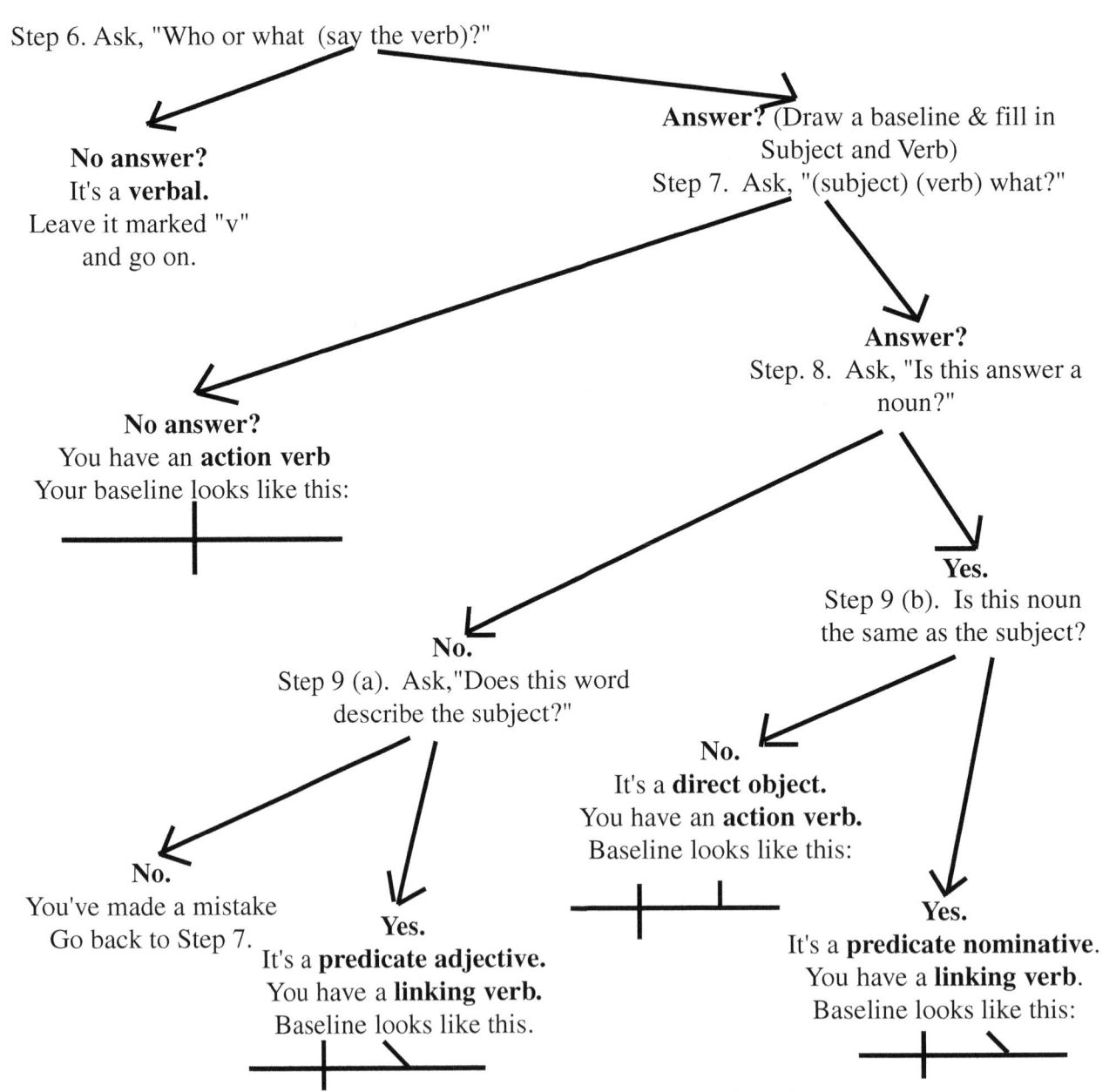

Step 6. Ask, "Who or what (say the verb)?"

No answer?
It's a **verbal.**
Leave it marked "v"
and go on.

Answer? (Draw a baseline & fill in Subject and Verb)
Step 7. Ask, "(subject) (verb) what?"

Answer?
Step. 8. Ask, "Is this answer a noun?"

No answer?
You have an **action verb**
Your baseline looks like this:

Yes.
Step 9 (b). Is this noun the same as the subject?

No.
Step 9 (a). Ask, "Does this word describe the subject?"

No.
It's a **direct object.**
You have an **action verb.**
Baseline looks like this:

No.
You've made a mistake
Go back to Step 7.

Yes.
It's a **predicate adjective.**
You have a **linking verb.**
Baseline looks like this.

Yes.
It's a **predicate nominative.**
You have a **linking verb.**
Baseline looks like this:

Step 10. Add articles, adjectives, prep. phrases, adverbs, and conjunctions to the diagram.

Step 11. Pat yourself on the back! You've successfully "parsed" and diagramed the sentence!

Photocopying this product is strictly prohibited by copyright law.

ANALYTICAL GRAMMAR (UNIT #8)   EXERCISE #1

PATTERNS 4 & 5: EXERCISE #1

NAME:_____DATE:_____

DIRECTIONS: *All the sentences below are teither the N-LV-N or N-LV-ADJ pattern. Parse and diagram the sentences.*

1. Jewish-Americans are important <u>contributors</u> to American culture.

2. George Burns was one of America's most beloved <u>comedians</u>.

3. The <u>extremely</u> talented Barbra Streisand is a great popular singer.

4. Henry Kissinger <u>was</u> America's powerful Secretary of State during the Nixon administration.

5. One influential Jewish-American publisher was <u>Joseph Pulitzer</u>.

6. Dr. Jonas Salk's polio <u>vaccine</u> was terribly important.

7. Albert Einstein's mind was more <u>brilliant</u> than any other.

8. Baseball Hall of Fame's Sandy Koufax was greatly respected.

Photocopying this product is strictly prohibited by copyright law.

ANALYTICAL GRAMMAR (UNIT #8)   EXERCISE #1 - PAGE 2

9. George Gershwin's music was incredibly beautiful.

10. The history of <u>Jews</u> in America is indeed great.

DIRECTIONS: Write what job the underlined words are doing. Choose your answers from among the following:

	SUBJECT	PREDICATE NOMINATIVE	OBJECT OF THE PREPOSITION
	MODIFIER	VERB	PREDICATE ADJECTIVE

SENTENCE #	WORD	JOB
1	contributors	
2	comedians	
3	extremely	
4	was	
5	Joseph Pulitzer	
6	vaccine	
7	brilliant	
10	Jews	

ANALYTICAL GRAMMAR (UNIT #8) EXERCISE #2

PATTERN 4 & 5: EXERCISE #2

NAME: _____ DATE: _____

DIRECTIONS: *All of the sentences below are either N-LV-N or N-LV-ADJ. Parse and diagram the entire sentence.*

1. The young girl was terrified by the <u>guns</u> of the Nazi prison guards.

2. The <u>members</u> of her family were <u>prisoners</u> of the anti-Jewish German government in the early 1940's.

3. She was a helpless inmate of Camp Mittelsteine in Germany.

4. The prisoner identification number on her arm was 55082.

5. Riva <u>grew</u> weaker from hunger.

6. This young girl felt desperately lonely for her <u>parents</u>.

7. They were prisoners of a death camp in a <u>different</u> place.

8. The guards at Riva's camp were almost unbelievably <u>cruel</u>.

(over)

Photocopying this product is strictly prohibited by copyright law.

ANALYTICAL GRAMMAR (UNIT #8) — EXERCISE #2 - PAGE 2

9. The mere idea of escape looked hopeless.

10. Riva felt less <u>miserable</u> in the secret world of her poetry.

DIRECTIONS: Write what job the following words are doing. Choose your answers from among the following:

SUBJECT   PREDICATE NOMINATIVE   OBJECT OF THE PREPOSITION

MODIFIER   PREDICATE ADJECTIVE   VERB

SENTENCE #	WORD	JOB
1	guns	_____
2	members	_____
2	prisoners	_____
5	grew	_____
6	parents	_____
7	different	_____
8	cruel	_____
10	miserable	_____

PATTERNS 4 & 5: EXERCISE #3

NAME:_____DATE:_____

DIRECTIONS: *The sentences below represent all five sentence patterns: N-V, N-V-N, N-V-N-N, N-LV-N, and N-LV-ADJ. Parse and diagram the entire sentence.*

1. The first group of Jews in America <u>came</u> from Brazil to New Amsterdam in 1654.

2. The second Jewish <u>settlement</u> in the American colonies was the <u>village</u> of Newport in Rhode Island in 1658.

3. Jews were "an alien nation" according to some <u>ignorant</u> settlers.

4. The <u>first</u> Jews in Pennsylvania traded with the Indians along the Delaware River in 1655.

5. The devout Jews of Philadelphia built <u>themselves</u> a very beautiful <u>synagogue</u> in 1770.

6. At the time of the American Revolution, approximately 2,500 Jews lived in the American colonies.

7. This tiny Jewish <u>minority</u> became historically important during the days of our fight for freedom from Great Britain.

(over)

ANALYTICAL GRAMMAR (UNIT #8) EXERCISE #3 - PAGE 2

8. Jews played an <u>important</u> part in the revolutionary struggle from the start.

9. Jews from Europe also joined into the fight for freedom.

10. Be <u>proud</u> of these early Jewish patriots!

DIRECTIONS: *Write what job the underlined words are doing. Choose your answers from among the following:*

SUBJECT   DIRECT OBJECT   INDIRECT OBJECT   PREDICATE NOMINATIVE

OBJECT OF THE PREPOSITION   MODIFIER   PREDICATE ADJECTIVE   VERB

SENTENCE #	WORD	JOB
1	came	
2	settlement	
2	village	
3	ignorant	
4	first	
5	themselves	
5	synagogue	
7	minority	
8	important	
10	proud	

SKILLS SUPPORT

DIRECTIONS: *Below is a poem written by a young girl in a German concentration camp during World War II. Parse and diagram lines 1 and 13. Then paraphrase the entire poem.*

WHY?

Written by Riva Minska, Number 55082
Camp Mittelsteine, Germany
January 14, 1945

Translated from the Yiddish
by Ruth Minsky Sender, Free Person
New York City, U.S.A.
1980

All alone, I stare at the window

Feeling my soul in me cry

Hearing the painful screams of my heart

Calling silently: Why?

Why are your dreams scattered, destroyed?

Why are you put in this cage?

Why is the world silently watching?

Why can't they hear your rage?

Why is the barbed wire holding me prisoner,

Blocking to freedom my way?

Why do I still keep waiting and dreaming

Hoping...maybe...someday...

I see above me the snow-covered mountains

Majestic, proud, and high.

If like a free bird I could reach their peaks

Maybe from there the world will hear my cry...

Why?

ANALYTICAL GRAMMAR (UNIT #8)   TEST

PATTERNS 4 & 5: TEST

NAME:_____ DATE:_____

(RAW SCORE: _____ /248 GRADE: _____ POINTS: ____/20____)

DIRECTIONS: *The sentences below represent all five sentence patterns. Parse and diagram the entire sentence.*

1. We find the <u>history</u> of the Jews in the Bible.

2. The first of the Jewish <u>patriarchs</u> was Abraham from the land of Canaan.

3. According to the story in the Bible, God <u>gave</u> Abraham this <u>land</u> for all time.

4. Abraham's great-grandson became a <u>slave</u> to the Egyptian pharaoh.

5. Later this pharaoh became <u>dependent</u> upon Joseph for advice.

6. In time another Egyptian pharaoh enslaved all the <u>Israelites</u>.

7. This pharaoh murdered all <u>Jewish</u> male babies except one.

(over)

ANALYTICAL GRAMMAR (UNIT #8)   TEST-PAGE 2

8. That one lucky <u>baby</u> was <u>Moses</u>.

9. Moses gave the <u>Children of Israel</u> their freedom once again.

10. Moses also gave the world God's <u>Ten Commandments</u>.

DIRECTIONS: *Write what job the underlined words are doing. Choose your answers from among the following:*

SUBJECT   PREDICATE NOMINATIVE   OBJECT OF THE PREPOSITION   VERB

DIRECT OBJECT   INDIRECT OBJECT   MODIFIER   PREDICATE ADJECTIVE

SENTENCE #	WORD	JOB
1	history	_____
2	patriarchs	_____
3	gave	_____
3	land	_____
4	slave	_____
5	dependent	_____
6	Israelites	_____
7	Jewish	_____
8	baby	_____
8	Moses	_____
9	Children of Israel	_____
10	Ten Commandments	_____

ANALYTICAL GRAMMAR (UNIT #9)   NOTES-PAGE 17

HELPING VERBS

DEFINITION: A word (or words) which comes before an action or linking verb and helps form different tenses. The helping verb and the main verb make up the VERB PHRASE. (Helping verbs are sometimes called "auxiliary verbs.")

EXAMPLES: (main verb)   CRAWL
             (verb phrase)   will crawl   (*will* is the helping verb)

             (main verb)   LISTEN
             (verb phrase)   has been listening   (*has* and *been* are helping verbs)

             (main verb)   FIND
             (verb phrase)   would have been found   (*would, have,* and *been* are helping verbs)

THE BEST WAY TO LEARN HELPING VERBS IS TO MEMORIZE THEM. THEY ARE LISTED BELOW:

is	has	will	may
am	have	would	might
are	had	shall	must
was	do	should	
were	does	can	
be	did	could	
being			
been			

You may have noticed that some of the helping verbs listed above were taught to you as ACTION VERBS (such as DO and HAVE). If one of these verbs is the LAST word in the verb phrase, then it is an action verb. If, however, it is NOT the last word in the verb phrase, it is a helping verb.

              pro hv av adj   n
EXAMPLE: I will do my homework.   (*will do* is the verb phrase and *do* is an action verb.)
              pro hv adv av   adj   n
              I do not want any lunch.   (*do want* is the verb phrase and *do* is a helping verb)

You may also have noticed helping verbs in the list above which were taught to you as LINKING VERBS (is, am, are, etc.). If one of these words is the LAST word in the verb phrase, it is a linking verb; otherwise, they are helping verbs.

              pn   hv lv art   n
EXAMPLE: John will be a senior.   (*will be* is the verb phrase and *be* is a linking verb)
              pn   hv hv av   pp   n
              John will be going (to college).   (*will be going* is the verb phrase & *be* is a helping verb)

NOTE: A favorite spot for adverbs to "live" is between a helping verb and the main verb. (I should *really* do my homework.) That's why you need to know those helping verbs by heart; otherwise, you might mistake an adverb for a helping verb.

HOW TO DIAGRAM HELPING VERBS: Helping verbs are just part of the verb, so they are diagramed like this:
           pn   hv lv adj adj   n   pp adj   n
           Josephine will be my study partner (in algebra class).

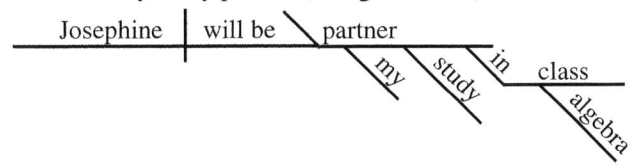

(over)

ANALYTICAL GRAMMAR (UNIT #9)   NOTES - PAGE 18

HOW TO DIAGRAM QUESTIONS: Most of the questions in our language are formed by moving the words in a statement around and putting them in a different order. Look at the following examples:

EXAMPLES: (statement)   I should do my homework.
            (question)   Should I do my homework?

Notice that, in order to form a question, the helping verb is simply moved in front of the subject.

            (statement)   He walked to school.
            (question)   Did he walk to school?

In this case, because the original statement did not have a helping verb, a helping verb is added to the sentence - again in front of the subject.

To diagram a question, the helping verb still goes in the verb slot, but it is capitalized to show that it came first in the sentence. Look at the diagram below:

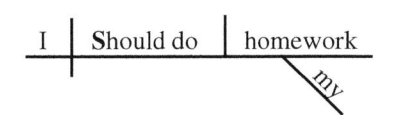

```
    I  |  Should do  |  homework
       |             \my
```

HELPING VERBS: EXERCISE #1

NAME: _____ DATE: _____

DIRECTIONS: *Parse and diagram the sentences below.*

1. Santha Rama Rau was born in India in 1923.

2. She has been writing novels for a long time.

3. Santha Rama Rau has long been famous for her superb essays.

4. She could easily have been popular for her novels also.

5. In "By Any Other Name" she has portrayed the cultural conflict in India because of the English colonization.

6. Do you know anything about cultural conflicts?

7. This essay might help you to an understanding of such conflicts.

8. Two Indian sisters were sent to a school for English children.

(over)

ANALYTICAL GRAMMAR (UNIT #9) — EXERCISE #1 - PAGE 2

9. This Anglo-Indian school had been taught by British teachers for years.

10. This British-run school must have caused many cultural problems for its Indian students.

ANALYTICAL GRAMMAR (UNIT #9)   EXERCISE #2

HELPING VERBS: EXERCISE #2

NAME: _____ DATE: _____

DIRECTIONS: *Parse and diagram the sentences below.*

1. The two sisters had been given two beautiful <u>Indian</u> names by their parents.

2. On the first day of school, the <u>teacher</u> had indicated her helplessness with Indian names.

3. Santha's new name would become <u>Cynthia</u>.

4. Premila would be known as <u>Pamela</u>.

5. The girls could not understand the reason for these <u>new</u> names.

6. They would soon understand the <u>reasons</u> for their mother's anxiety about this new English school.

7. <u>Four</u> other Indian children had been assigned to the same class with the two sisters.

(over)

Photocopying this product is strictly prohibited by copyright law.

ANALYTICAL GRAMMAR (UNIT #9)   EXERCISE #2 - PAGE 2

8. One of the other Indian girls was wearing a cotton dress instead of her native Indian <u>clothes</u>.

9. The girls <u>would ask</u> their mother about the possibility of English-style dresses for themselves.

10. Did <u>they</u> have a good reason for their desire for different clothes?

DIRECTIONS: *Write what job the underlined words are doing. Choose your answer from among the following:*

SUBJECT   DIRECT OBJECT   VERB   MODIFIER   OBJECT OF THE PREPOSITION

INDIRECT OBJECT   PREDICATE NOMINATIVE   PREDICATE ADJECTIVE

SENTENCE #	WORD	JOB
1	Indian	
2	teacher	
3	Cynthia	
4	Pamela	
5	new	
6	reasons	
7	Four	
8	clothes	
9	would ask	
10	they	

DEFINITIONS:

1. Helping verbs are verbs that come _____ main verbs to form different _____

2. Adjectives are words that _____

3. A pronoun is a word that _____

4. The helping verb and the main verb together make up the _____

ANALYTICAL GRAMMAR (UNIT #9)   EXERCISE #3

HELPING VERBS: EXERCISE #3

NAME: _____ DATE: _____

DIRECTIONS: *Parse and diagram the sentences below.*

1. That first <u>day</u> of school for the two sisters had been very difficult.

2. Santha <u>had been asked</u> by the teacher for her new name.

3. She could not remember <u>it</u>!

4. The rest of the <u>class</u> had laughed at her.

5. She had been a very embarrassed <u>girl</u>!

6. At <u>lunchtime</u> the other Indian students were eating sandwiches instead of normal Indian food.

7. At recess she could not understand the competitive <u>games</u>.

(over)

Photocopying this product is strictly prohibited by copyright law.   105

ANALYTICAL GRAMMAR (UNIT #9)   EXERCISE #3 - PAGE 2

8. At home the <u>girls</u> had been taught kindness to younger children in their games.

9. These English children did not return the <u>same</u> courtesy!

10. The two sisters would feel <u>glad</u> at the close of school on that first day.

DIRECTIONS: *Write what job the underlined words are doing. Choose your answer from among the following:*

SUBJECT   DIRECT OBJECT   VERB   MODIFIER   OBJECT OF THE PREPOSITION

INDIRECT OBJECT   PREDICATE NOMINATIVE   PREDICATE ADJECTIVBE

SENTENCE #	WORD	JOB
1	day	_____
2	had been asked	_____
3	it	_____
4	class	_____
5	girl	_____
6	lunchtime	_____
7	games	_____
8	girls	_____
9	same	_____
10	glad	_____

DEFINITIONS:

1. An antecedent is _____

2. In a noun - linkingverb - noun pattern the second noun is called the
   _____

3. In a noun - linking verb - adjective pattern the adjective is called the
   _____

4. A noun is _____

5. What are the modifiers in this sentence? _____

6. The verb phrase is made up of the _____

ANALYTICAL GRAMMAR (UNIT #9) — SKILLS SUPPORT

SKILLS SUPPORT

DIRECTIONS: Below is an exerpt from Santha Rama Rau's essay "By Any Other Name." Mark all the parts of speech that you know in the passage. Diagram "He still remains insular." Then paraphrase the entire passage.

...Mother had refused to send Premila to school in the British-run establishment of that time, because, she would say, "You can bury a dog's tail for seven years and it still comes out curly, and you can take a Britisher away from his home for a lifetime, and he still remains insular."

ANALYTICAL GRAMMAR (UNIT #9)   TEST

HELPING VERBS: TEST

NAME: _____ DATE: _____

(RAW SCORE: _____ /253 GRADE: _____ CLASS POINTS: _____ /20)

DIRECTIONS: *Parse and diagram the sentences below.*

1. On the day of Premila's first test, the girls' <u>lives</u> would change in a big way.

2. Premila had marched suddenly through the <u>door</u> of Santha's classroom.

3. "We <u>are leaving</u> this place now!"

4. Santha had been completely <u>dumbfounded</u> by Premila's behavior.

5. She could not disobey her <u>sister</u>, however.

6. "I can never attend <u>that</u> school again!"

7. On the way to their home, Santha was wondering about the reason for their sudden <u>departure</u>.

(over)

Photocopying this product is strictly prohibited by copyright law.

109

ANALYTICAL GRAMMAR (UNIT #9)   TEST - PAGE 2

8. At home, <u>Mother</u> would ask for a reason.

9. The British teacher <u>had accused</u> all the Indian students of cheating on tests!

10. To happy little Santha, however, this bad thing had happened to a girl by the name of <u>Cynthia</u>!

PART II: DIRECTIONS: *Write what jobs the underlined words are doing. Choose your answer from among the following:*   SUBJECT   VERB   DIRECT OBJECT   INDIRECT OBJECT   MODIFIER
OBJECT OF THE PREPOSITION   PREDICATE NOMINATIVE   PREDICATE ADJECTIVE

SENTENCE #	WORD	JOB
1	lives	
2	door	
3	are leaving	
4	dumbfounded	
5	sister	
6	that	
7	departure	
8	Mother	
9	had accused	
10	Cynthia	

DEFINITIONS:

1. A helping verb helps the main verb form different _____.

2. A verb is not a verb unless it has a _____.

3. Which word in this sentence is the predicate nominative? _____

4. An adjective is a word that _____.

5. A pronoun is a word that _____.

6. What is an antecedent? _____

7. What kind of noun can consist of more than one word? _____

8. The helping verb & the main verb make up the _____.

ANALYTICAL GRAMMAR (UNIT #10)　　　　　　　　　　　　　　　NOTES-PAGE 19

CONJUNCTIONS & COMPOUND SITUATIONS

A conjunction is a word (or words) that joins grammatical equals (noun to noun, verb to verb, etc.)

THERE ARE THREE KINDS OF CONJUNCTIONS:

    Coordinating conjunctions
        Correlative conjunctions
            Subordinating conjunctions (these will be covered later in Unit #16)

COORDINATING CONJUNCTIONS

and	or	for (when it means *because*)
but	nor	yet (when it means *but*)

EXAMPLES:
              conj
Anne cleaned the kitchen and the bedroom. (*and* joins 2 nouns: *kitchen* and *bedroom*)
              conj
We will go to the store and then to the cleaners. (*and* joins 2 prepositional phrases: *to the store* and *to the cleaners*)

CORRELATIVE CONJUNCTIONS

These conjunctions are always found in pairs with other words in between. They are....

either....or	both....and
neither....nor	not only....but (also)

EXAMPLES: Take special note of the way correlative conjunctions are marked.

You can take either the pie or the cake. (*either...or* joins 2 nouns: *pie* and *cake*)
          conj

The girl was both beautiful and kind. (*both...and* joins 2 predicate adjectives: *beautiful* and *kind*)
        conj

COMPOUND SITUATIONS:

A "compound situation" is when there are two (or more) of something joined by a conjunction in a sentence. Two (or more) subjects is called a "compound subject" and two or more verbs is called a "compound verb" and so forth. When you have a compound situation in a sentence diagram, you go to the place where that word (if it were only one word) would be diagramed - and then you "branch off." You make as many branches as you need to illustrate the compound situation in the sentence; so if you have a sentence with a **quadruple** subject (Kim, Tracy, Jean, and Mary all wore the same dress to the Prom), you would need four separate lines in the subject place in the diagram!

On the following pages of notes, you will find a sample diagram for all the possible compound situations you might encounter.

(over)

ANALYTICAL GRAMMAR (UNIT #10)   NOTES - PAGE 20

A. <u>COMPOUND SUBJECT:</u>   *pn conj pn   av   adv*
John and Jim walked home.

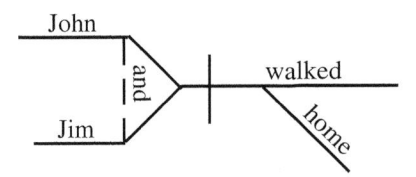

B. <u>COMPOUND VERB:</u>   EXAMPLE #1: *pn hv   av   conj   av   art   n*
John was washing and waxing the car.

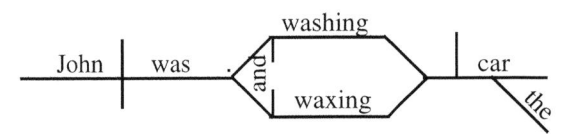

EXAMPLE #2:   *pn   av   art n conj   av   art   n*
John washed the car and mowed the lawn.

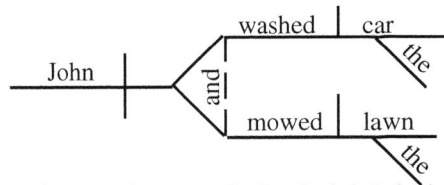

NOTE: In the first diagram above, we had to "rejoin" the base line after the compound verb because both verbs shared a direct object. In the second diagram each verb has its own direct object.

C. <u>COMPOUND DIRECT OBJECT:</u>   *pn   av   art   n   conj art adj   n*
Mom cleaned the kitchen and the living room.

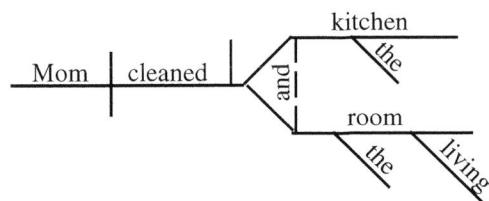

D. <u>COMPOUND INDIRECT OBJECT:</u>   *pn   av adj   n   conj pro art n*
Sally sent my brother and me a present.

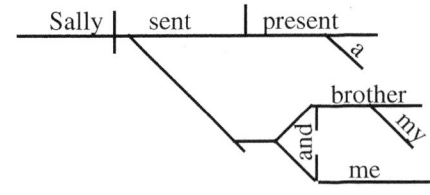

E. <u>COMPOUND PREDICATE NOMINATIVE OR PREDICATE ADJECTIVE:</u>

pro   lv   p-adj conj p-adj
She felt hungry and tired.

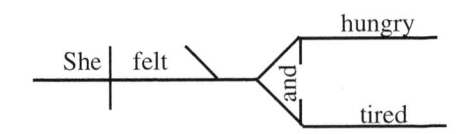

ANALYTICAL GRAMMAR (UNIT #10)   NOTES-PAGE 21

F. COMPOUND PREPOSITIONAL PHRASES:
pro av pp art n conj pp art n
We rode (over the river) and (through the woods).

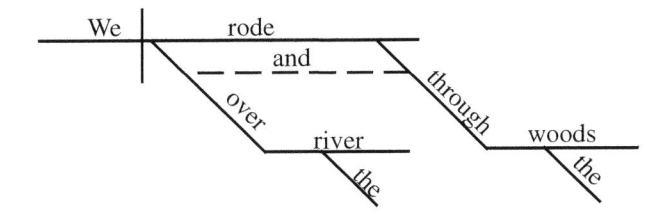

G. PREPOSITIONAL PHRASE WITH COMPOUND OBJECT: *pro av pp art adj n conj n*
She dusted (under the new table and chairs).

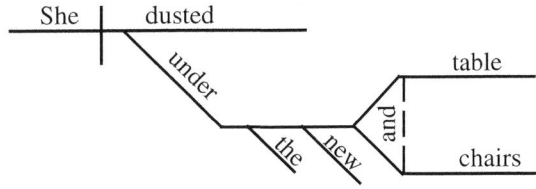

Notice that *the* and *new* are diagramed on the line that is shared by *table* and *chairs*. That's because these two modifiers modify both nouns.

H. COMPOUND SENTENCE: *pn av art n conj pn av pro*
John washed the car and Jim waxed it.

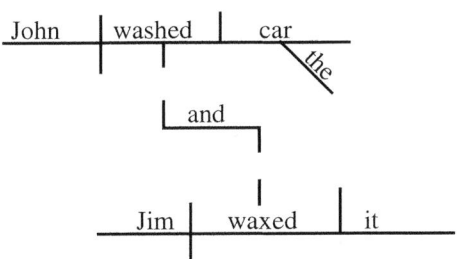

I. MULTIPLE COMPOUND SITUATIONS: *pn conj pn av conj av art n*
John and Jim washed and waxed the car.

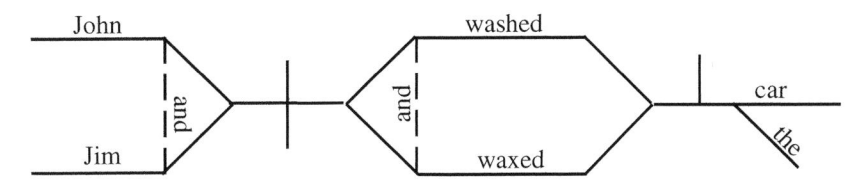

J. DIAGRAMING CORRELATIVE CONJUNCTIONS:
pn pn av adj n adv
Both Sean and Jason left their bikes outside.
↘*conj*↙

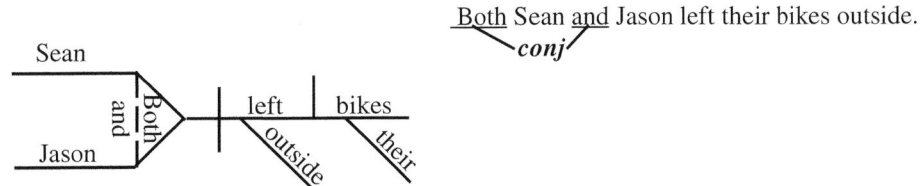

(over)

Photocopying this product is strictly prohibited by copyright law.   113

ANALYTICAL GRAMMAR (UNIT #10) NOTES - PAGE 22

K. **COMPOUND MODIFIERS:**

You learned how to diagram compound modifiers in Unit #4: Subject and Verb.

L. **THREE OR MORE OF SOMETHING:** *pn pn conj pn av n*
John, Joe, and Jim ate lunch.

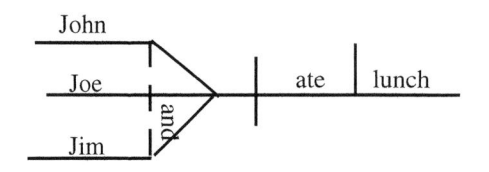

ANALYTICAL GRAMMAR (UNIT #10)   EXERCISE #1

COMPOUND SITUATIONS: EXERCISE #1

NAME: _____ DATE: _____

DIRECTIONS: *Parse and diagram the sentences below.*

1. Fairy tales and nursery rhymes entertain most American children. (See Notes A)

2. Our parents either read or tell us these favorite stories. (See Notes B - 1 & J)

3. Our first teachers tell the stories and sing the nursery rhymes with us. (See Notes B-2)

4. I loved nursery rhymes and fairy tales. (See Notes C)

5. My mother would read my brothers and me stories before bedtime. (See Notes D)

6. We were always quiet and spellbound. (See Notes E)

7. She would read them either in the living room or in our bedrooms. (See Notes F & J)

(over)

Photocopying this product is strictly prohibited by copyright law.

ANALYTICAL GRAMMAR (UNIT #10) — EXERCISE #1 - PAGE 2

8. She had special voices for the animals and characters in the stories. (See Notes G)

9. I loved "Little Red Riding Hood" and my brothers loved "Pinnochio." (See Notes H)

10. Billy, George, and I were always perfect children during story time! (See Notes L)

ANALYTICAL GRAMMAR (UNIT #10)   EXERCISE #2

COMPOUND SITUATIONS: EXERCISE #2

NAME: _____ DATE: _____

DIRECTIONS: *Parse and diagram the sentences below.*

1. Little Red Ridinghood and her mother packed her <u>basket</u> with cookies for her grandma.

2. The <u>path</u> to grandma's house went through the forest and up the hill.

3. Little Red Ridinghood ran and <u>skipped</u> down the forest path.

4. The big bad wolf waited behind a tree, and Little Red Ridinghood skipped <u>past</u>.

5. The big bad wolf jumped from the <u>bushes</u> and in front of Little Red Ridinghood.

6. The <u>wolf</u> asked Little Red Ridinghood the purpose and destination of her journey.

7. "I am going to my <u>grandma's</u>, and I am not <u>afraid</u> of you!"

(over)

Photocopying this product is strictly prohibited by copyright law.

ANALYTICAL GRAMMAR (UNIT #10)   EXERCISE #2 - PAGE 2

8. Little Red Ridinghood grabbed her basket and continued her <u>journey</u>.

9. Her grandma looked both <u>big</u> and strange to her.

10. The big bad <u>wolf</u> jumped on Little Red Ridinghood and gobbled her up!

DEFINITIONS:

1. Two or more subjects in a sentence is called a _____.

2. When the noun in front of the verb is the same thing as the noun after the verb, what kind of verb do you have?
_____

3. An adverb modifies _____, _____, and _____.

DIRECTIONS: *Write what job the underlined words are doing. Choose your answer from among the following:*

SUBJECT   DIRECT OBJECT   INDIRECT OBJECT   MODIFIER   VERB

PREDICATE NOMINATIVE   PREDICATE ADJECTIVE   OBJECT OF THE PREPOSITION

SENTENCE #	WORD	JOB
1	basket	
2	path	
3	skipped	
4	past	
5	bushes	
6	wolf	
7	grandma's	
7	afraid	
8	journey	
9	big	
10	wolf	

ANALYTICAL GRAMMAR (UNIT #10)　　　　　　　　　　　　　　　EXERCISE #3

COMPOUND SITUATIONS: EXERCISE #3

NAME: _____ DATE: _____

DIRECTIONS: *Parse and diagram the sentences below.*

1. Not only fairy tales but also nursery rhymes teach <u>children</u> values and lessons in life.

2. <u>Many</u> of our most beloved tales were written by Hans Christian Anderson and the Brothers Grimm.

3. Hans Christian Anderson <u>wrote</u> "The Ugly Duckling" and "The Little Mermaid."

4. The Brothers Grimm gave us "Little Red Ridinghood" and "<u>Hansel and Gretel</u>."

5. Hans Christian Anderson was born in <u>Denmark</u>, and the Brothers Grimm were born in Germany.

6. These fairy tales and nursery rhymes are <u>examples</u> of the strong European influence in our country's culture.

7. Most of our fairy tales come from <u>Europe</u>, but children's stories have been told in all countries and in all cultures.

(over)

Photocopying this product is strictly prohibited by copyright law.

ANALYTICAL GRAMMAR (UNIT #10) — EXERCISE #3 - PAGE 2

8. <u>Popular</u> stories come from China, India, and the Middle East.

9. <u>Interestingly,</u> all of them teach the same values and lessons to children.

DEFINITIONS:

1. A noun is a word that _____.

2. The articles in our language are _____, _____, and _____.

3. An antecedent is _____.

4. In a noun - linking verb - adjective pattern, the adjective is _____

5. List 3 jobs that a noun can do: _____
   _____

DIRECTIONS: Write what job the underlined words are doing. Choose your answer from among the following:

SUBJECT   DIRECT OBJECT   INDIRECT OBJECT   OBJECT OF THE PREPOSITION

PREDICATE NOMINATIVE   PREDICATE ADJECTIVE   MODIFIER   VERB

SENTENCE #	WORD	JOB
1	children	
2	Many	
3	wrote	
4	"Hansel and Gretel"	
5	Denmark	
6	examples	
7	Europe	
8	Popular	
9	Interestingly	

SKILLS SUPPORT

DIRECTIONS: Parse all the words in the poem below and diagram the second sentence. Then write your own version of this nursery rhyme - only this time the names are Dick and Jane. The more rhymes you change, the higher your score, so try to come up with NEW RHYMES instead of all the old ones! (NOTE: For now, treat "tumbling" as a noun.)

Jack and Jill

Went up the hill

To fetch a pail of water.

Jack fell down

And broke his crown,

And Jill came tumbling after!

ANALYTICAL GRAMMAR (UNIT #10)   TEST

COMPOUND SITUATIONS: TEST

NAME: _____ DATE: _____

(RAW SCORE: _____ /329 GRADE: _____ POINTS: _____ /20)

DIRECTIONS: *Parse and diagram the sentences below.*

1. <u>Parents</u> should read fairy tales and nursery rhymes to their <u>children</u>.

2. Not only do children love these <u>stories</u>, but they learn many valuable lessons too.

3. "The Ugly Duckling" can teach <u>children</u> kindness and tolerance of others' differences.

4. Cinderella was always <u>good</u> and patient, and she was rewarded in the end.

5. Two little pigs <u>built</u> their houses of straw and wood, but the third pig built his house of brick.

6. Good planning and hard work saved all three little <u>pigs'</u> lives.

(over)

Photocopying this product is strictly prohibited by copyright law.   123

ANALYTICAL GRAMMAR (UNIT #10)   TEST - PAGE 2

7. Snow White helped the dwarfs and escaped the evil queen's plot at the same <u>time</u>.

8. Pinocchio's lies and stories led him <u>away</u> from his father and lengthened his nose!

9. "The Emperor's New Clothes" is a story about the dangers of dishonesty and false pride.

10. <u>We</u> learn many valuable life lessons in our childhood stories and rhymes.

PART II: DIRECTIONS: *Write what job the underlined words are doing. Choose your answers from among the following:*

SUBJECT   DIRECT OBJECT   INDIRECT OBJECT   OBJECT OF THE PREPOSITION

PREDICATE NOMINATIVE   PREDICATE ADJECTIVE   VERB   MODIFIER

SENTENCE #	WORD	JOB
1	Parents	
1	children	
2	stories	
3	children	
4	good	
5	built	
6	pigs'	
7	time	
8	away	
10	We	

ANALYTICAL GRAMMAR (UNIT #10) — TEST - PAGE 3

DEFINITIONS:

1. A noun is a word that _____.

2. The articles in our language are _____

3. An adjective is a word that _____

4. A pronoun is a word that _____

5. An antecedent is _____.

6. A verb isn't a real verb unless it has a _____.

7. True or False: A direct object occurs with a linking verb. _____

8. In a N-LV-N sentence, the 2nd noun is called the _____.

9. An adverb is a word that _____.

10. Prepositional phrases do the job of _____.

11. A word can't be a preposition unless it's in a _____.

12. Two or more subjects in a sentence is called a _____.

13. The helping verb(s) and the main verb make up the _____.

14. Write an example of a correlative conjunction: _____.

15. The adjective following a linking verb is called _____.

Congratulations on completing the first season of Analytical Grammar! If you are spreading the program out over two or three years, make sure you stop here and do worksheets from the Reinforcement & Review book according to the timeline. You can find the timelines in our catalog or at www.analyticalgrammar.com.

Season Two

PARTICIPIAL PHRASES

For the next three units we'll be learning about those verbals we talked about back in Unit #4. There are three verbals in our language: participles, gerunds, and infinitives. This unit is about the participle.

DEFINITION: A participial phrase is a group of words beginning with a participle which acts as an ADJECTIVE.

    A participle is a verb form that acts like an adjective. There are two kinds of participles:
1.) PRESENT PARTICIPLES are verbs that end in "ing." (giving, taking, being, etc.)
2.) PAST PARTICIPLES are verbs that will fit into the phrase "I have ____" (walked, given, done, been, etc.)

If you found a participle all by itself in a sentence, you would call it an adjective because that is how it acts. You would also diagram it as a regular adjective.

EXAMPLE: art adj   n   av pro
                  A smiling policeman helped us.

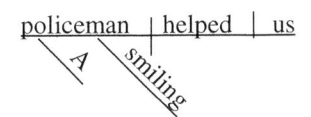

If, however, your participle comes in a PHRASE, it must be diagramed in a special way. You know you have a PARTICIPIAL PHRASE when your verb form acts like a verb as well as an adjective. For example, it may have a direct object, etc.

Since a participial phrase acts like an adjective, it is attached in the diagram to the noun or pronoun it modifies. The pattern looks like this (it's called a "dogleg"):

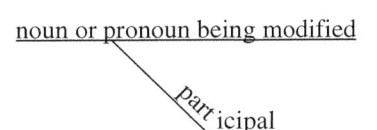

The following example diagrams show you what to do when you have a—

A.   PARTICIPLE WITH DIRECT OBJECT:

    EXAMPLE: art n   v   art adj   n   hv   av
                        A box containing a birthday gift was delivered.

(notice that the participle is marked "v" - not "av" - because it's a verbal.)

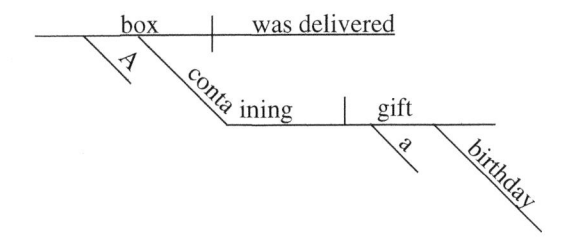

(over)

B. PARTICIPLE WITH MODIFIERS:

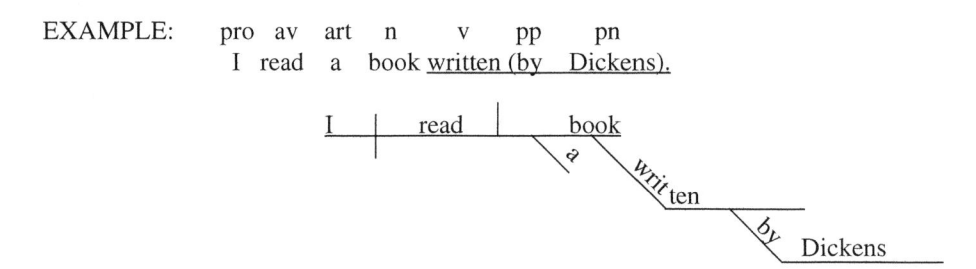

EXAMPLE: pro av art   n   v   pp   pn
                 I   read   a   book <u>written (by   Dickens)</u>.

C. PARTICIPIAL PHRASE WITH PREDICATE NOMINATIVE OR ADJECTIVE:

EXAMPLE: v   p-adj   art   n   hv   av   pp   pn
                <u>Smelling delicious</u>, the turkey was carved (by Dad).

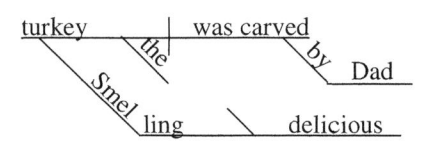

IMPORTANT: A participial phrase is an adjective. It can modify any noun or pronoun in the sentence. By the way, when a participial phrase is INTRODUCTORY (in other words, it comes at the beginning of the sentence), it is set off from the rest of the sentence by a comma.

ANALYTICAL GRAMMAR (UNIT #11)   EXERCISE #1

PARTICIPIAL PHRASES: EXERCISE #1

NAME:_____ DATE:_____

PART I: DIRECTIONS: *Look at each verb below. If it looks like a PRESENT PARTICIPLE, mark "pres" in the space at the left. If it looks like a PAST PARTICIPLE, mark "past." If the verb could not possibly be a participle, write "verb."*

_____1. spinning   _____6. win

_____2. was   _____7. behave

_____3. heard   _____8. placed

_____4. has gone   _____9. look

_____5. having   _____10. could

PART II: DIRECTIONS: *Parse the sentences below and put prepositional phrases in parentheses. Underline the participial phrases. Diagram the sentences. CHECK THE BACK FOR ADDITIONAL WORK.*

1. Outrunning the hounds, the fox easily escaped.

2. I saw him fishing contentedly by the river.

3. Tackled on the one-yard line, the quarterback fumbled the ball.

4. Wildly cheering for the team, we celebrated their victory.

5. The clerk handed the customer a box wrapped in white paper and tied with red ribbon.

6. Balancing a book on her head, the girl walked slowly across the room.

7. The professor wrote a note expressing her approval of the plan.

8. The children found an arrowhead buried on the riverbank.

PART III: DIRECTIONS:
   1.) *Make up a participial phrase to modify the SUBJECT of the following sentence. Diagram your completed sentence.*

          THE COACH SIGNALLED A TIME-OUT.

   2.) *Make up a participial phrase to modify the DIRECT OBJECT of the following sentence. Diagram your completed sentence.*

          I HAVE THREE FRIENDS.

(over)

Photocopying this product is strictly prohibited by copyright law.

ANALYTICAL GRAMMAR (UNIT #11) EXERCISE #1 - PAGE 2

Write what job the following words are doing in the sentences in PART II. Choose your answers from among the following:

SUBJECT   PREDICATE NOMINATIVE   OBJECT OF THE PREPOSITION   DIRECT OBJECT   VERB

INDIRECT OBJECT   PREDICATE ADJECTIVE   MODIFIER

SENTENCE #	WORD	JOB
1	fox	_____
2	contentedly	_____
3	line	_____
4	Wildly	_____
5	customer	_____
5	box	_____
6	girl	_____
7	wrote	_____

ANALYTICAL GRAMMAR (UNIT #11)   EXERCISE #2

PARTICIPIAL PHRASES: EXERCISE #2

NAME:_____DATE:_____

PART I: DIRECTIONS: *Parse the sentences below and put prepositional phrases in parentheses. Underline the participial phrases. Diagram the entire sentence.*

1. Smiling happily at the audience, the actress accepted the flowers.

2. Did you see Fred riding his bicycle today?

3. The cake, baked by a master chef and beautifully decorated, was the hit of the party.

4. Being a devout coward, I naturally avoid any contact with violent people.

5. Please read three books written by American authors during this year.

6. Screeching at the top of her lungs, Tillie hit the man with her bag.

7. Give the lady seated by my mother this glass of lemonade.

8. Choosing a huge piece of chocolate from the box, Mimi yawned lazily and continued her reading.

PART II: DIRECTIONS: *Make up a participial phrase to modify the INDIRECT OBJECT of the following sentence.*

        I TOLD THE STUDENTS A STORY.

(over)

ANALYTICAL GRAMMAR (UNIT #11)   EXERCISE #2 - PAGE 2

DIRECTIONS: Write what job the following words are doing in the sentences in PART I. Choose your answers from among the following:

SUBJECT	PREDICATE NOMINATIVE	OBJECT OF THE PREPOSITION
DIRECT OBJECT	INDIRECT OBJECT	MODIFIER	PREDICATE ADJECTIVE	VERB

SENTENCE #	WORD	JOB
1	flowers	_____
2	bicycle	_____
3	hit	_____
4	coward	_____
4	contact	_____
5	books	_____
6	lungs	_____
7	lady	_____
7	glass	_____
8	lazily	_____

ANALYTICAL GRAMMAR (UNIT #11)   EXERCISE #3

PARTICIPIAL PHRASES: EXERCISE #3

NAME:_____ DATE:_____

PART I: DIRECTIONS: *Parse the sentences below and put prepositional phrases in parentheses. Underline the participial phrases. Diagram the entire sentence.*

1. Carrying a large package, the messenger stumbled across the room.

2. The dog, attracted by the smell of meat, trotted over to the stranger.

3. The men playing golf at the country club helped us.

4. We noticed an old cowboy tanned deeply by the sun.

5. The store was packed with customers Christmas shopping and looking for bargains.

6. Feeling suddenly bored by her guests, the hostess stifled a yawn.

7. Which of those men wearing suits is your boss?

8. Bring me a sundae smothered in hot fudge and whipped cream.

9. Did a lady carrying a baby just run by this house?

10. Easily tired since her operation, Emily rested after lunch in her room.

PART II: DIRECTIONS:
　　1.) *Make up a participial phrase to modify the PREDICATE NOMINATIVE of the following sentence. Diagram your completed sentence.*

　　　　HE WAS AN OLD MAN.

　　2.) *Make up a participial phrase to modify the OBJECT OF THE PREPOSITION in the following sentence. Diagram your completed sentence.*

　　　　I SENT A LETTER TO MY AUNT.

(over)

Photocopying this product is strictly prohibited by copyright law.

ANALYTICAL GRAMMAR (UNIT #11)   EXERCISE #3 - PAGE 2

DIRECTIONS: Write what job the following words are doing in the sentenceS in PART I. Choose your answers from among the following:

SUBJECT   OBJECT OF THE PREPOSITION   PREDICATE NOMINATIVE

DIRECT OBJECT   INDIRECT OBJECT   MODIFIER   PREDICATE ADJECTIVE   VERB

SENTENCE #	WORD	JOB
1	package	_____
2	meat	_____
2	stranger	_____
3	men	_____
3	us	_____
4	deeply	_____
5	was packed	_____
6	bored	_____
7	suits	_____
8	hot	_____
9	house	_____
10	Emily	_____

ANALYTICAL GRAMMAR (UNIT #11) — TEST

PARTICIPIAL PHRASES: TEST

NAME:_____ PERIOD:_____ DATE:_____

(Raw Score:_____/309 Grade:_____ Points:_____/20)

PART I: DIRECTIONS: *Parse the sentences below and put parentheses around the prepositional phrases. Underline the participial phrases. Diagram the sentences. CHECK THE BACK FOR MORE WORK.*

1. Please introduce me to that man wearing the blue sweater.

2. The thief was either that man carrying the briefcase or that boy with the bike.

3. Painted in oils, the picture was very beautiful.

4. Yesterday we heard speeches given by the major political candidates.

5. I sent my cousin living in Germany a graduation announcement.

6. Winding the clock and putting the cat out, the old man prepared for bed.

7. It was a marriage made in heaven.

8. Becoming conscious of the smoke, the boy looked around him for a fire.

9. Is the woman wearing that fur coat your aunt?

10. The boy, munching on a large roll, ambled slowly down the street.

(over)

ANALYTICAL GRAMMAR (UNIT #11)   TEST - PAGE 2

PART II: DIRECTIONS: Write what job each word is doing. Choose your answers from among the following:

SUBJECT   DIRECT OBJECT   PREDICATE NOMINATIVE   INDIRECT OBJECT

OBJECT OF THE PREPOSITION   MODIFIER   PREDICATE ADJECTIVE   VERB

SENTENCE #	WORD	JOB
1	introduce	
1	sweater	
2	man	
3	beautiful	
4	we	
4	speeches	
5	cousin	
5	announcement	
6	clock	
7	It	
7	marriage	
8	conscious	
9	fur	
9	aunt	
10	boy	
10	roll	

ANALYTICAL GRAMMAR (UNIT #12) NOTES-PAGE 25

GERUND PHRASES

DEFINITION: A **GERUND** is a verb ending in "ing" which is used as a noun.

    EXAMPLE: **v or n**   **lv**   **adj**   **n**
                    Walking   is   good   exercise.

"Walking," which is usually thought of as a verb, is the subject of the above N-LV-N sentence.

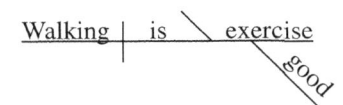

    A gerund can do any job a noun can do: subject, direct object, predicate nominative, indirect object, or object of the preposition.

    But sometimes gerunds behave like verbs, too. They can, for example, take a direct object, etc. When they behave like verbs - as well as nouns - they are called **GERUND PHRASES** and must be diagramed in a special way.

    The gerund phrase goes on a little "stilt" up above the place in the sentence for the noun the gerund phrase is substituting. For example, if the gerund phrase is a subject, the stilt goes in the subject space; if it is a direct object, the stilt goes in the direct object space; etc. Here are some examples of various types of gerund phrases doing various types of jobs:

A. <u>GERUND PHRASE AS A SUBJECT</u>

        v   adj   n   adv   lv   adj   n
    Walking your dog daily is good exercise.

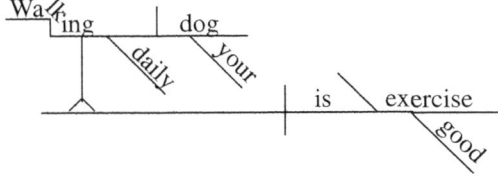

B. <u>GERUND PHRASE AS DIRECT OBJECT</u>

    pn   av   v   art   n
    John loves walking the dog.

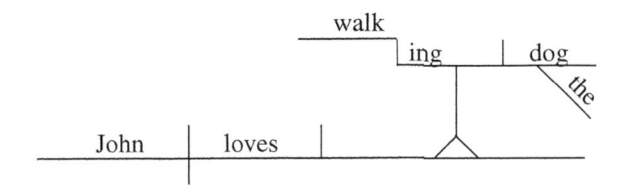

(over)

ANALYTICAL GRAMMAR (UNIT #12) NOTES - PAGE 26

C. GERUND PHRASE AS PREDICATE NOMINATIVE

```
    adj     adj    n   lv   v    art   n
John's favorite chore is walking the dog.
```

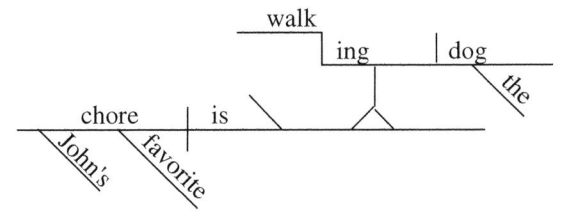

D. GERUND PHRASE AS OBJECT OF THE PREPOSITION

```
 pn   lv   p-adj    pp    v    art  n
John  is  crazy ( about walking the dog.)
```

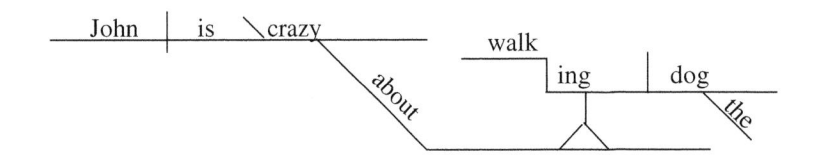

E. GERUND PHRASE AS INDIRECT OBJECT

```
 pn    av      v     art  n   adj    adj    n
John calls walking the dog his favorite chore.
```

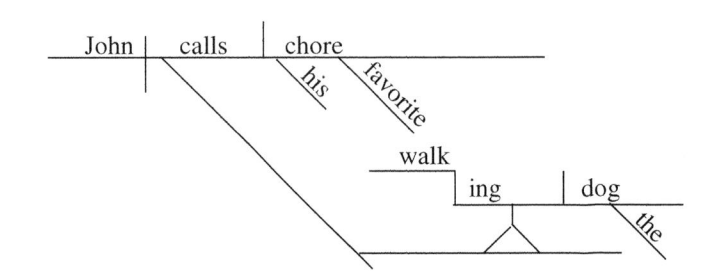

138 *Photocopying this product is strictly prohibited by copyright law.*

GERUND PHRASES: EXERCISE #1

NAME:_____ DATE:_____

DIRECTIONS: *Parse the sentences below and put prepositional phrases in parentheses. Underline the gerund phrases. Diagram the sentences.*

1. Writing essays is a major part of our course.

2. Playing the radio at night may disturb others.

3. I have always enjoyed playing chess.

4. The thief got in by telling the guard a lie.

5. His hobby has always been arguing politics heatedly with his friends.

6. The class gave me practice in speaking Spanish.

7. Mortimer gives playing the guitar a bad name.

8. Molly's rattling the dishes in the kitchen awakened the baby.

9. Her favorite pastime is telling everyone her troubles.

10. I dislike teasing the little boy.

(over)

ANALYTICAL GRAMMAR (UNIT #12) — EXERCISE #1 - PAGE 2

DIRECTIONS: *Write what jobs the following words are doing. Choose your answers from among the following:*

SUBJECT   PREDICATE NOMINATIVE   DIRECT OBJECT   INDIRECT OBJECT

OBJECT OF THE PREPOSITION   PREDICATE ADJECTIVE   MODIFIER   VERB

SENTENCE #	WORD	JOB
1	essays	
1	part	
2	others	
3	I	
4	guard	
5	heatedly	
6	me	
7	guitar	
8	Molly's rattling the dishes in the kitchen	
9	pastime	
9	everyone	
10	boy	

ANALYTICAL GRAMMAR (UNIT #12) EXERCISE #2

GERUND PHRASES: EXERCISE #2

NAME:_____ DATE:_____

DIRECTIONS: *Parse the sentences below and put prepositional phrases in parentheses. Underline the participial phrases ONCE and the gerund phrases TWICE. Diagram the sentences.*

1. Being a man with a big heart, Jim likes helping people.

2. Giving a dollar to the man begging in the street was the wealthy woman's act of charity for the day.

3. My counselor, carefully trained in psychology, considers sharing your troubles with a friend a good idea.

4. Being an incurable romantic, I love walking in the moonlight.

5. Crying in the movies usually embarrasses people caught in the act.

6. The last act of their day spent in the desert was watching the sunset from the mesa.

(over)

Photocopying this product is strictly prohibited by copyright law. **141**

ANALYTICAL GRAMMAR (UNIT #12) — EXERCISE #2 - PAGE 2

SUBJECT   PREDICATE NOMINATIVE   DIRECT OBJECT   INDIRECT OBJECT

OBJECT OF THE PREPOSITION   PREDICATE ADJECTIVE   MODIFIER   VERB

SENTENCE #	WORD	JOB
1	man	
1	people	
2	man	
2	woman's	
2	charity	
3	idea	
4	incurable	
4	romantic	
5	usually	
5	act	
6	desert	

GERUND PHRASES: EXERCISE #3

NAME:_____ DATE:_____

DIRECTIONS: *Parse the sentences below and put parentheses around the prepositional phrases. Underline the participial phrases ONCE and the gerund phrases TWICE. Diagram the sentences.*

1. Flowers picked especially for the occasion were used for decorating the ballroom.

2. My hobby, developed over many years, is embroidering samplers on linen.

3. Mr. Gardner enjoys reading books written in the 18th century.

4. Fluently speaking a foreign language gives anyone interested in a diplomatic career a distinct advantage.

5. Many students attending college in the Thirties made swallowing goldfish a huge fad.

6. I helped Mrs. Willows by visiting her little boy cooped up in the hospital.

(over)

ANALYTICAL GRAMMAR (UNIT #12)   EXERCISE #3 - PAGE 2

DIRECTIONS: *Write what jobs the following words are doing. Choose your answers from among the following:*

SUBJECT   PREDICATE NOMINATIVE   DIRECT OBJECT   INDIRECT OBJECT

OBJECT OF THE PREPOSITION   PREDICATE ADJECTIVE   MODIFIER   VERB

SENTENCE #	WORD	JOB
1	occasion	
1	ballroom	
2	hobby	
2	many	
3	books	
4	language	
4	advantage	
5	made	
5	fad	
6	boy	
6	hospital	

ANALYTICAL GRAMMAR (UNIT #12)　　　　　　　　　　　　　　　TEST

GERUND PHRASES: TEST

NAME:_____DATE:_____

(Raw Score:_____ /398 Grade:_____Points:_____ /20)

DIRECTIONS: *Parse the sentences below and put parentheses around the prepositional phrases. Underline the participial phrases once and the gerund phrases twice. Diagram the sentences.*

1. Photographing big game in Africa is the profession of that man wearing the brown jacket.

2. The students seated in the auditorium hated hearing the bell for class.

3. Ringing the church bells is the danger signal chosen by the villagers.

4. His excuse for breaking the law sounded ridiculous to the officer writing the ticket.

5. I was sick of studying algebra, but I expected a good grade on the test given by Mr. Wolf.

6. My cousin going to boarding school makes playing tricks on people his major pastime.

7. The car, speeding down a narrow road, just missed hitting a child.

8. By ironing her dress, Jan helped her friend catching the early plane.

9. My horse, recently broken to the saddle, enjoys exploring the bridle paths with me.

10. Mother, accustomed to large groups of people, adores planning parties.

(over)

Photocopying this product is strictly prohibited by copyright law.　　145

ANALYTICAL GRAMMAR (UNIT #12) — TEST - PAGE 2

PART II: DIRECTIONS: Write what jobs the following words are doing. Choose your answers from among the following:

SUBJECT	PREDICATE NOMINATIVE	DIRECT OBJECT	INDIRECT OBJECT
OBJECT OF THE PREPOSITION	PREDICATE ADJECTIVE	MODIFIER	VERB

SENTENCE #	WORD	JOB
1	game	____
1	Africa	____
1	profession	____
1	brown	____
2	hated	____
3	signal	____
4	excuse	____
4	law	____
4	ridiculous	____
5	sick	____
5	expected	____
5	grade	____
6	boarding	____
6	people	____
7	missed	____
7	child	____
8	Jan	____
9	horse	____
10	people	____

INFINITIVE PHRASES

DEFINITION: An infinitive is a verb form, almost always preceded by "to," which is used as a noun, adjective, or adverb.

    EXAMPLES: Lydia refused to help. ("to help" is the direct object, a noun's job)

    That was a day to remember. ("to remember" modifies "day," an adjectives job)

    The senator rose to speak. ("to speak" modifies the verb "rose," an adverb's job)

Sometimes an infinitive behaves like a verb, too. It may take, for example, a direct object or be modified by an adverb. When this occurs, we call it an INFINITIVE PHRASE. Infinitives and infinitive phrases must be diagramed in a special way, depending on the job they are doing.

A.   WHEN AN INFINITIVE IS A NOUN:

    EXAMPLE: -v-   pp art pn lv adj n
                    To enlist (in the Navy) is his plan.

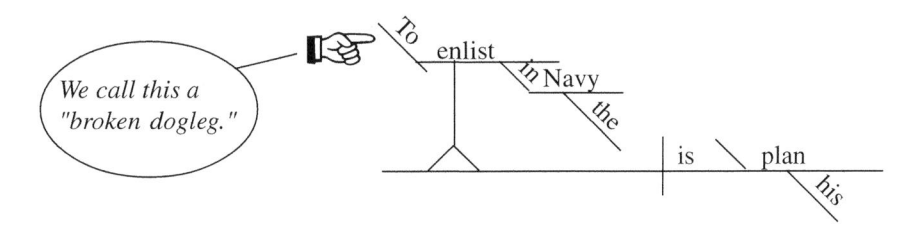

We call this a "broken dogleg."

When an infinitive is a noun, your "stilt" and "broken dogleg" go above the space where that noun would go ordinarily. It can be a subject, a direct object, or a predicate nominative. The other parts of the infinitive phrase are diagramed as if the infinitive were the verb of a sentence (for example, the infinitive's direct object is diagramed as a direct object, etc.)

B.   WHEN AN INFINITIVE IS A MODIFIER:

    EXAMPLE: pro hv av -v- art n
                    We are going to see the parade.

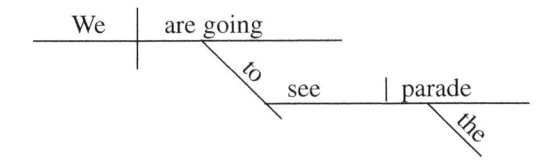

When an infinitive is a modifier, your "broken dogleg" goes underneath the word that the infinitive modifies.

(over)

ANALYTICAL GRAMMAR (UNIT #13) NOTES - PAGE 28

C. **INFINITIVE WITHOUT THE "TO"**:

Sometimes the "to" is "understood" in an infinitive.

EXAMPLE: pn   av   v   art n
               Dad helped <u>bake the cake</u>.

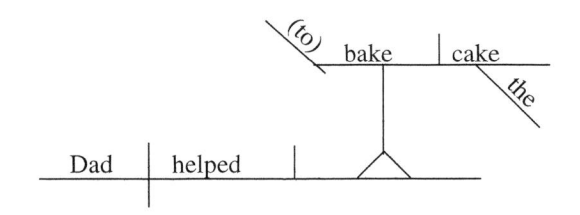

D. **WHEN AN INFINITIVE HAS A SUBJECT**:

The infinitive is the only one of the VERBALS which may have a subject. When it does, it is called an INFINITIVE CLAUSE. (We'll discuss clauses further in Units 19 - 21.) See below how to diagram it.

EXAMPLE: pro   av   pro -v- pro   pp   adj   n
               I wanted <u>him to help me (with my algebra</u>.)

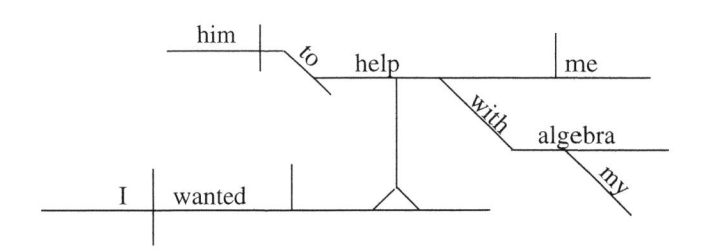

HINT: Whenever you spot a noun or a pronoun in front of your infinitive, always ask yourself, "Is that noun or pronoun DOING THE ACTION of the infinitive?" If the answer is yes, then you have a subject for your infinitive; in other words, you have an infinitive clause.

ANALYTICAL GRAMMAR (UNIT #13) EXERCISE #1

INFINITIVE PHRASES: EXERCISE #1

NAME:_____ DATE:_____

DIRECTIONS: *Parse the sentences below and put parentheses around the prepositional phrases. Underline the infinitives and infinitives phrases. Diagram the sentences. CHECK THE BACK FOR MORE WORK.*

1. To give advice is a simple matter.

2. We were hoping to solve the puzzle.

3. James plans to go.

4. I went to the library to look for him.

5. The best way to keep a secret is to forget it.

6. They started to discuss the plans for the dance.

7. I could feel the impulse to scream.

8. To be a good friend is an important thing.

9. Phil and Claude helped move the couch.

10. The door is difficult to open.

(over)

Photocopying this product is strictly prohibited by copyright law. **149**

ANALYTICAL GRAMMAR (UNIT #13)   EXERCISE #1 - PAGE 2

DIRECTIONS: Write what job the following words are doing. Choose your answers from among the following:

| SUBJECT | PREDICATE NOMINATIVE | DIRECT OBJECT | INDIRECT OBJECT |
| OBJECT OF THE PREPOSITION | PREDICATE ADJECTIVE | MODIFIER | VERB |

SENTENCE #	WORD	JOB
1	To give advice	
1	matter	
2	were hoping	
3	to go	
4	him	
5	to keep a secret	
6	plans	
7	impulse	
8	important	
9	move the couch	
10	difficult	

INFINITIVE PHRASES: EXERCISE #2

NAME:_____DATE:_____

DIRECTIONS: *Parse the sentences below and put parentheses around the prepositional phrases. Underline the infinitives and infinitive phrases. Diagram the sentences. CHECK THE BACK FOR MORE WORK.*

1. We hope to leave immediately after school.

2. Cathy did not dare tell us the bad news.

3. We are going to see the parade coming down Main Street.

4. Hearing our footsteps, Fido ran to greet us.

5. To reach the fifth floor, take the other stairs.

6. After hearing her speech, I decided to become a doctor.

7. Have we done everything except wash the dishes?

8. The man digging in the quarry helped find our baseball.

9. The girls living in my neighborhood want to start a softball team.

10. It is sometimes embarrassing to ask directions.

(over)

ANALYTICAL GRAMMAR (UNIT #13) EXERCISE #2 - PAGE 2

DIRECTIONS: *Write what job the following words are doing. Choose your answers from among the following:*

SUBJECT   PREDICATE NOMINATIVE   DIRECT OBJECT   INDIRECT OBJECT

OBJECT OF THE PREPOSITION   PREDICATE ADJECTIVE   MODIFIER   VERB

SENTENCE #	WORD	JOB
1	immediately	_____
2	tell us the bad news	_____
3	parade	_____
4	Hearing our footsteps	_____
5	stairs	_____
6	hearing her speech	_____
7	everything	_____
8	baseball	_____
9	to start a softball team	_____
10	embarrassing	_____

ANALYTICAL GRAMMAR (UNIT #13)   EXERCISE #3

INFINITIVE PHRASES: EXERCISE #3

NAME:_____DATE:_____

DIRECTIONS: *Parse the sentences below and put parentheses around the prepositional phrases. Underline the infinitives and infinitive phrases. Diagram the sentences. CHECK THE BACK FOR MORE WORK.*

1. Persons untrained in scuba diving are not allowed to demonstrate the equipment.

2. To write poetry requires a good vocabulary.

3. We are helping Bob to paint his house.

4. We are learning to diagram sentences containing phrases.

5. To interrupt a person speaking to you is impolite.

6. We needed the vet to see Prince's leg at once.

7. She is the person to see about the job advertised in the paper.

8. Did you see the center foul our man?

9. They were glad to hear his voice coming over the phone.

10. Mom will not let us swim immediately after lunch.

(over)

Photocopying this product is strictly prohibited by copyright law.   153

ANALYTICAL GRAMMAR (UNIT #13)　　　　　　　　　　EXERCISE #3 - PAGE 2

DIRECTIONS: *Write what job the following words are doing. Choose your answers from among the following:*

SUBJECT　　　　PREDICATE NOMINATIVE　　　DIRECT OBJECT　　　INDIRECT OBJECT

OBJECT OF THE PREPOSITION　　　PREDICATE ADJECTIVE　　　MODIFIER　　VERB

SENTENCE #	WORD	JOB
1	untrained in scuba diving	
2	To write poetry	
3	Bob	
4	phrases	
5	speaking to you	
6	the vet to see Prince's leg at once	
7	advertised in the paper	
8	man	
9	glad	
10	lunch	

ANALYTICAL GRAMMAR (UNIT #13)   TEST

INFINITIVE PHRASES: TEST

NAME:_____ DATE:_____

(Raw Score:_____/308 Grade:_____Points:_____/20___)

PART I: DIRECTIONS: *Parse the sentences below and put prepositional phrases in parentheses. Underline the INFINITIVE PHRASES and INFINITIVE CLAUSES. Diagram the sentences. CHECK THE BACK FOR MORE WORK.*

1. My father helped me to wash the car.

2. Dad does not want to go out after dinner.

3. Did you hear Rochelle sing your favorite song yesterday?

4. I am expecting to meet the six-o'clock train arriving here today.

5. To see movie stars was our main motive for going to Hollywood.

6. It is often necessary in a crowded bus to step very carefully.

7. The young lady wearing the plaid coat is trying to look interested in the game.

8. Did you see the team play their championship game?

9. Jack dared us to walk by the haunted house at midnight.

10. Jim wanted to tell us a ghost story especially designed for scaring people.

(over)

ANALYTICAL GRAMMAR (REVIEW UNIT #13) TEST - PAGE 2

PART II: DIRECTIONS: Write what job each of the following words is doing. Choose your answers from among the following:

SUBJECT   PREDICATE NOMINATIVE   DIRECT OBJECT   INDIRECT OBJECT

OBJECT OF THE PREPOSITION   PREDICATE ADJECTIVE   MODIFIER   VERB

SENTENCE #	WORD	JOB
1	me	
2	not	
2	dinner	
3	yesterday	
4	am expecting	
4	arriving here today	
5	To see movie stars	
5	going to Hollywood	
6	It	
6	necessary	
6	very	
7	wearing a plaid coat	
8	you	
8	game	
9	house	
10	us	
10	scaring people	

156

ANALYTICAL GRAMMAR (UNIT #14)   NOTES-PAGE 29

APPOSITIVE PHRASES

DEFINITION: An **APPOSITIVE** is a noun or a pronoun which usually follows another noun or pronoun and **RESTATES** it to help identify or explain it. When the appositive has modifiers, it is called an **APPOSITIVE PHRASE.**

   EXAMPLE: Jimmy, a star athlete, will surely get a scholarship to college.

   "a star athlete" restates who Jimmy is. It is an appositive phrase.

   Occasionally, the appositive or appositive phrase comes in front of the noun being restated.

   EXAMPLE: A man of integrity, Mr. Aldritch never cheats anyone.

THE PATTERN FOR DIAGRAMING AN APPOSITIVE PHRASE IS BELOW:

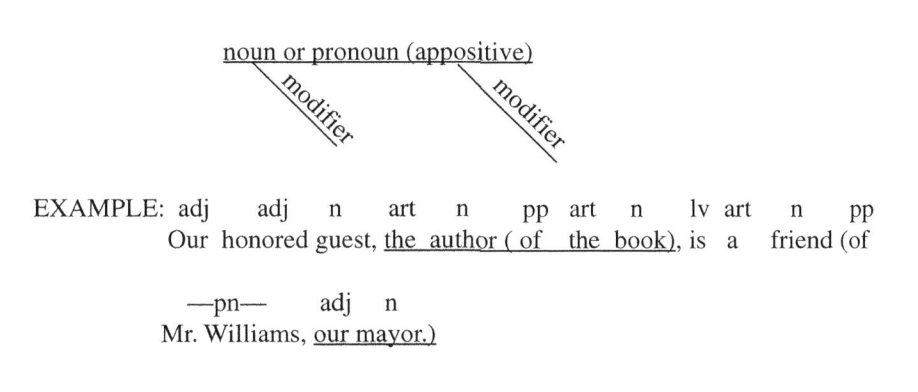

                noun or pronoun (appositive)
                   /   \
              modifier   modifier

   EXAMPLE: adj   adj   n   art   n   pp art   n   lv art   n   pp
             Our honored guest, the author (of the book), is   a   friend (of

             —pn—   adj   n
             Mr. Williams, our mayor.)

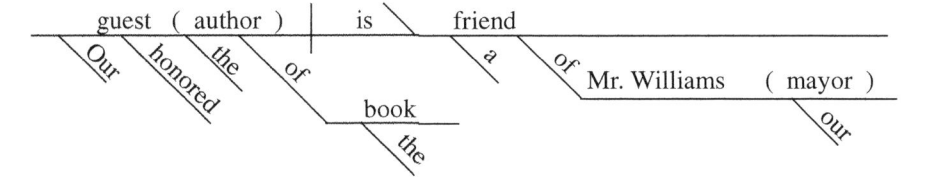

```
       guest ( author )  |  is  \  friend
      /  /    /   \         \         \
    Our honored the  of       a         of  Mr. Williams  ( mayor )
                      \                                      \
                      book                                    our
                       \
                       the
```

APPOSITIVE PHRASES: EXERCISE #1

NAME:_____DATE:_____

DIRECTIONS: *Parse the sentences below and put prepositional phrases in parentheses. Underline the appositives and appositive phrases. Diagram the sentences. CHECK THE BACK FOR MORE WORK.*

1. Our school has a dramatic club, the Thespian Society.

2. Mrs. Hinckley, an English teacher, is the club sponsor.

3. Officers of the club, mostly upperclassmen, planned a program for the next assembly.

4. The program was presented on Tuesday, the day of our weekly meeting.

5. Jim Carson, the program chairman, introduced David Haynes, director of the city's repertory company.

6. From Nina Mason, president of the Thespian Society, Mr. Haynes received our award of merit, a plaque designed by club members.

(over)

ANALYTICAL GRAMMAR (UNIT #14) EXERCISE #1 - PAGE 2

DIRECTIONS: Write what job each of the words below is doing. Choose your answers from among the following:

SUBJECT   PREDICATE NOMINATIVE   DIRECT OBJECT   INDIRECT OBJECT

OBJECT OF THE PREPOSITION   PREDICATE ADJECTIVE   MODIFIER   VERB

SENTENCE #	WORD	JOB
1	school	_____
2	English	_____
2	sponsor	_____
3	program	_____
4	Tuesday	_____
5	introduced	_____
6	Nina Mason	_____

ANALYTICAL GRAMMAR (UNIT #14)	EXERCISE #2

APPOSITIVE PHRASES: EXERCISE #2

NAME:_____DATE:_____

DIRECTIONS: *Parse the sentences below and put prepositional phrases in parentheses. Underline the appositives and appositive phrases. Diagram the sentences. CHECK THE BACK FOR MORE WORK.*

1. Jason, my little nephew, still enjoys hearing nursery rhymes.

2. My friend Mary Jo will visit us before leaving for Europe.

3. Carolyn Keene, the author of the Nancy Drew stories, is a popular writer with young people interested in mysteries.

4. Have you met Marie Ritterman, my best friend?

5. Science, my favorite class taken this year, gets more fascinating with each month.

6. The Randolph twins, members of the track team, have to report for practice soon.

7. Archimedes, a Greek physicist, supposedly made one of his discoveries in the bathtub.

(over)

Photocopying this product is strictly prohibited by copyright law. 161

ANALYTICAL GRAMMAR (UNIT #14)   EXERCISE #2 - PAGE 2

DIRECTIONS: Write what job each of the following words is doing. Choose your answers from among the following:

SUBJECT   DIRECT OBJECT   INDIRECT OBJECT   PREDICATE NOMINATIVE

OBJECT OF THE PREPOSITION   PREDICATE ADJECTIVE   MODIFIER   VERB

SENTENCE #	WORD	JOB
1	hearing nursery rhymes	
2	will visit	
3	writer	
3	mysteries	
4	best	
5	Science	
5	fascinating	
6	soon	
7	supposedly	

APPOSITIVE PHRASES: EXERCISE #3

NAME:_____DATE:_____

DIRECTIONS: *Parse the sentences below and put parentheses around the prepositional phrases. Underline the appositives and appositive phrases. Diagram the sentences. CHECK THE BACK FOR MORE WORK.*

1. The boy living next door loved to work on his car, a dilapidated old wreck.

2. Only two of the animals, a horse and a cow, were saved from the fire started by lightning.

3. A black funnel-shaped cloud, sign of a tornado, forced the family to hide in the cellar.

4. *Little Women*, a favorite book for young people, was a part of my education considered absolutely necessary.

5. Mr. Chang, my geography teacher, once visited natives living deep in the jungles of the Amazon Valley.

6. Catching a sailfish is the goal of my uncle, Ray Belson of Richmond, Virginia.

(over)

ANALYTICAL GRAMMAR (UNIT #14)   EXERCISE #3 - PAGE 2

DIRECTIONS: *Write what job each of the following words is doing. Choose your answers from among the following:*

SUBJECT   PREDICATE NOMINATIVE   DIRECT OBJECT   INDIRECT OBJECT

OBJECT OF THE PREPOSITION   PREDICATE ADJECTIVE   MODIFIER   VERB

SENTENCE #	WORD	JOB
1	living next door	_____
2	two	_____
2	lightning	_____
3	family	_____
4	part	_____
4	considered absolutely necessary	_____
5	natives	_____
6	Catching a sailfish	_____
6	uncle	_____

ANALYTICAL GRAMMAR (UNIT #14)   TEST

APPOSITIVE PHRASES: TEST

NAME:_____ DATE: _____

(RAW SCORE:_____ /374 GRADE:_____ POINTS:____/20___)

DIRECTIONS: *Parse the sentences below and put prepositional phrases in parentheses. Underline appositives and appositive phrases. Diagram the sentences. CHECK THE BACK FOR MORE WORK.*

1. After seeing *Gone With the Wind*, my very favorite movie, I usually want to re-read the book.

2. The story's main character, Scarlett O'Hara, is a beautiful, spoiled southern belle living on a plantation named Tara.

3. To marry Ashley Wilkes, heir to a neighboring plantation, is her one desire.

4. Ashley is engaged to marry Melanie, a sweet young woman beloved by everyone.

5. Rhett Butler, a gambler, meets and falls in love with Scarlett.

6. The Civil War, that tragic struggle to free the slaves, comes along and destroys their privileged way of life.

7. Tara is destroyed and Scarlett, head of the O'Haras, must struggle to feed her family.

8. Scarlett marries Rhett Butler, a rich man yearning for respectability.

9. Their marriage, an unhappy one, ends at the death of their only child, a daughter.

10. Rhett, a good man at heart, finally leaves, and Scarlett, now realizing her mistakes, decides to return to Tara.

(over)

Photocopying this product is strictly prohibited by copyright law.

ANALYTICAL GRAMMAR (UNIT #14)   TEST - PAGE 2

PART II: Write what job the following words are doing. Choose your answers from among the following:

SUBJECT   PREDICATE NOMINATIVE   DIRECT OBJECT   MODIFIER

OBJECT OF THE PREPOSITION   VERB   INDIRECT OBJECT   PREDICATE ADJECTIVE

SENTENCE #	WORD	JOB
1	to re-read the book	
2	main	
2	belle	
2	named Tara	
3	To marry Ashley Wilkes	
3	neighboring	
4	Melanie	
5	Rhett Butler	
5	Scarlett	
6	slaves	
6	privileged	
7	must struggle	
8	Rhett Butler	
8	respectability	
9	unhappy	
9	child	
10	to return to Tara	

# ADJECTIVE CLAUSES

Before discussing ADJECTIVE CLAUSES in particular, it is necessary to discuss CLAUSES in general. A CLAUSE is a group of words that contains a verb <u>and its subject</u> and is used as part of a sentence. If a clause expresses a <u>complete thought</u>, then we call it a SENTENCE (if it's all by itself) or an INDEPENDENT CLAUSE (if it's attached to another clause). If a clause does NOT <u>express a complete thought</u>, then we call it a DEPENDENT or SUBORDINATE CLAUSE.

DEPENDENT or SUBORDINATE clauses need INDEPENDENT clauses to complete their meaning.

    EXAMPLE: <u>After it stopped raining</u>, we played softball.

The subordinate clause "After it stopped raining" is not a complete thought by itself. Put together with the independent clause "we played softball," it has meaning.

(EXERCISE #1 IS BASED ON THE ABOVE INFORMATION ABOUT CLAUSES IN GENERAL.)

We will now discuss ADJECTIVE CLAUSES. Obviously, an adjective clauses is a clause that does the work of an adjective. In other words, it modifies a noun or pronoun. The easiest way to spot an adjective clause is to look at the FIRST WORD OF THE CLAUSE. Adjective clauses are introduced by RELATIVE PRONOUNS. You must memorize them. They are WHO, WHOM, WHOSE, WHICH, and THAT. Use WHICH or THAT when referring to things and WHO, WHOM, or WHOSE when referring to people.

The relative pronoun does two things at once. First, it "stands for" or relates to the word in the independent clause that the adjective clause is modifying. Second, it serves as part of the clause. For example, the relative pronoun might be the subject of the clause or its direct object. The following sample diagram will show you how these adjective clauses work:

    EXAMPLE: pn   pro   av   pp   pn   adv   av   pn
                  Yvette, <u>who lived (in France)</u>, quickly learned English.

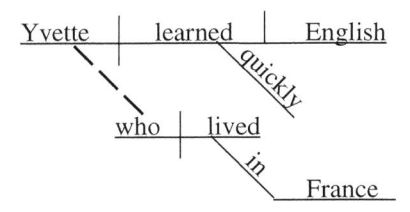

The relative pronoun "who" (1) acts as the subject of the subordinate clause, and (2) shows that "who" stands for "Yvette."

Study the following sample diagrams:

    EXAMPLE: art   n   pro   pro   av   adv   av   art   n
                  The man <u>whom you met yesterday</u> bought a house.

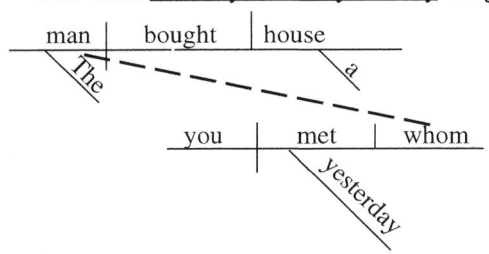

The relative pronoun "whom" (1) acts as the direct object of the subordinate clause and (2) shows you that "whom" stands for "man" in the independent clause.

                                                                                           (over)

ANALYTICAL GRAMMAR (UNIT #15)   NOTES - PAGE 32

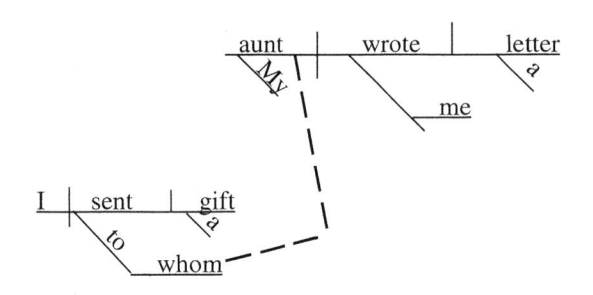

```
EXAMPLE:   adj   n     pp    pro    pro av  art  n    av  pro  art   n
           My  aunt, ( to   whom )  I  sent  a  gift, wrote me   a  letter.
```

```
         aunt  |  wrote  |  letter
           \My         \me      \a

    I  |  sent  |  gift
          \to        \a
           \whom
```

The relative pronoun "whom" (1) acts as the object of the preposition "to" and (2) shows you that "whom" stands for "aunt" in the independent clause.

```
EXAMPLE:  pro    av    art   n  * pro/adj    n    pro  hv    av
          We  thanked  the  man  whose    shovel  we  had  borrowed.
```

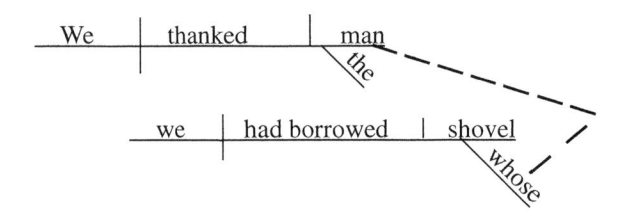

```
  We  |  thanked  |  man
                      \the

        we  |  had borrowed  |  shovel
                                  \whose
```

The relative pronoun "whose" (1) acts as a modifier for "shovel" and (2) shows you that "whose" stands for "man" in the independent clause.

"Whose" is the relative pronoun, but it's acting like an adjective, so it's also correct to call it an adjective. Either answer is correct here.

ANALYTICAL GRAMMAR (UNIT #15)   EXERCISE #1

ADJECTIVE CLAUSES: EXERCISE #1

NAME:_____DATE:_____

DIRECTIONS: *In each sentence below, underline the subordinate clause. Look at each clause and see if you can tell whether the clause is acting like an adjective (answering the question "Which?" about a noun) or acting like an adverb (answering the questions "How?" "When?" "Why?" "Where?" about a verb, an adjective, or an adverb).*

1. When my family went to New York last summer, we visited the Theodore Roosevelt museum.

2. The museum has been established in the house in which Roosevelt was born.

3. It is located on the basement floor of Roosevelt's birthplace, which is on East Twentieth Street.

4. The museum contains books, letters, and documents that pertain to Roosevelt's public life.

5. There are mounted heads of animals, a stuffed lion, and zebra skins from big-game hunts that Roosevelt went on in Africa.

6. Because Roosevelt was once a cowboy, there are also branding irons.

7. Before Theodore Roosevelt became President, he fought in the Spanish-American War.

8. During the war he led the Rough Riders, who made the charge up San Juan Hill.

(over)

Photocopying this product is strictly prohibited by copyright law.

ANALYTICAL GRAMMAR (UNIT #15) EXERCISE #2

ADJECTIVE CLAUSES: EXERCISE #2

NAME:_____ DATE:_____

DIRECTIONS: *Parse the sentences below. Underline the subordinate clause and circle the relative pronoun. Diagram the entire sentence. CHECK THE BACK FOR MORE WORK.*

1. Mrs. Dalton recommended the movie that I am seeing.

2. Here is the letter that I wrote to you.

3. People who want to learn languages must study every day.

4. Students who read a great deal usually write well.

5. Some of the paintings that were done by students sold for big money.

6. Mercury, who was the messenger of the gods, wore winged sandals.

7. The man whom the policeman wants is Jake the Snake, a petty thief.

8. Will the person whose lights are on please report to the desk?

9. A person who knows nothing about a topic should not express an opinion.

10. He is the man from whom I bought the car.

(over)

Photocopying this product is strictly prohibited by copyright law. 171

ANALYTICAL GRAMMAR (UNIT #15)   EXERCISE #2 - PAGE 2

DIRECTIONS: *Write what job the following words are doing. Choose your answers from among the following:*

SUBJECT   PREDICATE NOMINATIVE   DIRECT OBJECT   INDIRECT OBJECT

OBJECT OF THE PREPOSITION   PREDICATE ADJECTIVE   MODIFIER   VERB

SENTENCE #	WORD	JOB
1	that	
2	Here	
3	languages	
4	Students	
5	that	
5	money	
6	messenger	
7	whom	
8	please	
9	nothing	
9	not	
10	whom	

ANALYTICAL GRAMMAR (UNIT #15)   EXERCISE #3

ADJECTIVE CLAUSES: EXERCISE #3

NAME:_____DATE:_____

DIRECTIONS: *Parse the sentences below. Underline the adjective clauses, circle the relative pronouns, and diagram the sentences. CHECK THE BACK FOR MORE WORK.*

1. I did well on the test that Mrs. Freeman gave yesterday.

2. My cousin, who enjoys practical jokes, put pepper into my popcorn.

3. Dad disappeared into the shed in which he kept his gardening tools.

4. My sister, whose horsebackriding skills are amazing, won seven blue ribbons.

5. This dress, which is too long for you, may fit Mary.

DIRECTIONS: *The following pairs of sentences are short and choppy. Re-write them and combine the two sentences into one sentence using ADJECTIVE CLAUSES. You may change words, add words, delete words — your sentence must (1) contain ALL the ideas that were in the original two and (2) contain an adjective clause.*

1. Morris drove the white convertible. The convertible led the parade.

2. Einstein did not do well in school. He was a genius.

3. I ordered this hamburger. It is cold!

4. That man is my uncle. I have admired him for a long time.

5. The policeman's badge is lost. He is retiring in 2008.

(over)

Photocopying this product is strictly prohibited by copyright law.

ANALYTICAL GRAMMAR (UNIT #15)   EXERCISE #3 - PAGE 2

Write what job the following words are doing. Choose your answers from among the following:

SUBJECT   DIRECT OBJECT   INDIRECT OBJECT   PREDICATE NOMINATIVE

OBJECT OF THE PREPOSITION   PREDICATE ADJECTIVE   MODIFIER   VERB

SENTENCE #	WORD	JOB
1	well	
1	that	
2	who	
3	which	
4	ribbons	
5	long	

ANALYTICAL GRAMMAR (UNIT #15)   TEST

ADJECTIVE CLAUSES: TEST

NAME:_____ DATE:_____

(RAW SCORE:_____ /381 GRADE:_____ POINTS:____ /20)

PART I: DIRECTIONS: *Parse the sentences below. Underline the adjective clauses, circle the relative pronouns, and diagram the sentences. CHECK THE BACK FOR MORE WORK.*

1. Antonyms are <u>words</u> which have opposite meanings.

2. Scuba diving is a sport that is now becoming very <u>popular</u>.

3. Pluto, which is the farthest planet from Earth, takes <u>248</u> years to revolve once around the <u>sun</u>.

4. A scholarship was awarded to the one <u>whose</u> short story was best.

5. We invited everyone <u>whom</u> we knew to the party.

6. <u>Words</u> in our language which begin with "th" are often <u>hard</u> for <u>foreigners to pronounce.</u>

7. Robert Frost, who for many <u>years</u> was our unofficial national <u>poet</u>, died in 1963.

8. In her diary Jane kept a <u>record</u> of everything that she did and thought.

(over)

ANALYTICAL GRAMMAR (UNIT #15) — TEST - PAGE 2

9. Achilles was the Greek <u>warrior</u> who <u>could be wounded</u> only in the heel.

10. <u>Here</u> is a <u>picture</u> of the man for <u>whom</u> the police are searching.

PART II: DIRECTIONS: Write what job the following words are doing. Choose your answers from among the following: SUBJECT, PREDICATE NOMINATIVE, DIRECT OBJECT, INDIRECT OBJECT, OBJECT OF THE PREPOSITION, PREDICATE ADJECTIVE, MODIFIER, VERB.

SENTENCE #	WORD	JOB
1	words	
2	popular	
3	248	
3	sun	
4	whose	
5	whom	
6	Words	
6	hard	
6	foreigners to pronounce	
7	years	
7	poet	
8	record	
9	warrior	
9	could be wounded	
10	Here	
10	picture	
10	whom	

ANALYTICAL GRAMMAR (UNIT #15)

PART III: DIRECTIONS: *The following pairs of sentences are short and choppy. Re-write them and combine the* two *sentences into* one *sentence using ADJECTIVE CLAUSES. You may change words, add words, delete words — your sentence must (1) contain ALL the ideas that were in the original two and (2) contain an adjective clause. Remember: you use* which *or* that *when referring to things, and* who/whom *when referring to people.*

1. My cousin loves old movies. He stayed home this afternoon to watch TV.

2. Dad built a "worm fence." It has zigzagging rails.

3. The dress once belonged to my aunt. It has a poodle on the skirt.

4. Johnny is too old to play with you. He wants to play with Jimmy.

5. Mary wrote a book. It was on the best-seller list.

6. I fell madly in love with the artist. He lives next door.

7. I stumbled over the scooter. It was lying on the sidewalk.

8. My father paid $100 for that chair. It once belonged to the mayor.

9. The little boy had lost his temper. He was screaming at his sister.

10. That tall man coaches our football team. You met him yesterday.

ANALYTICAL GRAMMAR (UNIT #16)   NOTES-PAGE 33

ADVERB CLAUSES

DEFINITION: An **ADVERB CLAUSE** is a group of words with a subject and a verb that modifies a verb, an adjective, or an adverb. It answers the questions "How?" "When?" "Where?" or "Why?" about one of those words located in the independent clause.

EXAMPLE: <u>Before the game started</u>, we ate lunch.

The subordinate clause "Before the game started" tells you WHEN we ate. It is an adverb clause modifying the verb "ate."

EXAMPLE: I am glad <u>that you are coming</u>.

The subordinate clause "that you are coming" tells WHY I am glad. It is an adverb clause modifying the predicate adjective "glad."

Adverb clauses are introduced by <u>SUBORDINATING CONJUNCTIONS</u>. You should become very familiar with these words:

after	before	unless
although	if	until
as	in order that	when
as if	since	whenever
as long as	so that	where
as soon as	than	wherever
because	though	while

(WHEN YOU PARSE A SUBORDINATING CONJUNCTION, MARK IT "<u>S C</u>.")

HERE'S A TRICK: If you think a group of words is an adverb clause, but you're not sure, try this: cover up the subordinating conjunction with one thumb. Cover up the independent clause with the other thumb. What's left over? If what is left over is a little sentence, you have an adverb clause. Try it with the example sentences above. The little sentence left over in the first example is "the game started." In the second example, it's "you are coming." This is called the <u>Mrs. Finley's Never-Fail Thumb Test</u>.

HOW TO DIAGRAM A SENTENCE WITH AN ADVERB CLAUSE:

EXAMPLE: s c   art n   av art n   pro   av   adj n
Before the guests left the ballroom, they thanked their hosts.

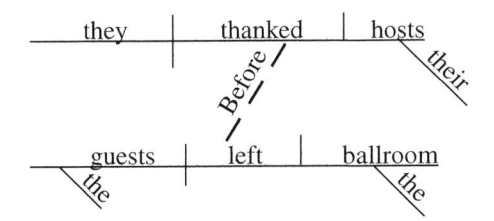

The subordinating conjunction is on a dotted line which goes from the verb of the subordinate clause to whatever word in the independent clause it modifies.

(over)

ADVERB CLAUSES: EXERCISE #1

NAME:_____ DATE:_____

DIRECTIONS: *Parse the sentences below and put parentheses around the prepositional phrases. Remember to parse subordinating conjunctions as "s c." Underline the adverb clauses. Diagram the sentences.*

1. Because the present came from her aunt, Diane opened it immediately.

2. I will attend the party if it starts by seven.

3. My brother slept later than I did.

4. Although I am not a Sherlock Holmes, I enjoy solving difficult puzzles.

5. He saw the author of the play when he was leaving the theatre.

6. After you add the eggs to the mixture, beat for ten minutes.

7. John looked as if he had seen a ghost.

8. The driveway will not set if the concrete has too much water in it.

9. Can you plan the party so that it will be a complete surprise?

10. Unless my dad changes his mind, I can not go to the dance.

ADVERB CLAUSES: EXERCISE #2

NAME:_____DATE:_____

DIRECTIONS: *Parse the sentences below and put parentheses around the prepositional phrases. Underline the adverb clauses. Diagram the sentences.*

1. If you wish to ruin a friendship, watch my friend Morris.

2. When the other person is speaking, Morris interrupts him.

3. As soon as someone starts telling a joke, he gives the punch line away.

4. Then he acts as if the joke was not funny.

5. He changes the subject so that he can brag about himself.

6. While he is talking about his heroic deeds and great intelligence, he always goes into lengthy and uninteresting detail.

7. Before he describes saving a child's life, he mentions the other heroic things that he has done in his life.

8. Whenever he gets a chance, he criticizes his other friends.

9. Unless he monopolizes every conversation, he gets angry and sulks.

10. Remember to act like Morris, if you never want to have any friends!!

ANALYTICAL GRAMMAR (UNIT #16)   EXERCISE #3

ADVERB CLAUSES: EXERCISE #3

NAME:_____ DATE:_____

DIRECTIONS: *Underline the adjective & adverb clauses in the sentences below. Circle the relative pronouns and the subordinating conjunctions. Above the clause write whether it's an adverb or adjective clause and what word in the main clause it modifies. This is what you will have to do on the test, so be sure you know what you're doing!*

1. Since I did not have my math book, I borrowed one from Mary, who is always prepared for class.

2. This class, which is considered to be the hardest in the school, will not seem so hard after it is finished.

3. My science teacher, who loves to build strange machines, and my math teacher, who gets his kicks from solving difficult puzzles, will be the recipients of the state Teacher of the Year award because they are such excellent teachers.

4. The girl who was sitting in the back row acted as if she had not heard the teacher's instructions.

5. When I finally graduate from high school, the idea of going to college, which seems like a dream, will actually become a reality.

6. Before I left the auditorium, I asked the man who had given the speech for an autograph.

7. I always get a souvenir which my little brother will like whenever I am on a trip.

8. Students who read directions carefully usually do well when they are tested.

9. Whenever I go on vacation, I like to buy something that reminds me of the place.

10. Since I had no homework, I decided to read a book which I had been wanting to read.

ANALYTICAL GRAMMAR (UNIT #16) TEST

SUBORDINATE CLAUSES: TEST

NAME:_____ DATE:_____

(RAW SCORE:_____ /100 GRADE:_____ POINTS:____/20___)

DIRECTIONS: There are twenty subordinate clauses in the story below. On a separate sheet of paper, do the following things: 1.) copy the entire subordinate clause, 2.) on the line below it, write either ADJECTIVE CLAUSE or ADVERB CLAUSE, whichever it is, 3.) circle the relative pronoun or the subordinating conjunction, and 4.) write the word in the main clause that the subordinate clause modifies. Try to number your clauses in the order in which they come in the story.

EXAMPLE: The old boxer who had retired from the ring was teaching the young fighter.

1. (who) had retired from the ring

    adjective clause   boxer

    Robert Browning, who was a poet of the Victorian period, wrote a poem about Childe Roland, a daring knight who set out on a dangerous quest for the Dark Tower. Many brave knights had been killed because they had searched for the Tower, but Roland was determined not to rest until he found it.

    After Roland had searched for years, he came upon an old man who pointed the way to the Tower. Following the old man's directions, Roland found himself in a land which was horrible beyond belief. As he passed across the eerie wasteland, he saw all around him the signs of savage struggles that had taken place here in the past. Although Roland now felt doomed, he rode on. He saw sights that would have convinced the bravest of men to turn back. But Roland would not give up while he had strength to continue.

    Finally, when he had become discouraged, a large black bird swooped down over his head. As he watched it fly away, he saw in the distance the place which the old man had described to him. A dark tower loomed up before him as if a huge stone had arisen out of the valley. He felt like a sailor looking at a rocky shelf at the very moment that his ship crashes into it. While Roland paused to look, he heard ringing in his ears the names of all those who had died in the quest for the Tower. Then, on the hillsides, he saw in a sheet of flame the figures of the knights who had perished. But, in spite of the horror, Roland raised his horn to his lips and blew: "Child Roland to the Dark Tower came!"

EXTRA CREDIT: In this story there are one appositive phrase, four infinitive phrases, and three participial phrases. Find as many as you can and copy them out on your test paper. Be sure to tell what each item is before writing it down. What is the appositive restating? What job is each infinitive doing? What is each participial phrase modifying? The example below shows you how to do this exercise.

EXAMPLE: Bowser, my three-legged dog, falls over in a stiff wind.

    my three-legged dog - appositive phrase - restates Bowser.

ANALYTICAL GRAMMAR (UNIT #16) TEST - PAGE 2

PART II: DIRECTIONS: *The sentences below are choppy and sound childish. Using ADJECTIVE and ADVERB CLAUSES, combine the pairs of sentences into one sentence. To get credit here, your sentence must 1.) contain an adjective or adverb clause, and 2.) contain all the ideas of the original two sentences. You may have to change words, delete words, and/or add words.*

1. Henry Borsini is getting bald. He is also overweight and out of shape.

2. I didn't have a warm coat. I borrowed one from a friend.

3. I was almost asleep. I heard a sound that jerked me awake.

4. Amy has never been outside the United States. She speaks German beautifully.

5. The Lawsons are our neighbors. They have gone to Hawaii for two weeks.

6. That glass has become chipped. It is dangerous.

7. Ray searched for many days. He found the perfect gift.

8. Jane wanted to talk to that man. He was eating lunch in the same restaurant.

9. The twins had never seen a waterfall. Their uncle took them to Niagara Falls.

10. The women couldn't walk very easily. They changed into flat-heeled shoes.

NOUN CLAUSES

DEFINITION: A NOUN CLAUSE is a subordinate clause which is used as a noun in the sentence. It may be a subject, a complement (direct object, indirect object, or predicate nominative), or the object of a preposition.

EXAMPLES:

1.)   pro pro av   av   pro
<u>What he said</u> surprised me.

(The noun clause "What he said" acts as the subject of the verb "surprised.")

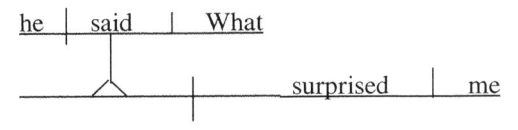

2.)   art   n   hv lv pro   av
The champion will be <u>whoever wins.</u>

(The noun clause "whoever wins" acts as the predicate nominative of "will be.")

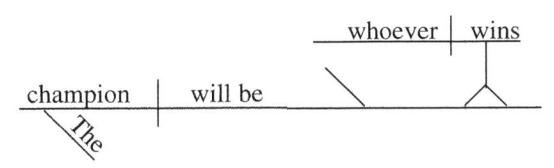

3.)   pn   av   pro adj n   lv
Jane knows <u>what your secret is.</u>

(The noun clause "what your secret is" is the direct object of "knows.")

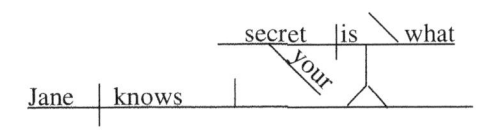

4.)   pro hv av   pro   av   art n
I will give <u>whoever comes</u> a ticket.

(The noun clause "whoever comes" is the indirect object of "give.")

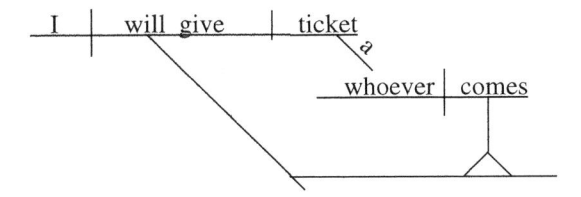

(over)

ANALYTICAL GRAMMAR (UNIT #17) NOTES - PAGE 36

5.)   pro   av   n   pp   pro   lv   p-adj
She brings food (to whoever is ill.)

(The noun clause "whoever is ill" is the object of the preposition "to.")

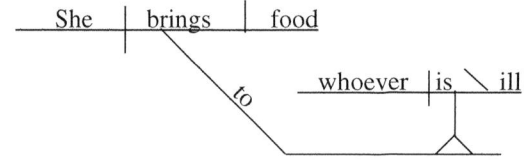

Noun clauses are usually introduced by the following pronouns:

that	what	who	whom
	whatever	whoever	whomever

And sometimes by the following adverbs:

where	when	why	how
wherever	whenever	whyever	however

THESE INTRODUCTORY WORDS HAVE NO SPECIAL NAME OF THEIR OWN; JUST PARSE THEM EITHER "PRO" OR "ADV."

IMPORTANT NOTE: Most of the time the introductory word has some job to do in the clause (see the above diagrams); however, sometimes (with the word "that") it has no function in the clause at all. Its only function is to connect the subordinate clause to the main clause.

EXAMPLE: pro   av   pro pro   lv   p-adj
She thought that I was sick.

NOUN CLAUSES: EXERCISE #1

NAME:_____ DATE:_____

DIRECTIONS: *Parse the sentences below. Underline the noun clauses. Diagram the sentences and, to the side of your diagram, indicate what job each clause is doing.*

1. What the club wanted was a spook house.

2. His message was that he would not be home for dinner.

3. A guide pointed to where the picture was.

4. The teacher gave whoever had read the story a short quiz.

5. Tammy always had a cheery hello for whomever she knew.

6. Whoever guesses the correct number of jellybeans will win a prize.

7. The outcome of the whole thing is what really matters.

8. A beekeeper explained to us how honey is made.

9. That she was not coming was quite obvious.

10. We were astonished by what happened here yesterday.

(over)

NOUN CLAUSES: EXERCISE #2

NAME:_____ DATE:_____

DIRECTIONS: *Below each sentence, underline and identify every phrase (participial, gerund, infinitive, or appositive) and every clause (adjective, adverb, or noun). If it's doing a job, write what job it's doing; if it's modifying something, write what it's modifying.*

EXAMPLE: When he heard Maria's speech, Mark felt that he should try harder.
         (Adverb clause - modifies "felt")   *(Noun clause - direct object)*

1. What he does best is playing the piano.

2. Mr. Allen is the man who taught us origami.

3. Screaming with fear, Jenny sat up suddenly when the tent collapsed.

4. My brother's family, our favorite relatives, surprise us whenever they arrive on time.

5. I could not understand what the directions said to do before entering the restricted area.

6. Where we sat was the row of seats located near the exit.

7. Wolfman Jack, who was a disc jockey, loved to play old songs on "The Midnight Special."

8. The oranges that we picked when we were in Florida were very juicy.

9. Gene, a thoughtful person, brought sandwiches for whoever was hungry.

10. Horses, considered stupid by many people, have strong feelings about where they go.

NOUN CLAUSES: EXERCISE #3

NAME:_____ DATE:_____

DIRECTIONS: *Below each sentence, underline and identify every phrase (participial, gerund, infinitive, or appositive) and every clause (adjective, adverb, or noun). If it's doing a job, write what job it's doing; if it's modifying something, write what it's modifying. It would probably be best to use a separate sheet of paper and copy the phrases and clauses out, since this is what will be required on the test.*

1. Joe, who was Mary's partner in the dance contest, refused to leave the dance floor when the judge tapped him on the shoulder.

2. Professor Watkins, lecturing about the Amazon, absentmindedly left the room after the break because he thought the class was over.

3. The argument was all about what Teresa had said when Jill told her a joke.

4. Although they were already exhausted, the first string players stayed in the game because the score was tied.

5. Jason, who is taller than Kyle, thinks that it would be funny if he played the part of Scarlett O'Hara in the *Gone With the Wind* parody.

6. Saving the environment had become an obsession with Tracy, whom I was telling you about.

7. Karen, burdened with a huge pile of books, was staggering down the hall, and Kevin, who is very thoughtful, offered to help her out.

8. I turned around and only had a moment to see a shadow, which I felt was that of a man, flitting past the open doorway.

Season Three

You completed the second season! Great work. If you are following the two or three year track, you need to take a break at this point and do the worksheets from the Reinforcement & Review book before you start Season Three.

ANALYTICAL GRAMMAR (UNIT #17)   TEST

NOUN CLAUSES: TEST

NAME:_____ DATE:_____

(RAW SCORE:_____/80 GRADE:_____ POINTS:____/20)

DIRECTIONS: PART I: *On a separate sheet of paper, write out the entire subordinate clause in each sentence below. Write what kind of a clause it is. If it is a noun clause, write what job it is doing. If it is an adjective or adverb clause, write what word it modifies.*

1. Len claims that he knows judo.

2. Amy blushed when she read the letter.

3. The bait that worked best was shrimp.

4. Everyone who travels needs a map.

5. No one saw Diane after she left practice.

6. The wolf attacked because it was trapped.

7. The robot will do whatever you ask.

8. The test, which was quite hard, lasted one hour.

9. We went to the circus when it came to town.

10. What I like best is talking on the phone with friends.

11. The champion beat whomever he fought.

12. A person who designs buildings is an architect.

13. Kenny Loggins is the one who plays guitar.

14. Whoever returns the stolen jewels will get a reward.

15. The dog followed Jeff wherever he went.

16. Although she prefers hockey, Grace plays center on the basketball team.

17. Many people watch television because they are bored.

18. We could see the lake from where we stood.

19. Slavery was what divided the country.

20. Radar, which locates distant objects, is used to track spacecraft.

(over)

Photocopying this product is strictly prohibited by copyright law.

ANALYTICAL GRAMMAR (UNIT #17) TEST - PAGE 2

PART II: DIRECTIONS: *On this test paper, copy out the clauses (adjective, adverb, or noun) and phrases (participial, gerund, infinitive, or appositive) that you find in the sentences below. Identify what kind of clause or phrase it is. (These sentences were taken from "The Hound of the Baskervilles" by Sir Arthur Conan Doyle) BE SURE TO COPY OUT THE ENTIRE PHRASE OR CLAUSE!!! (If the phrase or clause is too long to fit on the line provided below, write the first word of it, and ellipses [...], and the last word).*

EXAMPLE: On the night of Sir Charles's death, Barrymore the butler, who made the discovery, sent Perkins the groom on horseback to me. (3 items in this sentence)

Example	"the butler"	Appositive phrase
Example	"who....discovery"	Adjective clause
Example	"the groom"	Appositive phrase

1. I whisked round and had just time to catch a glimpse of something which I took to be a large black calf passing at the head of the drive. (4 items in this sentence)

2. A hound it was, an enormous coal-black hound, but not such a hound as mortal eyes have ever seen. (2 items in this sentence)

3. With long bounds the huge black creature was leaping down the track, following hard upon the footsteps of our friend. (1 item in this sentence)

4. Never have I seen a man run as Holmes ran that night. (1 item in this sentence)

5. The gleam of the match which he struck shone upon his clotted fingers and upon the ghastly pool which widened from the crushed skull of the victim. (2 items in this sentence)

(Up to 5 points extra credit for correctly diagraming sentence #5 in Part II)

SENTENCE #	WORD GROUP	IDENTIFICATION
1	_____	_____
1	_____	_____
1	_____	_____
1	_____	_____
2	_____	_____
2	_____	_____
3	_____	_____
4	_____	_____
5	_____	_____
5	_____	_____

ANALYTICAL GRAMMAR (COMMA SPLICES)   NOTES- PAGE 37

COMMA ERRORS

There are two kinds of comma errors: comma SPLICES and comma SPLITS.

A comma SPLICE is a comma which incorrectly joins two sentences. Sometimes you write two sentences next to each other that just *feel* like they ought to go together, so you just *put* them together with a comma.   Such as --

We could prove we'd spent the whole day at the beach, we had the sunburn to prove it!

But what you've got there is a comma splice, which is a "no-no." In the case of the above sentences, you could fix the "no-no" in one of three ways:

1. Just write two separate sentences.
2. Join the two sentences with a subordinating conjunction, such as "because."
3. Join the two sentence with a semicolon (See Unit #26)

A comma SPLIT is when you put a comma where it doesn't belong. *The following is a list of places where a comma should not be:*

1. There should never be ONE comma separating the SUBJECT AND VERB.

    EXAMPLE: The butler carrying a tray, walked into the room.

2. There should never be ONE comma separating the VERB AND ITS DIRECT OBJECT.

    EXAMPLE: We discovered after searching carefully, many things.

3. There should never be ONE comma separating a LINKING VERB AND ITS COMPLEMENT.

    EXAMPLE: James felt, absolutely wonderful.

4. There should never be ONE comma separating a MODIFIER AND ITS NOUN..

    EXAMPLE: The soft, cuddly, sweater was gorgeous.

5. There should never be ONE comma separating a VERB AND ITS INDIRECT OBJECT.

    EXAMPLE: I wrote, my aunt in Florida a letter.

6. There should never be ONE comma separating an INDIRECT OBJECT AND ITS DIRECT OBJECT.

    EXAMPLE: I wrote my aunt in Florida, a letter.

SO REMEMBER THE SIX DEADLY SPLITS!

1.	*Subject and verb*	*4.*	*Modifier and its noun*
2.	*Verb and direct object*	*5.*	*Verb and indirect object*
3.	*Linking verb and complement*	*6.*	*Indirect object and direct object*

Photocopying this product is strictly prohibited by copyright law.

COMMA RULES 1, 2, & 3

COMMA RULE 1: The "buzzword" for this rule is *ITEMS IN A SERIES*: use commas to separate items in a series of grammatical equals. This may be a series of nouns, verbs, prepositional phrases, adjective clauses, etc.

NOTE THAT THERE IS A COMMA SEPARATING THE LAST TWO ITEMS.

EXAMPLE: John, Uncle Hank, Aunt Jean, and Anne went to church. (nouns)

The happy, carefree, and enthusiastic kids enjoyed the picnic. (adjectives)

We searched under the desks, behind the shelves, and in the trashcan for the missing keys. (prepositional phrases)

NOTE: If all the items are separated by "and" or "or," do not use commas to separate them.

EXAMPLE: I bought jeans and a shirt and a sweater.

NOTE: When writing a sentence containing a series of items, make sure the sentence is PARALLEL.

EXAMPLE: A good bedtime routine is a hot shower, flossing and brushing your teeth, and to get your clothes ready for the next morning.

(The above sentence makes sense, but it is not PARALLEL because you don't have a series of grammatical equals. "a hot shower" is a noun with modifiers. "flossing and brushing your teeth" is a gerund phrase. "to get your clothes ready for the next morning" is an infinitive phrase. One way to improve it is to make all your items gerund phrases, like the sentence below. Or you could make all your items infinitives. Try that.)

A good bedtime routine is <u>taking</u> a hot shower, <u>flossing</u> and <u>brushing</u> your teeth, and <u>getting</u> your clothes organized for the next morning.

COMMA RULE 2: The "buzzword" for this rule is *TWO ADJECTIVES with "AND TEST"*: you SOMETIMES use a comma to separate two or more adjectives preceding a noun. The "and test" works like this: If it sounds very natural to put "and" between the two adjectives, you need a comma. If "and" sounds awkward at all, forget the comma.

EXAMPLE #1: That is a rough narrow dangerous road.

(...a rough and narrow road?...sounds okay - you need a comma)

(...a narrow and dangerous road?...sounds okay - you need a comma)

That is a rough, narrow, dangerous road.

EXAMPLE #2: I saw a little old man.

(...a little and old man?...sounds weird - forget it.)

(over)

ANALYTICAL GRAMMAR (UNIT #18)   NOTES - PAGE 40

COMMA RULE 3:   **The buzzword for this rule is** *COMPOUND SENTENCE:* use a comma before the conjunction when it joins independent clauses (or sentences).

EXAMPLE: Brian changed the oil on the old Chevy, and Joe checked the plugs on the Pontiac.

(There is a complete sentence on either side of the conjunction, so you need a comma.)

EXAMPLE: Brian changed the oil on the old Chevy and checked the plugs on the Ford.

(There is NOT a complete sentence on either side of the conjunction, so do not put a comma.)

EXCEPTION TO THIS RULE: IF....you are using the conjunction *and*

and

IF...either one of the sentences contains four words or less,

DO NOT USE A COMMA.

EXAMPLE: Brian changed the oil and Joe checked the plugs on the Pontiac.
(The first independent clause contains only FOUR WORDS and the conjunction is *and*; that's why there's no comma.)

WHEN YOU'RE USING ANY OTHER CONJUNCTION BESIDES *AND*, YOU MUST USE A COMMA IF YOU HAVE A COMPOUND SENTENCE.

ANALYTICAL GRAMMAR (UNIT #18)   EXERCISE #1

COMMA RULES 1, 2, & 3: EXERCISE #1

NAME:_____ DATE:_____

DIRECTIONS: *Insert commas where they are needed.*

1. We had lessons in swimming canoeing archery and handicrafts.

2. Mary and Frances and Ted dashed out of the car down the beach and into the water.

3. Our school has organized clubs for music art radio and computers.

4. The high school orchestra includes violins cellos clarinets saxophones trumpets and drums.

5. I've planted seedlings fertilized them carefully and watered them daily.

6. The children played happily on the swings on the slide and in the pool.

7. Science and Latin and algebra are all included in next year's curriculum.

8. Do you know how to pitch a tent how to build a campfire or how to cook outdoors?

9. I enjoy swimming boating and surfing more than skiing sledding or skating.

10. Find out who is going to the picnic what we must take and when we are going.

11. This morning Tom will wash the car Mary will pack the lunch and then we'll go for a drive.

12. In spite of bad predictions, the fog lifted the sun shone and everyone was happy.

13. Science teaches us how to conserve our forests how to prevent erosion of the soil and how to control our water supplies.

14. I would like to visit England France Spain and Norway, the "Land of the Midnight Sun."

15. Soccer basketball and football are all strenuous sports.

DIRECTIONS: *The sentence below is not parallel. Rewrite it.*

The smell of cookies, going Christmas shopping, and how to keep a secret are part of what the holidays are all about.

(over)

ANALYTICAL GRAMMAR (UNIT #18)   EXERCISE #1 - PAGE 2

DIRECTIONS: *In each sentence below there is a COMMA SPLIT. Write the number which is under the comma split in the space at the left. Then in the space below each sentence, write what the comma is splitting.*

EXAMPLE: __3__ The happy, carefree, enthusiastic kids, enjoyed the picnic.
                                  1   2   3

_____ ***subject and verb*** _____

- -

_____ 1. The old, dog trotted slowly into the beautiful, elegant, immaculate house.
                        1   2   3

_____

. _____ 2 The rain stopped, the sun came out, and the children continued their vigorous,
                                1   2   3

strenuous, game.
              4

_____

_____ 3. The gym teacher is carefully teaching during the course of this semester, wrestling, gymnastics,
                                                                                                                    1   2   3

and tumbling.

_____

204

COMMA RULES 1, 2, & 3: EXERCISE #2

NAME:_____ DATE:_____

DIRECTIONS: *Insert commas where they are needed.*

1. John was the popular efficient president of the senior class.

2. The cold dry northern air is very invigorating.

3. We loved running barefoot over the damp cool sand.

4. What a stern dignified manner that soldier has!

5. The dark dingy musty attic seemed spooky.

6. The noisy carefree fans cheered when they saw the bright blue uniforms of the band.

7. Have you read about the strong courageous man who climbed the sheer icy slopes of Mt. Everest?

8. An alert hard-working businesslike leader is needed.

9. A dark squatty-looking iron stove stood in the corner of the cabin.

10. Alfred Hitchcock fascinated us with his thrilling blood-curdling films.

11. It was a bright brisk beautiful autumn day.

12. A little old man knocked at the door.

13. That was a long hard exhausting train ride.

14. Jupiter is a large mysterious planet.

15. Althea Gibson played a powerful brilliant game.

DIRECTIONS: *The sentence below is not parallel. Rewrite it.*

I love to eat, playing with my kitten, and a good conversation with a friend.

(over)

ANALYTICAL GRAMMAR (UNIT #18)   EXERCISE #2 - PAGE 2

DIRECTIONS: *In each sentence below there is a COMMA SPLIT. Write the number which is under the comma split in the space at the left. Then in the space below each sentence, write what the comma is splitting.*

_____ 1. That, is a good, long, tough hike!
             1   2   3

            _____

_____ 2. The young, inexperienced boys are working on a new, innovative, computer.
                1   2   3

            _____

_____ 3. The dark, wet, musty tank smelled, terrible.
             1   2   3

            _____

ANALYTICAL GRAMMAR (UNIT #18) EXERCISE #3

COMMA RULES 1, 2, & 3: EXERCISE #3

NAME:_____DATE:_____

DIRECTIONS: *Insert commas where they are needed.*

1. There are many beautiful beaches along the coast but one must get used to the cold water.

2. Henry came over but Tom stayed at home.

3. I used steel traps to catch muskrats but my friend said that was cruel.

4. Astronomy is an old science yet it is now one of the most exciting.

5. Our teacher is using videos and cd-roms in our Social Studies class and we are really enjoying them.

6. She tried on eight pairs of shoes and didn't buy any of them!

7. A robin has a nest in a tree near our porch and we watch her feeding the baby birds.

8. Harry lived on a farm and had to get up early in the morning to do chores.

9. I will explain this theory once more but you must listen.

10. The teacher explained the project and we went to work.

11. I'd love to go to the movies but I have too much work to do.

12. The movie was excellent but I didn't enjoy waiting in line.

13. We stopped on the side of the road and ate our lunch.

14. On the moon the temperature rises to over 200 degrees in the daytime but drops far below zero at night.

15. There was an annoying noise in the car but we could not locate the cause.

16. The coach drew a diagram and the players studied it.

DIRECTIONS: *The sentence below is not parallel. Rewrite it.*

A car that is poorly maintained, operating it beyond the speed limit, and to drink and drive can all be very dangerous.

(over)

ANALYTICAL GRAMMAR (UNIT #18)   EXERCISE #3 - PAGE 2

DIRECTIONS: *In each sentence below there is a COMMA SPLIT. Write the number which is under the comma split in the space at the left. Then in the space below each sentence, write what the comma is splitting.*

_____1. The girl who was very verbal, talked too fast, but she told fascinating, interesting stories.
                              1   2   3

            _____

_____2. I craved a hot, delicious, cheesy pizza and drove in the pouring rain, ten miles.
                       1   2   3

            _____

_____3. My mother gave the girl who was just learning how to cook, the orders, but I followed them.
                                                                    1   2

            _____

ANALYTICAL GRAMMAR (UNIT #18)   TEST

COMMA RULES 1, 2, & 3: TEST

NAME:_____ DATE:_____

(RAW SCORE:_____ /79 GRADE:_____ POINTS:_____ /20)

PART I: DIRECTIONS: COMMA RULE #1: *Insert commas where they are needed.*

1. Students teachers parents and visitors attended the picnic.

2. They roamed over the hills through the fields down to the lake and across the bridge.

3. I bought a suit and a tie and a dress shirt yesterday.

4. George Washington Carver derived from the peanut such items as ink coffee beauty creams and pigments.

5. Do you want French or ranch or Catalina dressing on your salad?

6. Mosquitoes hummed crickets chirped and mockingbirds sang.

7. Robert Browning said that youth is good that middle age is better and that old age is best.

8. Those who had walked to the picnic who had brought small children who had no umbrellas or who had worn good clothes dashed to a nearby farmhouse.

9. The smell of peanuts the music of a calliope and the feel of sawdust under my feet always remind me of the circus.

10. I got <u>Gone With the Wind</u> <u>The Grapes of Wrath</u> and <u>The Hobbit</u> from the library.

PART II: COMMA RULE #2: *Insert commas where they are needed.*

1. My aunt is a kind generous warm-hearted person.

2. I need the help of three willing young men.

3. A vain talkative disc jockey annoys me.

4. Anna fluttered her gorgeous black eyelashes.

5. We chose a beautiful mahogany end table.

(over)

ANALYTICAL GRAMMAR (UNIT #18)

TEST - PAGE 2

6. Round deep craters and steep rugged mountains dot the surface of the moon.

7. We passed the warm humid afternoon playing "Monopoly."

8. What a wide smooth highway this is!

9. If one is not in a hurry, the quaint little streets of old Alexandria are very inviting.

10. The crowded uncomfortable dining car was no pleasure for anyone.

PART III: COMMA RULE #3: *Insert commas where they are needed.*

1. Everyone was at the game but Quincy arrived an hour late.

2. Either the gift was lost in the mail or he had forgotten to thank me.

3. Into the garbage pail she flung the burned cake and immediately started work on another.

4. The critics hated the play but it ran for six months.

5. Ethan whispered something to Philip and quickly left the stadium.

6. Jan picked the flowers and Mary arranged them.

7. Beaumont led in the first inning by two runs but Houston was leading in the second by a score of 6-2.

8. Rescue workers helped farmers to clear away debris and to replant their ruined crops after the flood.

9. The *Titanic* was considered an unsinkable ship but she sank in the North Atlantic on April 14, 1912.

10. At last the weather became more merciful and settled down to normal.

PART IV: ALL COMMA RULES: *Insert commas where they are needed.*

1. A beach party was planned for Saturday but the weather looked bad.

2. We had invited Mary Tom Jane and Jason.

3. Mom helped us with the refreshments and Jason brought a couple of videos.

4. We ate pizza played "Trivial Pursuit" and watched a funny old beach-blanket movie.

5. It was actually a fun lazy relaxing afternoon.

6. Tom said he was bored and tried to organize a game of touch football.

7. Before we could play, we had to look all over the house to find the football locate warm clothing and find some shoes for Mary.

8. After the football game Jane stretched out on the couch and took a brief blissful snooze.

ANALYTICAL GRAMMAR (UNIT #18)   TEST - PAGE #3

9. The boys waited until she was fast asleep and then painted a moustache on her upper lip.

10. Jane woke up saw the moustache and Jason and Tom both ran for cover!

PART V: NON-PARALLEL SENTENCES: *Re-write the following sentences to make them parallel.*

1. To learn some new words, writing a good essay, and how to analyze our language are major parts of Mrs. Finley's curriculum.

2. My home town has all the advantages: the weather is good, friendly neighbors, with excellent schools, and fine shopping.

PART VI: COMMA SPLItS: *In each sentence below there is a COMMA SPLIT. Write the number which is under the comma split in the space at the left. Then in the space below each sentence, write what the comma is splitting.*

_____1. The man who lives next door, wants his children to excel in school, but he fails to give them careful,
                            1   2   3
consistent help.

_____

_____2. The students in this class are reading in the spring semester, a wonderful book which contains
                                                                        1
adventure, fantasy, and romance.
        2   3

_____

_____3. The frigid, icy air made it difficult for people to breathe, but coach kept us out to practice for our
                 1   2
upcoming, match against South High.
        3

_____

COMMA RULE 4

The "buzzword" for this rule is *NONESSENTIAL MODIFIERS:* use a comma to separate nonessential adjective clauses and nonessential participial phrases from the rest of the sentence.

ADJECTIVE CLAUSES and PARTICIPIAL PHRASES are groups of words that act like adjectives. In other words, they MODIFY NOUNS AND PRONOUNS.

    EXAMPLE: My English teacher, who loves books, reads all the time.

The group of words "who loves books" is there to describe the noun "teacher." You will notice that the noun being described is almost always located in front of the phrase or clause that modifies it.

HOW TO IDENTIFY AN ADJECTIVE CLAUSE:
    An adjective clause almost always begins with a RELATIVE PRONOUN. The relative pronouns are **WHO, WHOSE, WHOM, WHICH,** and **THAT.**

HOW TO IDENTIFY A PARTICIPIAL PHRASE:
    A participial phrase begins with a PARTICIPLE. There are two kinds of participles:
    1.)   PRESENT PARTICIPLES are verbs that end in "ing."
    2.)   PAST PARTICIPLES are verbs that fit into the phrase "I have_____."

Once you have located the participial phrase or adjective clause, you have to decide if it's ESSENTIAL or NONESSENTIAL. If it's nonessential, the reader doesn't need it to understand what the sentence is really saying.

    EXAMPLE: Jim Riley, who skips school repeatedly, will be expelled.

    Try taking the modifier "who skips school repeatedly" out of the sentence. What is left? "Jim Riley will be expelled." Even without the adjective clause, we still know who will be expelled. That clause is therefore NONESSENTIAL and that's why we have commas around it.

    EXAMPLE: Students who skip school repeatedly will be expelled.

    Try taking the modifier "who skip school repeatedly" out of this sentence. What is left? "Students will be expelled." Do we know which students will be expelled without that modifier? No, we don't. It is therefore ESSENTIAL and that's why there are no commas around it.

HERE'S A TRICK: One way to tell if a clause is essential or not is to read the sentence with as much natural expression as you can (pretend you're a TV news announcer). If the modifier is nonessential, your voice will just naturally pause right where the commas go. If it is essential, there will be no tendency to pause at all.

ANALYTICAL GRAMMAR (UNIT #19)   EXERCISE #1

COMMA RULE 4: EXERCISE #1

NAME:_____ DATE:_____

DIRECTIONS: Underline the adjective clause or participial phrase in each sentence below. After each sentence, write "AC" if it's an adjective clause and "PART" if it's a participial phrase. Then separate all the NONESSENTIAL modifiers from the rest of the sentence with commas.

1. Senator Stewart hoping for a compromise began an impassioned speech.

2. I bought all the books written by John Grisham at a garage sale.

3. The Foresman Building which has become a firetrap will be torn down.

4. Sometimes I feel like throwing every outfit that I buy on sale into the trash!

5. Students who watch television until late at night are not going to do their best.

6. My grandfather Ben sitting in his favorite chair would always tell us stories before bedtime.

7. Give this note to the girl sitting on the sofa.

8. The senior representative from Zambia dressed in his native costume made a colorful sight.

9. The kids who sing in the choir enjoy performing for the other students.

10. The candidate of my choice kissing babies like a seasoned campaigner was learning about politics quickly.

(over)

Photocopying this product is strictly prohibited by copyright law.

ANALYTICAL GRAMMAR (UNIT #19)   EXERCISE #1 - PAGE 2

DIRECTIONS: *In each sentence below there is a comma split. In the spaces below each sentence are the numbers of all the commas in the sentence. Find the comma split and write its number in the space at the left. Write what it is splitting beside that comma's number below the sentence. By the other numbers, write the "buzzwords" of the correct commas.*

EXAMPLE:

__*1*__   Students who skip school repeatedly, will be expelled, but our enthusiastic, dedicated
                                              1   2   3
students never skip.

   #1   *splits subject and verb*

   #2   *compound sentence*

   #3   *two adjectives with "and test"*

- -

_____   1.   John Wilson, elected by a large majority, began planning, a huge victory celebration.
                             1   2   3

   #1 _____

   #2 _____

   #3 _____

_____   2.   We have, a soft, luxurious carpet in our living room, dining room, and hall.
                        1   2   3   4

   #1 _____

   #2 _____

   #3 _____

   #4 _____

_____   3.   Students, who have a lot of homework should budget their time, but often they waste
                         1   2
their energy in useless, futile procrastination.
                        3

   #1 _____

   #2 _____

   #3 _____

Photocopying this product is strictly prohibited by copyright law.

COMMA RULE 4: EXERCISE #2

NAME:_____DATE:_____

DIRECTIONS: *Underline the participial phrases and adjective clauses below. Identify them as you did on Exercise #1. Insert commas where they are needed.*

1. The pitcher thinking the runner was out started off the field.

2. Here is my cousin James whom you met yesterday.

3. Mary who enjoys her class in physics will be an excellent engineer.

4. Louis Pasteur striving to save a little boy from death by rabies used a vaccine which finally conquered that dread disease.

5. The man and woman who discovered radium were Pierre and Marie Curie.

6. E. T. Seton who was a famous artist-naturalist was born in England in 1860.

7. *Wild Animals I Have Known* which is one of his most popular works was his first book.

8. The boy or girl who enjoys reading usually does well in school.

9. The boy playing left end is our best tackle.

10. The winning runners breathing hard and visibly tired broke the tape at the same time.

11. Lake Superior covering an area of 30,000 square miles is the largest Great Lake.

12. The girl working next to you is my sister.

13. The students having gorged themselves on junk food called the picnic a huge success.

14. My turquoise and silver ring which we bought in Mexico is my favorite.

15. A meal cooked by my mother is always a treat.

16. Only the students gathered in the auditorium got to hear the guest speaker.

17. John cramming for the history exam wished he had kept up with his reading.

18. My parents always loved the gifts that I made myself.

19. Our new school library which has just been opened is a great asset to our school.

20. The cat took a snooze in the warm sunlight streaming through the living room window.

(over)

ANALYTICAL GRAMMAR (UNIT #19)   EXERCISE #2 - PAGE 2

DIRECTIONS: *In each sentence below there is a comma split. In the spaces below each sentence are the numbers of all the commas in the sentence. Find the comma split and write its number in the space at the left. Write what it is splitting beside that comma's number below the sentence. By the other numbers, write the "buzzwords" of the correct commas.*

_____ 1. I have a huge, overpowering urge to tell that rude man to go jump off the incredibly tall,
                            1   2
Empire State Building, which is located in New York City.
                      3

#1 _____
#2 _____
#3 _____

_____ 2. I was reading, a really thrilling, mysterious book, but my mom, my dad, and my big
                         1   2   3   4   5
sister told me how it came out!

#1 _____
#2 _____
#3 _____
#4 _____
#5 _____

_____ 3. The kids in the band, decided to raise money, and their idea was to have a dance, a bake
                                 1   2   3
sale, and a car wash.
    4

#1 _____
#2 _____
#3 _____
#4 _____

ANALYTICAL GRAMMAR (UNIT #19)   EXERCISE #3

COMMA RULE 4: EXERCISE #3

NAME:_____ DATE:_____

DIRECTIONS: *Insert commas where they are needed. Circle the word the phrase or clause modifies.*

1. Ruth Snyder who is my second cousin will visit me next year.

2. We take the *Shreveport Times* which is an excellent newspaper.

3. All highways that have eight lanes are very safe.

4. You're a lot like my dad who loves to tinker with old cars.

5. I think all girls who dye their hair platinum blonde look funny.

6. Hepzibah Humperdinck who has a short haircut looks funny.

7. I attend Cranford High School which has an enrollment of 598.

8. All contestants answering this question correctly will win a prize.

9. The hog-nosed snake feared by many is not poisonous.

10. In *The Man of Feeling* which is a very sentimental book the hero who is extremely romantic drops dead when his sweetheart says she loves him.

DIRECTIONS: *You are to write four sentences. In the first sentence, use the adjective clause "who passed this grammar unit" in a sentence where it is nonessential (with commas). In the second sentence use "who passed this grammar unit" as an essential adjective clause(no commas). In the third sentence the participial phrase "running in the house" must be nonessential (with commas). In the fourth sentence "running in the house" should be an essential phrase (no commas).*

DIRECTIONS: *Write four sentences of your own (try not to be boring...) in which you...*

1. ...demonstrate "items in a series"

2. ...demonstrate "two adjective with 'and test'"

3. ...demonstrate "compound sentence"

4. ...demonstrate "nonessential modifier"

(over)

ANALYTICAL GRAMMAR (UNIT #19) EXERCISE #3 - PAGE 2

DIRECTIONS: *In each sentence below there is a comma split. In the spaces below each sentence are the numbers of all the commas in the sentence. Find the comma split and write its number in the space at the left. Write what it is splitting beside that comma's number below the sentence. By the other numbers, write the "buzzwords" of the correct commas.*

_____ 1. The delicious, succulent turkey that was cooked by Chef Andre, won first
                              1   2

   prize, but Georgine's souffle won second prize.
         3

   #1 _____

   #2 _____

   #3 _____

_____ 2. The woman in the store looked, incredibly angry at the poor clerk, who
                                        1   2

   was trying desperately to wrap an awkward, bulky package.
                                             3

   #1 _____

   #2 _____

   #3 _____

_____ 3. Bruce Willis, Kevin Costner, and Tom Cruise, are all big stars now.
                           1   2   3

   #1 _____

   #2 _____

   #3 _____

Photocopying this product is strictly prohibited by copyright law.

ANALYTICAL GRAMMAR (UNIT #19)   TEST

COMMA RULE 4: TEST

NAME:_____DATE:_____

(RAW SCORE:_____ /80 GRADE:_____POINTS:_____ /20)

PART I: DIRECTIONS: *Underline the participial phrase or adjective clause in the sentences below. Circle the noun or pronoun each phrase or clause modifies. Insert commas where they are needed.*

EXAMPLE: My (brother), who is an excellent basketball player, got a scholarship to Temple.

1.   In my day a teenager liked to single out a hero who could sing or act.

2.   This hero worship which our parents said was a common affliction of teenagers took many forms.

3.   For example, when Elvis moaned and jerked his way through a song, his female audience reacting hysterically to his singing screamed or fainted.

4.   During his reign which lasted longer than anyone expected his followers imitated his hairstyle and way of speaking and moving.

5.   Then the Beatles blasting onto the rock-and-roll scene in the early 60's stole much of the limelight from Elvis who didn't have a cute English accent or a "choirboy" hairdo.

6.   Within a short time Beatle posters which were a necessity to every fan were pushing Elvis items off the shelves.

7.   Every young man who wanted to be "cool" had a Beatle haircut.

8.   In time, however, even the almighty Beatles had to make way for those who were now taking the music-buying public by storm.

9.   In my opinion, the attention that we paid to our singing idols was more beneficial than harmful.

10. A young person interested in guitars and music was probably less likely to get into serious trouble.

(over)

ANALYTICAL GRAMMAR (UNIT #19)   TEST - PAGE 2

PART II: *Insert commas where they are needed.*

1. All students planning to attend the Student Council meeting are excused at 2:00.

2. Louis Pasteur working in his laboratory took time out to treat people for rabies.

3. The fifty-story Civic Center located on the corner of Main and Daniels was evacuated this afternoon due to a small fire in the lobby.

4. Every child enrolling in school for the first time must have a smallpox vaccination.

5. Their youngest daughter loved by everyone is not at all spoiled.

6. Anyone seeing a suspicious character should notify police immediately.

7. A long-distance telephone call wishing you a happy birthday is always a nice surprise.

8. My left index finger badly bruised by the blow began to swell.

9. Miss Danby trying not to laugh offered to help us with the stage makeup.

10. The "House of Tiles" built in Mexico City in the sixteenth century is now known as Sanborn's.

DIRECTIONS: *In each sentence below there is a comma split. In the spaces below each sentence are the numbers of all the commas in the sentence. Find the comma split and write its number in the space at the left. Write what it is splitting beside that comma's number below the sentence. By the other numbers, write the "buzzwords" of the correct commas.*

_____   1.   The All-Breed Dog Show this weekend, will begin at 9:00 on Friday morning,
                                                    1   2
              10:00 on Saturday morning, and noon on Sunday.
                                        3

              #1 _____

              #2 _____

              #3 _____

_____   2.   The beautiful, elegant, model walked gracefully across the stage, but she stopped and
                            1   2   3
              posed when she saw the camera.

              #1 _____

              #2 _____

              #3 _____

ANALYTICAL GRAMMAR (UNIT #19)   TEST - PAGE 2

_____   3.   The winning student, who made a terrific speech, told me, a very funny story about how
                                     1   2   3
              he prepared for it.

              #1 _____

              #2 _____

              #3 _____

_____   4.   I am definitely, a real fan of old movies, early 50's rock-and-roll, and vintage clothes.
                            1   2   3
              #1 _____

              #2 _____

              #3 _____

_____   5.   John, having seen "Star Trek" four times, doesn't want, to see it again, but I could see it
                   1   2   3   4
              ten more times!

              #1 _____

              #2 _____

              #3 _____

              #4 _____

ANALYTICAL GRAMMAR (UNIT #20)　　　　　　　　　　　　　NOTES-PAGE 43

COMMA RULE 5

Use a comma to set off certain INTRODUCTORY ELEMENTS (things which come at the beginning of the sentence). There are four separate "buzzwords" for this rule.

A. **The "buzzword for this rule is *INTRODUCTORY SINGLE WORD:***

   This rule applies to words which come at the beginning of the sentence and serve no function in the sentence, words such as *yes*, *well*, *no*, *why*, etc.

   EXAMPLE: Why, you must be exhausted!

B. **The "buzzword" for this rule is *INTRODUCTORY PARTICIPIAL PHRASE:***

   Put a comma after an introductory participial phrase. (Remember, a participle is a verb that either ends in "ing" or fits into "I have _____.")

   EXAMPLE: Pausing for a moment in the doorway, the new student smiled timidly.

C. **The "buzzword" for this rule is *INTRODUCTORY ADVERB CLAUSE:***

   Put a comma after an introductory adverb clause. (Remember the "thumb test" for finding out if a group of words is an adverb clause. Try this with the sentence below: #1: Put your left thumb over the subordinating conjunction *After*. #2: Put your right thumb over everything that follows the comma. Between your thumbnails you have "Bill hit the ball," right? That's a sentence, isn't it? That's how the "Thumb Test" works: if what's left between your thumbnails is a sentence, then that introductory group of words is an adverb clause.)

   EXAMPLE: After Bill hit the ball, the crowd cheered.

D. **The "buzzword" for this rule is *TWO OR MORE INTRODUCTORY PREPOSITIONAL PHRASES:***

   Put a comma after TWO OR MORE introductory prepositional phrases.

   EXAMPLE: Near the gate at the end of the corral, the horse stood quietly.

   NOTE: If there is only one prepositional phrase at the beginning of the sentence, no comma is necessary **unless the sentence would be confusing without it.** Look at the sentence below and try to imagine it without the comma. Why would it be confusing if there were no comma in it?

   　　　In our state, sales tax is rather rare.

   If the comma were not there, would you - at first - think that this sentence is about "state sales tax"? If the last word of the prepositional phrase looks like it might modify the next word, then you need a comma there to avoid confusion.

ANALYTICAL GRAMMAR (UNIT #20) EXERCISE #1

COMMA RULE 5: EXERCISE #1

NAME:_____ DATE:_____

DIRECTIONS: *Underline and identify the introductory element in each sentence below. (sw=single word; part=participial phrase; prep=prepositional phrase(s); a.c.= adverb clause) Insert commas where they are needed.*

1. Yes Paula is my sister.

2. Climbing down a tree I ripped my pocket on a sharp twig.

3. Since you collect coins you might want this one.

4. While we were vacationing in Montreal we met many French-speaking people.

5. In the morning mail is delivered to our house.

6. When we entered the room was empty.

7. In a corner of the garden the dog had buried all his bones.

8. While she was painting my sister accidentally broke a window.

9. On the morning of the third day the stranded hikers began to worry.

10. Say do you know where the key to the clock is?

DIRECTIONS: *In each sentence below there is a comma split. In the spaces below each sentence are the numbers of all the commas in the sentence. Find the comma split and write its number in the space at the left. Write what it is splitting beside that comma's number below the sentence. By the other numbers, write the "buzzwords" of the correct commas.*

_____   1.   After Bill, hit the ball, the enthusiastic, exuberant crowd cheered, but the home team lost
                         1   2   3   4
                  anyway.

   #1 _____

   #2 _____

   #3 _____

   #4 _____

(over)

Photocopying this product is strictly prohibited by copyright law.

227

ANALYTICAL GRAMMAR (UNIT #20) EXERCISE #1 - PAGE 2

_____   2.   John, who scored the top grade on the math final, has been given, the opportunity to
                      1   2   3
                attend a special math camp this summer.

                #1 _____

                #2 _____

                #3 _____

_____   3.   Henry told Jill, a silly, ridiculous joke that really wasn't funny, but she laughed anyway.
                                   1   2   3
                #1 _____

                #2 _____

                #3 _____

ANALYTICAL GRAMMAR (UNIT #20)   EXERCISE #2

COMMA RULE 5: EXERCISE #2

NAME: _____ DATE: _____

DIRECTIONS: *Underline and identify the introductory elements in the sentences below, using the abbreviations you were given in Exercise #1. Insert commas where they are needed.*

1. Known in China thousands of years ago falconry is an ancient sport.

2. Like the hawk a falcon has a crooked beak.

3. Although falconry is an ancient art many people still enjoy it today.

4. Having sharp claws and hooked beaks falcons are naturally good hunters.

5. In the place of guns some sportsmen use falcons for hunting.

6. After she has learned to fly a female falcon is taken from the nest and tamed.

7. Until the falcon becomes accustomed to living around men she wears a hood.

8. Covering the eyes and head this leather hood helps the hunter control the bird.

9. When the falcon has the hood on the hunter carries the bird into the field.

10. In the field the desired game is located.

11. When the hunter sees his prey and takes the hood off the falcon instinctively attacks.

12. In addition to a hood other implements are used in falconry.

13. During a hunt a falconer usually wears a heavy leather gauntlet or glove.

14. When he is training a young falcon to hunt he also uses lures.

15. Used properly lures teach falcons to attack certain birds.

16. Containing pieces of meat and feathers the lure quickly attracts the falcon.

17. Within seconds a hungry falcon usually pounces upon the lure.

18. Yes falcons become trained hunters in a short time.

19. Since the falcon's speed and accuracy are extremely effective guns are unnecessary.

20. In a field with a falcon hunters often use a dog to retrieve the game.

(over)

ANALYTICAL GRAMMAR (UNIT #20)   EXERCISE #2 - PAGE 2

DIRECTIONS: *In each sentence below there is a comma split. In the spaces below each sentence are the numbers of all the commas in the sentence. Find the comma split and write its number in the space at the left. Write what it is splitting beside that comma's number below the sentence. By the other numbers, write the "buzzwords" of the correct commas.*

_____   1.   Three students in Mrs. Finley's 3rd hour class have received this month, awards for
                                                                                          1
                  attendance, courtesy, and academic excellence.
                         2   3

       #1 _____
       #2 _____
       #3 _____

_____   2.   The happy, excited, fans ran out onto the football field, and they carried the triumphant
                           1   2   3
                  coach around the track.

       #1 _____
       #2 _____
       #3 _____

_____   3.   In a drawer in my dresser, I keep my diary, which contains my innermost thoughts, but
                                           1   2   3
                  no one but me, is allowed to see it.
                                4

       #1 _____
       #2 _____
       #3 _____
       #4 _____

ANALYTICAL GRAMMAR (UNIT #20) EXERCISE #3

COMMA RULE 5: EXERCISE #3

NAME:_____ DATE:_____

DIRECTIONS: *Underline and identify the introductory elements in the sentences below, using the abbreviations you were given for Exercise #1. Insert commas where they are necessary.*

1. Why the entire story is false!

2. Washing and polishing the car for hours the boys found that they were tired.

3. While Mario put the costume on the accompanist played "Rhapsody in Blue."

4. At the edge of the deep woods near Lakeville in Cumberland County they built a small cabin.

5. Among the weak and cowardly competition is usually unpopular.

6. Oh I wouldn't be too sure of that!

7. Behaving like a spoiled child he sulked and pouted for hours.

8. When we had finished playing the piano was rolled offstage to make room for the next act.

9. On the afternoon of the first day of school the halls are filled with confused 7th graders.

10. Driven beyond her patience the teacher slammed her book upon the desk.

11. In a minute I will leave for home.

12. In the dark shadows can appear to be monsters.

PART II: DIRECTIONS: *Write sentences according to the following instructions.*

1. A sentence with a single-word introductory element.

2. A sentence with an introductory participial phrase.

3. A sentence with two or more introductory prepositional phrases.

4. A sentence with an introductory adverb clause.

5. A sentence demonstrating "items in a series."

6. A sentence demonstrating "two adjectives with 'and test.'"

7. A sentence demonstrating "compound sentence."

8. A sentence demonstrating "nonessential modifier."

(over)

ANALYTICAL GRAMMAR (UNIT #20)   EXERCISE #3 - PAGE 2

DIRECTIONS: *In each sentence below there is a comma split. In the spaces below each sentence are the numbers of all the commas in the sentence. Find the comma split and write its number in the space at the left. Write what it is splitting beside that comma's number below the sentence. By the other numbers, write the "buzzwords" of the correct commas.*

_____   1.   Speaking on the intercom, Mr. Campbell, who is our principal, read us in his clear
                                         1   2   3
                voice, the morning announcements.
                     4

                #1 _____
                #2 _____
                #3 _____
                #4 _____

_____   2.   Well, I have a particular reason, which I certainly don't have to explain, for not doing my
                    1   2   3
                boring, stupid, homework!
                      4   5

                #1 _____
                #2 _____
                #3 _____
                #4 _____
                #5 _____

_____   3.   The short, dumpy woman in the line at the bakery sounded completely, idiotic when she
                         1   2
                asked for some bread, which was the only product they sold in the store.
                                    3
                #1 _____
                #2 _____
                #3 _____

ANALYTICAL GRAMMAR (UNIT #20)   TEST

COMMA RULE #5: TEST

NAME:_____DATE:_____

(RAW SCORE:_____/104__GRADE:_____POINTS:_____/20__)

PART I: *ITEMS IN A SERIES:* Insert commas where they are needed.

1. She was formerly on the staff of the embassies in Moscow Berlin Vienna and Madrid.

2. There were toys for the children books for Mom and Dad and a stereo for me!

3. During the summer, workers installed a new gym floor an improved heating system and green chalkboards in the high school.

4. The weather forecaster predicted rain or sleet or snow for tomorrow.

5. We walked we played we ate and we had a great time.

PART II: *TWO ADJECTIVES WITH "AND TEST":* Insert commas where they are needed.

1. She is an alert lively girl.

2. We patiently sat through a long dull amateurish performance.

3. It was a raw cold dark November day.

4. She is a bright talented young woman.

5. He wore a new blue blazer to the concert.

PART III: *COMPOUND SENTENCE:* Insert commas where they are needed.

1. I grabbed the wet dog and Susie slammed the door before he could get away.

2. I gave some good advice to Jim and got some from him in return.

3. The first two acts were slow-moving but the third act is full of action.

4. You go ahead and I'll follow you.

5. The train pulled out of the station and left me stranded there with no luggage.

PART IV: *NONESSENTIAL MODIFIERS:* Insert commas where they are needed.

1. John Thomas who was offered scholarships to two colleges will go to Yale in September.

2. John Thomas is the only senior who was offered two scholarships.

3. My youngest brother who was playing in the street was almost struck by a car.

4. Animals frightened by thunder often try to hide.

5. Friends who do favors for you may expect you to do favors for them.

(over)

Photocopying this product is strictly prohibited by copyright law.

ANALYTICAL GRAMMAR (UNIT #20)   TEST - PAGE 2

PART V: *INTRODUCTORY ELEMENTS*: *Underline and identify the introductory element in each sentence below, using the following abbreviations:(sw=single word; part=participial phrase; prep=prepositional phrase; ac=adverb clause.) Insert commas where they are necessary.*

1. Well be sure to ask if you need help. _____

2. In the second half of the first period Johnson slam-dunked the ball to put our team in the lead. _____

3. Speaking in the assembly Katy Stover urged students to continue to keep the school clean. _____

4. In the newspaper writers seldom make grammatical errors. _____

5. When Bill was driving our truck lurched alarmingly. _____

6. Having studied the commas rules in detail Jean aced the test. _____

7. Why anyone can see the child is ill! _____

8. Since we were leaving in the morning we went to bed early. _____

9. By the end of the class the students were extremely restless. _____

10. Finished at the last minute the assignment was poorly done. _____

PART VI: *ALL COMMA RULES COMBINED*: *Insert commas where they are needed.*

1. Looking for the lost car keys we searched under the car in the house on the porch and among the weeds.

2. Well I guess that about does it!

3. Among the synonyms are "humor" "wit" "sarcasm" and "irony."

4. After we had placed an ad in the paper we found the owner of the puppy.

5. I sold three tickets Jason sold four Jill sold ten and Myra sold twelve.

6. Wanting to gain attention the child talked loudly and interrupted our conversation.

7. In the second section on page 23 notice the list of helping verbs.

8. Students going on the field trip must be at the bus at 9:00 sharp.

9. In the wild animals must kill for food.

10. The teacher read us an excerpt from the speech yet we were not able to recognize it later.

ANALYTICAL GRAMMAR (UNIT #20)   TEST - PAGE 3

PART IV: DIRECTIONS: *In each sentence below there is a comma split. In the spaces below each sentence are the numbers of all the commas in the sentence. Find the comma split and write its number in the space at the left. Write what it is splitting beside that comma's number below the sentence. By the other numbers, write the "buzzwords" of the correct commas.*

_____ 1.   The exhausted, exasperated, teacher walked quickly to the faculty lounge, which was the only
                                 1   2   3
             place where she could get away from kids for a while.

             #1 _____

             #2 _____

             #3 _____

_____ 2.   In a kingdom by the sea, the boy in the poem, loved the main character, who was called
                                           1   2   3
             Annabel Lee.

             #1 _____

             #2 _____

             #3 _____

_____ 3.   Determined to catch students running in the halls, Mr. Calderera suspended, John Griffith, Jason
                                                                           1   2   3
             McGrath, and Tina Matthews.
                          4
             #1 _____

             #2 _____

             #3 _____

             #4 _____

_____ 4.   The Great Bandini, who is undoubtedly the greatest magician on earth, showed his enraptured
                                 1   2
             audience, the most amazing trick of all time.
                          3
             #1 _____

             #2 _____

             #3 _____

Photocopying this product is strictly prohibited by copyright law.

ANALYTICAL GRAMMAR (UNIT #20)   TEST - PAGE 4

_____ 5.   The student who wrote the best essay was, the winner of the Literary Award, and he received a
                                                    1   2
            scholarship, a cash prize, and a certificate.
                    3   4

            #1 _____

            #2 _____

            #3 _____

            #4 _____

COMMA RULES 6, 7, & 8

These comma rules have to do with things that INTERRUPT the sentence. There are three things that, because they "interrupt" the structure of the sentence, are set off by commas.

RULE #6: **The "buzzword" for this rule is either *APPOSITIVES* or *APPOSITIVE PHRASES*.** These are usually set off by commas.

An APPOSITIVE is a noun or pronoun. An APPOSITIVE PHRASE is a noun or pronoun plus anything that modifies it. It is located (usually) after another noun or pronoun and helps to describe it by giving further information about it.

EXAMPLE: I often play tennis, a lively game. (The appositive phrase "a lively game" is another way of saying "tennis" and further describes it.)

NOTE: Sometimes an appositive is so closely related to the noun it restates that it should not be set off by commas. You can usually tell when this is the case by reading the sentence "a la network newscaster." If there is no <u>need</u> to pause, there should not be commas to set it off.

EXAMPLES: My sister Elizabeth is left-handed. (appositive=Elizabeth)
We girls are going shopping. (appositive=girls)
The writer Mark Twain is dead. (appositive=Mark Twain)

NOTE: If the appositive phrase is a title which is already "set off" by either italics or quotation marks, then the commas around that title should be eliminated.

EXAMPLE: My favorite book <u>Gone With the Wind</u> was a national sensation.

Since the title of the book is underlined (or in italics), it is already "set off" from the rest of the sentence, so no commas are necessary.

RULE #7: **The "buzzword" for this rule is *DIRECT ADDRESS*.** Words used in **direct address** are set off by commas.

DIRECT ADDRESS means any name you call someone when you are DIRECTLY ADDRESSING them.

EXAMPLES: The program, Jean, has been changed.(direct address = Jean)
Miss Bates, may I leave early? (direct address=Miss Bates)
Please answer the doorbell, Honey. (direct address=Honey)

RULE #8: **The "buzzword" for this rule is *EXPRESSIONS*.** Expressions are set off by commas.

This rule applies to EXPRESSIONS that are inserted into sentences - not really necessary information - but the kind of information you might put in parentheses. These are often commonly used expressions like "after all," or "on the other hand," or "I think."

EXAMPLES: He didn't, however, keep his promise.(expression=however)
After all, you won the contest! (expression = after all)
Men, in general, like dark suits. (expression = in general)

Photocopying this product is strictly prohibited by copyright law.

ANALYTICAL GRAMMAR (UNIT #21)　　　　　　　　　　　　　　　　EXERCISE #1

COMMA RULES 6, 7, & 8: EXERCISE #1

NAME:_____DATE:_____

DIRECTIONS: *Underline the appositive or appositive phrase, draw an arrow to the noun or pronoun it restates, and insert commas where they are necessary.*

1. Jack my little cousin still prefers nursery rhymes.

2. My friend Mary Jo will visit us soon.

3. Carolyn Keene author of the Nancy Drew stories is a popular writer.

4. Have you met Gail Phillips my best friend?

5. Science my favorite subject gets more fun each year.

6. The Smith twins members of the rugby team have to report for practice soon.

7. Archimedes the Greek physicist made a great discovery by placing a gold crown in a tub of water.

8. The boys had fun working on the car a dilapidated old wreck.

9. Only two of the animals a horse and a cow were saved from the fire.

10. A black funnel-shaped cloud sign of a tornado sent everyone running for shelter.

DIRECTIONS: *Rewrite each pair of sentences into a single sentence containing an appositive or appositive phrase.*

EXAMPLE:　　　Jill Douglas is mayor of our town. She will speak next.

　　　　　　　　Jill Douglas, mayor of our town, will speak next.

1. The fastest runner is Penny Tate. She is on the track team.

2. We have a favorite horse. Her name is Daisy and she won the race.

3. The author is Mark Twain. He knew a lot about people.

4. The girl in the third row is Paula. She likes to hike.

5. There was only one hit against Wills. It was a single.

DIRECTIONS: *Insert commas where they are needed.*

1. Mother have you met Mrs. Gillespie?

2. On the other hand I'd rather have the day off.

3. Dinner Madame is served.

(over)

ANALYTICAL GRAMMAR (UNIT #21) EXERCISE #1 - PAGE 2

DIRECTIONS: *In each sentence below there is a comma split. In the spaces below each sentence are the numbers of all the commas in the sentence. Find the comma split and write its number in the space at the left. Write what it is splitting beside that comma's number below the sentence. By the other numbers, write the "buzzwords" of the correct commas.*

_____ 1. Since the boy who was the winner of the skating competition, had only been training for a short
                                                                                          1
while, some of the other competitors were jealous, or at least they resented his apparently
   2   3
effortless, natural style.
          4

#1 _____

#2 _____

#3 _____

#4 _____

_____ 2. In a short, clear memo to his workers, Mr. Baldwin described all the things he thought were
                   1   2
wrong with the company, how they had gotten that way, and exactly what, could be done
                      3   4   5
about them.

#1 _____

#2 _____

#3 _____

#4 _____

#5 _____

_____ 3. Jackie, my little cousin, still enjoys nursery rhymes, yet he is growing every day, more and
           1   2   3   4
more mature.

#1 _____

#2 _____

#3 _____

#4 _____

ANALYTICAL GRAMMAR (UNIT #21) EXERCISE #2

COMMA RULES 6, 7, & 8: EXERCISE #2

NAME:_____DATE:_____

DIRECTIONS: *Underline the appositives and appositive phrases below. Insert commas where they are needed.*

Yesterday at dawn my family was startled out of bed by a loud screech of tires my uncle Jasper's car pulling into our driveway. Soon we heard voices in the hallway our relatives all talking at once. Sadie my aunt asked, "Oh, is this pretty house where your brother Bob lives? Won't they be surprised to see us their favorite relatives?"

Sparky our little cocker spaniel expressed our surprise by barking noisily at the intruders our uninvited and unexpected relatives. Then Bonecrusher their Saint Bernard lumbered forward and tried to make breakfast out of Sparky! Dad untangled the snarling animals and tied both of them Sparky and Bonecrusher in the backyard. Mortal enemies on sight the dogs spent the rest of the day growling and yapping at each other.

A minor incident that fight was only the beginning of the turmoil in our house. Wilbur Uncle Jasper's youngest boy took an immediate liking to a handpainted vase a treasured heirloom and dashed it to smithereens. While Aunt Sadie was apologizing for Wilbur, Uncle Jasper was chasing Sylvester his oldest boy. Sylvester, meanwhile, was chasing my sister Beth so he could cut her hair with the kitchen scissors!

Just before leaving the house a place I used to call "Home Sweet Home" Uncle Jasper said, "We're going to spend our vacation two whole weeks with you!" To be polite, we have to stay home and play nifty games particularly Monopoly and Chinese checkers. Even our family's bedtime formerly 10:00 has changed to midnight. And, since Aunt Sadie has insomnia a condition which prevents her from sleeping past 5:00 a.m. everybody gets up for an early breakfast. My stomach turns when I think about their visit a full two weeks.

But yesterday Mother a wonderfully wise person smiled at my complaints. "Take heart, Daniel my son," she said. "Remember that we will have our revenge! Our day will come at about 2:00 p.m. on a Thursday in November Thanksgiving when - totally unannounced - we'll just drop in on THEM!!!"

DIRECTIONS: *Use each of the following items as an APPOSITIVE or APPOSITIVE PHRASE in a sentence of your own. Write 10 separate sentences, one for each item below.*

1. Linda
2. a nuisance
3. my neighbor
4. a good teacher
5. Austin and Victor
6. the life of the party
7. a girl sitting near me
8. the candidate to select
9. a book for children
10. the man you should meet

EXAMPLE: Mrs. Finley, a good teacher, is also a wonderful person.(...your sentences don't have to be true...)

(over)

ANALYTICAL GRAMMAR (UNIT #21)   EXERCISE #2 - PAGE 2

DIRECTIONS: *In each sentence below there is a comma split. In the spaces below each sentence are the numbers of all the commas in the sentence. Find the comma split and write its number in the space at the left. Write what it is splitting beside that comma's number below the sentence. By the other numbers, write the "buzzwords" of the correct commas.*

_____ 1. My neighbor's relatives, an interesting group, visit them each summer with an
                              1   2
assortment of equally peculiar, friends.
                                3

#1 _____

#2 _____

#3 _____

_____ 2. During the early part of last June, they were looking forward to a few weeks of complete, total
                                          1   2
relaxation when they answered, an unwelcome knock at the door.
                              3

#1 _____

#2 _____

#3 _____

_____ 3. Standing there in all their splendor of baggy Bermuda shorts, knobby knees, and friendly grins
                                                                  1   2
were his uncle Herbert and his large, obnoxious, family.
                                    3   4

#1 _____

#2 _____

#3 _____

#4 _____

ANALYTICAL GRAMMAR (UNIT #21)   EXERCISE #3

COMMA RULES 6, 7, & 8: EXERCISE #3

NAME:_____ DATE:_____

DIRECTIONS: *Underline the interrupters in the sentences below. Identify them in the space below as follows: appos = appositive or appositive phrase, da = direct address, expr = expression. Insert commas where they are needed.*

1. The story in my opinion is much too long and complicated._____

2. You scoundrel what do you mean by trying to cheat your friends?_____

3. When Mr. Kean my geography teacher visited Indiana, he toured the campus of Purdue.
   _____

4. Richie leave the room and shut the door. _____

5. Mathematics I'm afraid is my hardest subject._____

6. *Little Women* a classic book for young people was part of my growing up._____

7. You will stay I hope as long as you possibly can. _____

8. Do you remember Patty what Romeo's last name was?_____

9. Modern highways for example are marvelous feats of engineering. _____

10. May I go to the movies Dad?_____

DIRECTIONS: *This is an activity you and your teacher will do tomorrow. You don't have to do anything for homework.*

1.	as I was saying	4.	for instance	7.	on the other hand
2.	on the contrary	5.	if you ask me	8.	however
3.	of course	6.	to tell the truth	9.	for example
				10.	in fact

(over)

ANALYTICAL GRAMMAR (UNIT #21)   EXERCISE #3 - PAGE 2

DIRECTIONS: *In each sentence below there is a comma split. In the spaces below each sentence are the numbers of all the commas in the sentence. Find the comma split and write its number in the space at the left. Write what it is splitting beside that comma's number below the sentence. By the other numbers, write the "buzzwords" of the correct commas.*

_____ 1. What, in your opinion, was the cause of the economic crash of 1929, and why didn't the people in
              1   2   3
charge of the Stock Market, do anything about it?
                           4

#1 _____

#2 _____

#3 _____

#4 _____

_____ 2. My hair dryer, which I bought three years ago, has put out more hot air than all Presidential
                        1   2
candidates put together, but this morning, if you can believe it, it decided, to poop out on me!
                       3   4   5   6

#1 _____

#2 _____

#3 _____

#4 _____

#5 _____

#6 _____

_____ 3. Anybody who has ever tried to eat spaghetti at a fancy restaurant, knows that, no matter what,
                                                                            1   2   3
you'll end up with spots of sauce all over your chin, down your shirt, and on the tablecloth.
                                                    4   5

#1 _____

#2 _____

#3 _____

#4 _____

#5 _____

Photocopying this product is strictly prohibited by copyright law.

PLAYING WITH TRANSITIONAL DEVICES

What you see below is a conversation about Mrs. Dragonbottom, the evil grammar teacher. Do you find it difficult to follow? Doesn't it appear to be saying one thing and then saying just the opposite? Now, using the transitional devices at the bottom of Exercise #3, put the first expression in front of the first sentence below; put the second expression in front of the second sentence, and so on. Is it hard to follow now? That's how valuable these transitional devices are; you should make an effort to use them in your writing until they become second nature.

SAMPLE CONVERSATION

Mrs. Dragonbottom is the meanest teacher in this whole school!

She's an absolute sweetiepie!

She can be rather vindictive when she is crossed.

She gave me a detention just for setting fire to Martha Sue's pigtails!

She's a mean old witch!

I don't think I've ever known anybody as mean as Mrs. Dragonbottom.

She rescued that poor little lost puppy last week.

That doesn't excuse all the other stuff she does.

When Billy knocked over the outhouse, she called his mom!

Billy was grounded until his 21st birthday!

NOW - TRY IT WITH THE EXPRESSIONS!

ANALYTICAL GRAMMAR (UNIT #21)   TEST

COMMA RULES 6, 7, & 8: TEST

NAME:_____ DATE:_____

(RAW SCORE:____/82 GRADE:_____ POINTS:____/20)

PART I: DIRECTIONS: *Insert commas where they are needed.*

1. Shana Alexander one-time editor of <u>McCall's</u> was the main speaker.

2. We have a figurine made of clay from Kilimanjaro Africa's highest mountain.

3. The whole class listened to my best friend Jane give her speech.

4. Saint Augustine the oldest city in the United States has many very narrow streets.

5. Sugar cane an important Florida crop may be shipped refined or raw.

6. Do you own a thesaurus a dictionary of synonyms and antonyms?

7. At North Cape the northernmost point of Europe the sun does not set from the middle of May until the end of July.

8. The American mastodon an extinct, elephantlike animal was hunted by primitive man.

9. John F. Kennedy's brother Robert was assassinated during a Presidential campaign.

10. At Thermopylae a narrow pass in Eastern Greece a band of three hundred Spartans faced an army of thousands from Persia.

PART II: DIRECTIONS: *Insert commas where they are needed.*

1. Sandra why do you call your cat Cleopatra?

2. Stop this incessant chatter class.

3. We my fellow graduates of the class of 2000 will be the leaders of the 21st century.

4. Professor Adams when was the Battle of Marathon?

5. What is your opinion of the candidates Laura?

6. Dad may I borrow the car?

7. Where my dear Mr. Ditherington do you think you are going?

8. Senator Smith I have a proposal for improving our state.

9. Lisa you really must apologize.

10. You know that dogs aren't allowed on the couch Snoopy!

(over)

ANALYTICAL GRAMMAR (UNIT #21) — TEST - PAGE 2

PART III: DIRECTIONS: *Insert commas where they are needed.*

1. Yes there are many constellations visible in the summer.

2. For instance on a summer night you can see the Scorpion and the Serpent.

3. To be sure we should not fail to mention the Milky Way.

4. The Milky Way in fact is more impressive in the summer than at any other time.

5. Of course Hercules is an interesting constellation.

6. Studying the constellations is in my opinion a most interesting pastime.

7. It does take some imagination however to pick out some of them.

8. The Archer for example is hard to perceive.

9. The Scorpion on the other hand is quite clearly outlined.

10. Astronomy I think is a fascinating science.

PART IV: DIRECTIONS: *Insert commas where they are needed.*

1. The whole family several friends and some relatives from out-of-state came for dinner on Sunday.

2. Mom made a delicious gourmet meal and we sat down to a table loaded with food.

3. Yes we all ate way too much!

4. I especially loved the golden-brown piping-hot home-baked rolls.

5. My dad who is trying to lose a few pounds started off with a generous serving of salad.

6. Since he'd eaten only salad he decided to have a "tiny taste" of everything else.

7. The "tiny taste" a generous serving of everything edible on the table filled his plate!

8. His diet needless to say was blown sky-high for the day.

9. Cutting himself a large piece of lemon-meringue pie Dad declared that his diet would start first thing the next morning.

10. Dinners eaten on festive occasions in our house are always fatal to Dad's diet!

****

DIAGRAM FOR 5 POINTS EXTRA CREDIT:

Any student of this course in grammar should know the structure of the sentence and the function of every word in it.

ANALYTICAL GRAMMAR (UNIT #21) TEST - PAGE 3

DIRECTIONS: *In each sentence below there is a comma split. In the spaces below each sentence are the numbers of all the commas in the sentence. Find the comma split and write its number in the space at the left. Write what it is splitting beside that comma's number below the sentence. By the other numbers, write the "buzzwords" of the correct commas.*

_____ 1. Yes, we all sat around looking at old yearbooks, laughing at the funny hair styles we wore, and
           1   2   3
secretly wishing with all our hearts, that we could go back to those good old days for a while.
                                    4

#1 _____
#2 _____
#3 _____
#4 _____

_____ 2. The character in the play who had all the money and fame, was the one whom we most suspected,
                                                                1   2
but the real murderer was a quiet, mousy person that no on even noticed!.
                                 3

#1 _____
#2 _____
#3 _____

_____ 3. John, the most able debater on the team, appeared to be stumped for an answer until one of the
       1   2
youngest, least-experienced, members of the team saved the day.
        3   4

#1 _____
#2 _____
#3 _____
#4 _____

_____ 4. Before Albert was old enough to get a license, he had already picked out his car, a used Chevrolet
                                                     1   2
with 40,000 miles on it, and started with his own money, a savings account for the down payment.
                       3   4

#1 _____
#2 _____
#3 _____
#4 _____

COMMA RULES 9, 10, & 11

COMMA RULE #9: **The "buzzword" for this rule is *DATES & ADDRESSES*:** use commas to separate items in dates and addresses.

    EXAMPLE: My family moved to Knoxville, Tennessee, on Monday, May 4, 1964.

    On May 4, 1964, I changed my address to 645 Commerce Street, Knoxville, Tennessee 20200.

(NOTE: There is no comma between the state and zip code.)
(ALSO NOTE: When a date or an address is part of a sentence, you must put a comma AFTER the last item in the date or address, if the sentence continues on. Look at the comma after "Tennessee" and the one after "1964" in the sentences above.)

COMMA RULE #10: *The "buzzword" for this rule is SALUTATIONS & CLOSINGS:* use a comma after the salutation of a friendly letter (use a colon after the salutation of a business letter) and after the closing of any letter.

    EXAMPLE:
Dear Jim, (friendly letter)
Dear Mr. Jones: (business letter)
Truly yours,
Loves and kisses,

COMMA RULE #11: *The "buzzword" for this rule is NAMES & ABBREVIATIONS:* use a comma between a name and Jr., Sr., M.D., etc.

    EXAMPLE:
Allen Davies, Jr.
Stanley Browne, M. D.

(NOTE: Do not use a comma between a name and a Roman numeral - Jonathan Sanders III; Henry VIII; Elizabeth I)

Photocopying this product is strictly prohibited by copyright law.

COMMA RULES 9, 10, & 11: EXERCISE #1

NAME:_____ DATE:_____

DIRECTIONS: *Insert commas where they are needed.*

1. 443 North University Avenue Lansing Michigan 48103

2. 1900 Logan Road Linden New Jersey 07036

3. Monday August 5 1991

4. after January 1 1984

5. 379 Scott Avenue Salt Lake City Utah 85115

6. Michigan Avenue at Twelfth Street Chicago Illinois

7. Thanksgiving Day 1978

8. from June 23 1989 to January 2 1990

9. either Tuesday September 3 or Saturday September 7

10. Box 147 Rapid City South Dakota

11. The building on the corner of Market Street and Highland Avenue in Akron Ohio is where my grandfather was born.

12. Sincerely yours

13. Dear Jean   (in a letter thanking her for a baby shower gift.)

14. Dear George   (in a letter asking your tax man for information on the stock market)

15. The Founding Fathers of our nation signed the Declaration of Independence in Philadelphia Pennsylvania on July 4 1776.

16. The party will be on Friday July 9 in Wheeling West Virginia at 7:00 in the evening.

(over)

ANALYTICAL GRAMMAR (UNIT #22) — EXERCISE #1 - PAGE 2

DIRECTIONS: *In each sentence below there is a comma split. In the spaces below each sentence are the numbers of all the commas in the sentence. Find the comma split and write its number in the space at the left. Write what it is splitting beside that comma's number below the sentence. By the other numbers, write the "buzzwords" of the correct commas.*

_____ 1. In July, 1776, Thomas Jefferson and the other Founding Fathers, gave us the Declaration of
        1   2   3
Independence.

#1 _____

#2 _____

#3 _____

_____ 2. The men at the Continental Congress in Philadelphia, voted on a document which remains to this
                                                   1
day one of the most famous, revered writings of all time, but they probably didn't realize that at
                          2   3
the time.

#1 _____

#2 _____

#3 _____

_____ 3. When the Declaration was finally signed on July 4, 1776, they surely thought, that the world
                                                  1   2   3
would soon forget what they had done on that hot, humid day.
                                               4

#1 _____

#2 _____

#3 _____

#4 _____

ANALYTICAL GRAMMAR (UNIT #22) EXERCISE #2

COMMA RULES 9, 10, & 11: EXERCISE #2

NAME:_____ DATE:_____

DIRECTIONS: *Insert commas where they are needed.*

1. The first Boston Marathon was held on April 19 1897.

2. Are you talking about Kansas City Kansas or Kansas City Missouri?

3. Sherlock Holmes supposedly lived at 221B Baker Street London England.

4. Send your reply to Campbell and Jones, Inc. 135 South LaSalle Street Chicago Illinois 60603.

5. He was born on April 3 1963 which makes him an Aries.

6. Ed's address is 4652 Orchard Street Oakland California.

7. We're going to the museum on Thursday May 5.

8. Does this address say Gary Indiana or Cary Illinois?

9. My older brother hasn't had many birthdays because he was born on February 29 1960.

10. Someday my address will be 1600 Pennsylvania Avenue Washington D. C.

DIRECTIONS: *Insert commas where they are needed and be prepared to tell why you used each comma.*

1. Since Susan's visit was to be a short one we wanted to do something special each day.

2. A luncheon was held in her honor and all of her high school buddies were there.

3. Claiming to be totally surprised Susan had a terrific time.

4. At her table were Marie Stacey Beth and Renee.

5. Since no one had plans for the evening we talked until it was quite late.

6. The waiter cleared our table but we sat over our coffee and talked for hours.

7. Susan who was a very appreciative guest said she had never had so much fun.

8. On Saturday June 10 we got together with some of our old neighbors.

9. Yes even old Mrs. Bates was there!

10. After many hours of gossip memories and laughter we took Susan to the airport.

(over)

ANALYTICAL GRAMMAR (UNIT #22)   EXERCISE #2 - PAGE 2

DIRECTIONS: *In each sentence below there is a comma split. In the spaces below each sentence are the numbers of all the commas in the sentence. Find the comma split and write its number in the space at the left. Write what it is splitting beside that comma's number below the sentence. By the other numbers, write the "buzzwords" of the correct commas.*

_____ 1.   John, my next-door neighbor, is giving a party this weekend, but he is extremely, nervous about
                     1   2   3   4
the arrangements.

#1 _____

#2 _____

#3 _____

#4 _____

_____ 2.   He has invited, all his closest, most intimate friends to a gathering on Friday, February 6th.
                             1   2   3

#1 _____

#2 _____

#3 _____

_____ 3.   The refreshments, the music, and all the games, have been gathered together, and we all expect
                                    1   2   3   4
to have a wild, crazy time.
                5

#1 _____

#2 _____

#3 _____

#4 _____

#5 _____

ANALYTICAL GRAMMAR (UNIT #22)				EXERCISE #3

COMMA RULES 9, 10, & 11: EXERCISE #3

NAME:_____ DATE:_____

DIRECTIONS: *Insert commas where they are needed.*

1. My cousins were both born on September 6 1962.

2. Why is 10 Downing Street London famous?

3. Eleanor Roosevelt was born on October 11 1884 and died on November 7 1962.

4. Where were you on Friday June 23 2000?

5. Reno Nevada is farther west than Los Angeles California.

6. Saturday July 26 is Kathryn's birthday party.

7. The best hot dogs on earth are at Petey's 110 Washington Street Elm Forest Illinois.

8. Address your letter to the *Chicago Sun-Times* 401 North Wabash Avenue Chicago Illinois 60611.

9. We lived at 130 Rand Road Austin Texas from May 1 1993 to April 30 1997.

10. The only historical date I can remember is July 4 1776.

DIRECTIONS: *Insert commas where they are needed and be prepared to tell which rule is used.*

1. Completely exhausted by our day outdoors we were happy to tumble into bed early.

2. Susan lived on a farm and she invited us to visit her on another weekend.

3. Although we had seen many farms visiting one was a new experience.

4. It was great fun in my opinion to see all the cows horses pigs and chickens.

5. When the roosters began to crow at dawn the farm seemed to come to life.

6. Breakfast was very early so that we could get to the barn to see the milking machine feed the pigs and scatter feed for the chickens.

7. Dinner was at noon and we had never had such heaping platters of mashed potatoes fried chicken fresh peas and homemade blueberry muffins.

8. After we had eaten our dessert we stretched out under a big leafy tree and went to sleep.

9. Since it was a warm humid afternoon we were glad to go for a cool refreshing swim.

10. Getting ready for bed that night we decided that the farm was the perfect vacation spot.

(over)

ANALYTICAL GRAMMAR (UNIT #22)   EXERCISE #3 - PAGE 2

DIRECTIONS: *In each sentence below there is a comma split. In the spaces below each sentence are the numbers of all the commas in the sentence. Find the comma split and write its number in the space at the left. Write what it is splitting beside that comma's number below the sentence. By the other numbers, write the "buzzwords" of the correct commas..*

_____ 1. Sherlock Holmes, who is one of my favorite fictional characters, solved with the help of
                          1   2
Dr. Watson, hundreds of difficult mysteries.
           3

#1 _____
#2 _____
#3 _____

_____ 2. Holmes and Watson were, extremely clever when it came to dealing with dangerous, vicious
                       1   2
criminals, and they put their share of them behind bars.
         3

#1 _____
#2 _____
#3 _____

_____ 3. Since the middle of the 19th century, readers have thrilled to the workings of Holmes' precise,
                                              1   2
computer-like, mind as he solved crime after crime.
              3

#1 _____
#2 _____
#3 _____

ANALYTICAL GRAMMAR (UNIT #22) NOTES

ALL COMMA RULES TEST

NAME:_____ DATE:_____

(RAW SCORE:_____ /138 GRADE:_____ POINTS:_____ /100)

PART I: Items in a Series: *Insert commas where they are needed.*

1. Jim and Ted and Bill are my best friends among all my classmates.

2. Today's symbols of success in the home include personal computers VCR's and electronic games.

3. A considerate person listens when others are speaking thinks carefully before saying anything and tries not to hurt anyone's feelings.

4. We noticed unsightly beer cans candy wrappers and refuse paper all along the road.

5. I want a stereo or a mountain bike or cross-country skis for my birthday.

PART II: Two Adjectives with "And Test": *Insert commas where they are needed.*

1. Everyone stared at the king's priceless crown.

2. The wagon train approached wild lonely mountainous country.

3. Port Townsend is a friendly unsophisticated little town.

4. The beautiful blond lady had a short peculiar-looking older brother.

5. The old grandfather clock struck midnight.

PART III: Compound Sentence: *Insert commas where they are needed.*

1. The long drought that had worried the farmers and ranchers finally ended and day after day the rain came down in sheets.

2. The beds of streams that had been dry came to life and the caked soil became green again.

3. Small streams became raging rivers and greedily engulfed the countryside.

4. The levees broke and towns were flooded.

5. We thought the drought would never end but it finally did.

(over)

Photocopying this product is strictly prohibited by copyright law.

ANALYTICAL GRAMMAR (UNIT #22)   TEST - PAGE 2

PART IV: Nonessential Modifiers: *Insert commas where they are needed*

1. Students who cut school should be expelled.

2. Senator Stevens hoping for passage of his bill talked to several legislators.

3. All buildings which had been declared unsafe were torn down.

4. I wish the boy that I met at Sandy's party would call me.

5. The young salesman trying desperately to make a sale talked for five minutes.

PART V: Introductory Elements: *Insert commas where they are needed.*

1. Why everyone knows what happened in 1776!

2. When we were watching television last night I felt an earthquake.

3. In a dark corner of the deserted building a kitten was crying pathetically.

4. Walking slowly through the museum the man searched for a particular painting.

5. For walking shoes should be comfortable and sturdy.

PART VI: Appositives, Direct Address, Expressions: *Underline the interrupter in each sentence below. Insert commas where they are needed. Identify the interrupter in the space provided. (appos = appositive; da = direct address; expr = expression)*

1. Today's movies if you want my opinion contain too much violence. _____

2. John Glenn America's first astronaut to orbit the earth became a United States Senator. _____

3. Class today we'll be studying the use of the semicolon. _____

4. Your room sir is ready for you. _____

5. The Waldorf one of New York's oldest hotels has all the charm of yesteryear. _____

6. By the way have you met my aunt? _____

7. It is after all your turn to wash the dishes. _____

8. Last fall I read *Tom Sawyer* by Mark Twain America's foremost 19th century humorist. _____

9. Have you seen the car keys Mom? _____

10. The final game however was called because of rain. _____

ANALYTICAL GRAMMAR (UNIT #22)   TEST - PAGE 3

PART VII: Dates & Addresses, Salutations & Closings, Names & Abbreviations: *Insert commas where they are needed.*

1. Our idea was to hold a reunion on June 22 2001 at the old high school.

2. Write to me at 222 Oak Road Akron Ohio 81007 after the first of March.

3. Their baby was born on Monday May 1 1959 in Baltimore Maryland.

4. It was on May 10th in 1948 that they began work on the project.

5. She lived at 330 Main Street in Westfield New Jersey.

6. Henry III was a monarch about whom Shakespeare wrote plays.

7. Maria had moved to Tampa Florida on November 19 1995 and in 1996 she moved again to Columbus Ohio.

8. Present at the reception for Senator and Mrs. Stevens were Mr. and Mrs. Henry Worth Jr. and Martin Feldstein M. D.

9. The Constitution of the United States was signed on September 17 1787 in Philadelphia Pennsylvania.

10. Dear John

    Last night I heard what I thought was a cat in severe pain outside my window. Imagine my surprise when my mother told me it was you serenading me! If you promise never to sing to me again for as long as we live, I accept your proposal of marriage!

                                                                  Love and kisses

                                                                       Marcia

PART VIII: All Comma Rules: *Insert commas where they are needed.*

1. We left Moravia which is a resort town in New York and drove to Owasco Lake which is near Syracuse.

2. Michael you know I hate tea parties receptions and formal dinners!

3. This letter is addressed to Mr. Nick Walters P. O. Box 429 Culver City California 90014 and is dated July 14 1991.

4. When people say I resemble my mother I always feel flattered.

5. A simple clear writing style is always appropriate.

6. The class studied all the comma rules in detail and the teacher gave them a big test.

7. A boy riding a red bicycle was seen leaving the scene of the accident.

8. That dress my dear Miss Ames looks like a dream on you!

9. Paul Bunyan the legendary giant of the Northwest had a blue ox for a pet.

10. Mrs. Hood said she wasn't mad about the window and invited us in for cookies.

(over)

ANALYTICAL GRAMMAR (UNIT #22) — TEST - PAGE 4

DIRECTIONS: *In each sentence below there is a comma split. In the spaces below each sentence are the numbers of all the commas in the sentence. Find the comma split and write its number in the space at the left. Write what it is splitting beside that comma's number below the sentence. By the other numbers, write the "buzzwords" of the correct commas.*

_____ 1. On our trip around the country, we were really and truly, disgusted to see the litter that
                                          1   2
thoughtless, selfish people had dropped along the wayside.
           3

#1 _____

#2 _____

#3 _____

_____ 2. We saw beer cans, candy wrappers, and all sorts of filthy, unsightly, garbage.
                      1   2   3   4

#1 _____

#2 _____

#3 _____

#4 _____

_____ 3. Because of public awareness of this problem, people all over the country, are getting fed up with
                                                  1   2
litterers, who should know better.
        3

#1 _____

#2 _____

#3 _____

_____ 4. Signs, commercials, and articles have increased in recent years, our determination to do
              1   2   3
something about this problem.

#1 _____

#2 _____

#3 _____

_____ 5. Hoping the message will get out, the media is trying to convince "litterbugs" to leave us, a
                                       1   2
cleaner, more beautiful country, but we all have to help.
       3   4

#1 _____

#2 _____

#3 _____

#4 _____

PUNCTUATING QUOTATIONS

First of all, there are four terms we will be using in this unit which you must understand: they are DIRECT QUOTE, INDIRECT QUOTE, DIALOGUE, and NARRATIVE. The following four lines should make these terms clear to you.

DIRECT QUOTE: Jackie said, "I am going to Palmer on Saturday."
(DIALOGUE is what we call the words that Jackie is saying = *I am going to Palmer on Saturday*)
(NARRATIVE is what we call what the narrator is saying = *Jackie said*)

INDIRECT QUOTE: Jackie said that she is going to Palmer on Saturday.

I. You use quotation marks ("-open quotes," - close quotes) to enclose a person's exact words.

    EXAMPLE: "We're learning about punctuation," said Joe.

II. A direct quote begins with a capital letter *if the quote is a sentence*.

    EXAMPLE: Maria said, "The frame is not strong enough."

III. THE BROKEN QUOTE: When a quoted <u>sentence</u> of dialogue is divided into two parts by narrative, the second part of the dialogue begins with a lower case letter.

    EXAMPLE: "The time has come," said Joe, "to finish my term paper." (note the lower case *t* in *to*)

IV. When you go from dialogue to narrative or from narrative to dialogue - unless other punctuation is present - you need a comma to "change gears" from one to the other.

    EXAMPLE: "Science is more interesting than history," said Bernie.
    (note the location of the comma after "history")

    I asked, "Who is your science teacher?"
    (note the location of the comma after "asked")

    "Does she let you do experiments?" asked Debbie.
    (note that no comma is necessary after "experiments" because there is other punctuation there.)

V. A period or comma following a quotation is ALWAYS placed INSIDE the close quotes.

    EXAMPLE: "It's time to go," said the guide.

    The man replied, "I'm ready."

See how the period and comma are <u>inside</u> the close quote?

(over)

VI. Question marks and exclamation marks should be placed <u>inside</u> the close quotes IF THE DIALOGUE IS A QUESTION OR EXCLAMATION. Question marks and exclamation marks should be place <u>outside</u> the close quotes IF THE NARRATIVE IS A QUESTION OR EXCLAMATION. Study the following quotations very carefully.

    EXAMPLE: "How far have we come?" asked the man. (dialogue is a question)

                     Who said, "Go west, young man"? (narrative is a question)

                     "Jump!" screamed the woman. (dialogue is an exclamation)

                     I nearly died when he said, "Time's up"! (narrative is an exclamation.)

VII. When your dialogue consists of several sentences, open quotes at the beginning and don't close them until the end of the dialogue.

    EXAMPLE: "I'll wait for you at the Mall. Get there as soon as you can. Try not to be late," he said and rushed off down the hill.

VIII. A QUOTE WITHIN A QUOTE: Use single quotes (' - open quote,'- close quote) to enclose dialogue inside other dialogue.

    EXAMPLE: "Let's all yell, 'You won!' when Jack comes in," said Dad.

                     "Did I really hear Mrs. Neuman say, ' You may use books on the test'?" asked Sally.

A good way to handle quotations is to think of them as sentences inside other sentences. In the sentence -

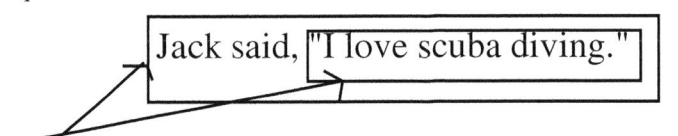

                     Jack said, "I love scuba diving."

The "inside" sentence is "I love scuba diving." Any punctuation for the inside sentence goes <u>inside the quotes.</u>

   I is the subject, *love* is the verb, and *scuba diving* is the direct object.

The "outside" sentence is "Jack said, 'I love scuba diving.'" Any punctuation for this sentence goes <u>outside the double quotes</u>, unless it is a period or a comma which go inside the close quote no matter what.

   Jack is the subject, *said* is the verb and the quoted sentence is the direct object.

Be sure, when you're dealing with quotations, that you punctuate each sentence - both the inside one and the outside one - correctly.

A couple of handy items: You never have two "end marks" of punctuation together, unless one of them is a question mark and one of them is an exclamation mark. Example: *Did Jane scream, "Help!"? asked Mr. Bates.* Notice that Mr. Bates is asking a question, so his sentence needs a question mark. Jane is screaming, so her sentence needs an exclamation mark.

In any other situation, a question or exclamation mark would "cancel out" a period or comma. Example: *Did Jane say, "I'm going out"? asked Mr. Bates.* Notice that Jane's sentence loses its punctuation to the question mark.

ANALYTICAL GRAMMAR (UNIT #23) — EXERCISE #1

PUNCTUATING QUOTATIONS: EXERCISE #1

NAME:_____ DATE:_____

DIRECTIONS: *Copy the following sentences in the space provided below each sentence, inserting commas, quotation marks, and capitals where they are needed. Do not recopy the ones that are correct as they are.*

1. The librarian told me to be quiet.

2. At the same time Mike whispered hush up!

3. He asked can't you see that people are trying to study?

4. I replied in a whisper I'm sorry that I disturbed you.

5. I should have known better, I said to myself, than to raise my voice.

6. Next I quietly asked the girl across from me for her science book.

7. She whispered I'll give it to you in a minute.

8. But I need it now I explained.

9. She muttered something about people who can't remember to bring their stuff.

10. About that time the bell rang and the librarian called out it's time to go, kids.

PUNCTUATING QUOTATIONS: EXERCISE #2

NAME:_____ DATE:_____

DIRECTIONS: *Rewrite the following sentences in the space provided, inserting proper punctuation and capitalization.*

1. What do you know about the life of Mark Twain our teacher asked Lydia.

2. Did you mean it when you said I'll help you with that assignment

3. Look out screamed the man on the dock.

4. What a relief it was to hear the timekeeper say put down your pencils now *(Sentences worded in this manner [What a day it was!] should be treated as exclamations.)*

5. Do you remember asked Mrs. Bates the story of the tortoise and the hare

6. I leaned over and whispered are you going to be busy this afternoon

7. Did anybody notice that sign that said last chance for gas for 100 miles

8. If you think shouted Bill I'm going to help you now, you're crazy

9. When was the last time you heard a teacher say no homework tonight, class

10. The next person who says loan me a pen is going to regret it

ANALYTICAL GRAMMAR (UNIT #23)   EXERCISE #3

PUNCTUATING QUOTATIONS: EXERCISE #3

NAME:_____ DATE:_____

DIRECTIONS: *Rewrite the following sentences, punctuating them correctly. Be careful, they're sneaky!*

1. Noel, have you seen my catcher's mitt asked Jim it's been missing since Monday. I need it for practice today.

2. In what poem did Longfellow write the thoughts of youth are long, long thoughts asked Bill

3. Is his motto still stay in the game and pitch I asked Bob

4. How I laughed when my science teacher referred to Bob as the young Einstein in my class exclaimed Tip

5. Did Jack shout bring my book or did he yell ring my cook asked the Duke

DIRECTIONS: *If a sentence below is an INDIRECT QUOTE, rewrite it to be a DIRECT QUOTE. If it's a DIRECT QUOTE, rewrite it to be an INDIRECT QUOTE.*

1. My brother said he would miss the rehearsal.

2. "What is your excuse?" asked the principal.

3. "Sam," asked Mia, "why aren't you playing soccer this year?"

4. The thief finally admitted that he stole the furs.

5. I told Dad I needed fifteen dollars.

6. "How did you manage to get that answer?" asked the teacher.

7. Bill yelled that the score was tied again.

8. Grandpa said he could feel snow in the air.

9. Jim said he thought he could win.

10. "That," said Mr. Turner with a grin, "is the first mistake I've made in ten years!"

ANALYTICAL GRAMMAR (UNIT #23)   TEST

PUNCTUATING QUOTATIONS: TEST

NAME:_____ DATE:_____

(RAW SCORE:_____ /185 GRADE:_____ POINTS:____ /20)

PART I: DIRECTIONS: *Rewrite the following sentences NEATLY on a separate sheet of paper. Put in the necessary capitalization and punctuation. Keep in mind, as you do this, that this is a story which BEGINS WITH NARRATIVE and contains a conversation between TWO PEOPLE.*

1. do you often hear your fellow students complain my teachers give too much homework

2. have you ever heard students shout down with homework

3. I'm drowning in homework I hear students cry

4. How pathetic it is to hear a student say I can't do any more

5. the first thing you usually hear a student say is what's the homework tonight

6. I think I have homework tonight said Jean

7. Bob, do we have any homework tonight in Mr. Gaal's class she asked

8. sure Bob replied he told us to read Chapter Twelve and answer the questions

9. Chapter Twelve shrieked Jean doesn't that man think we have personal lives

10. that man replied Bob is a sadist

11. I know that Bob groaned Jean I wish there was a way to get him locked up

12. I know what we could do we could drive him right over the edge shouted Bob

13. How asked Jean, looking hopefully at Bob tell us how

14. If we all did our homework every single night said Bob, rubbing his hands gleefully together he'd probably have a nervous breakdown trying to keep up with the grading

15. Jean stared at Bob with disgust. Is THAT your great idea she asked

16. When you said is THAT your great idea it means you're not thrilled with it, right said Bob

17. Bob said Jean go soak your head. Your idea stinks

Photocopying this product is strictly prohibited by copyright law.

ANALYTICAL GRAMMAR (UNIT #23) — TEST - PAGE 2

PART II: DIRECTIONS: *Recopy the following sentences on a separate sheet of paper, punctuating and capitalizing them properly. If the sentence is correct as it is, write the letter C next to that number on your paper.*

1. Did you notice Inspector Brewer asked anything peculiar about the suspect

2. Just that he wore a raincoat and a hat that hid his face I replied.

3. Right said the Inspector

4. I also believe he limped on his left foot I said

5. Did you say he was tall Brewer asked and are you certain about the limp

6. I reminded the Inspector that I had only caught a glimpse of the man.

7. Oh by the way I added he was carrying a small suitcase too

8. Would you mind coming down to the station to make a statement Brewer asked

9. I told him I didn't mind, but that I preferred to keep my name out of the papers.

10. No need to worry he remarked as he opened the squadcar door for me

11. I thanked him for his courtesy and got in.

PART III: DIRECTIONS: *Rewrite the following sentences on a separate sheet of paper. Be careful; they're sneaky!*

1. Jack asked are you sure Mr. Phillips said hand in your term papers tomorrow, class

2. Who said I wear the chain I forged in life in Dickens' famous story asked Mrs. Bailey

3. I always crack up when James asks what page are we on exclaimed Sue

ANALYTICAL GRAMMAR (UNIT #24)　　　　　　　　　　　　　　　　　NOTES-PAGE 51

PUNCTUATING DIALOGUE

I.　When you write dialogue (two or more persons having a conversation), begin a new paragraph each time the speaker changes. Remember, the narrator is a speaker too. Pay special attention to which narrative goes in a paragraph by itself and which narrative goes in the same paragraph with the dialogue.

"Hi," said Sean to the boy trying to open the locker next to him. "Need some help?"

The boy looked up. "Yeah," he said, "I'm new here and - I know this sounds dumb - but I've never had a locker before! I don't really understand how to open this thing!"

Sean stared at the new boy. He LOOKED normal. American accent, American clothes. How could he have gotten through junior high without having a locker? "I don't get it," said Sean. "Did you go to school on Mars?"

"You're not too far off!" laughed the boy. "My folks are with the Peace Corps in West Africa. I've never gone to school before. My mom and dad taught me at home. I feel like I am from Mars!" He blushed and glanced at Sean uneasily. He hoped this boy, the first person who'd spoken to him in the new school, wouldn't think he was weird. He really wanted to have some friends in this new place.

"Gosh!" said Sean. "People are really going to make a big deal out of you! Wait'll our Social Studies teacher hears about this!"

The two boys walked off together down the hall, Sean asking questions as fast as he could get them out of his mouth. The new boy, Eric, was answering them the best he could - a huge grin on his face. It was going to be all right!

NOTE: If you look at the above passage, you will notice that sometimes the narrative is in the same paragraph as a speech, and sometimes it's in a separate paragraph. Imagine that you are a television director and that each paragraph is a camera angle. In the first paragraph above, you would have one camera shot of Sean by himself. In the next sentence, which is narrative, you would change your camera angle (or paragraph) because it's about Eric and what he's doing and saying. The last paragraph would require a new "camera angle" because it's about what both boys are doing. So if you just visualize when a new camera angle would be needed, that's where you need a new paragraph!

II.　When a quoted passage consists of more than one paragraph, put quotation marks at the BEGINNING OF EACH PARAGRAGH and at the END OF THE ENTIRE PASSAGE. Do NOT put quotation marks at the end of any paragraph but the last.

EXAMPLE:

"After dinner this evening, " said Jack, leaning back contentedly in his easy chair, "Denise and I decided to make a list of all the jobs that need doing around here.

"We first inspected the house. The major jobs were the following: mending the hole in the sofa cushion, washing Grandma's crystal, sorting out the sheets and towels, dusting Mom's china collection, and re-potting the African violets. Of course, I insisted on helping. After all, I live here too!

"Well, I broke a crystal wine glass and a china teacup and dumped our favorite African violet out on the living room carpet. What can I say? I guess I'm just too clumsy to do delicate work like this! I tell ya," Jack said with a wink, as he watched Denise scurrying madly around the house, "a homeowner's work is NEVER done!"

Notice that there are "open quotes" at the beginning of each of Jack's three paragraphs, but the close quotes don't appear until the very end of his entire speech.

Photocopying this product is strictly prohibited by copyright law.

PUNCTUATING DIALOGUE: EXERCISE #1

NAME:_____DATE:_____

DIRECTIONS: *Copy the following story, using whatever paragraphing and punctuation are necessary. The punctuation marks which are already included in the exercise are correct.*

Christmastime had finally arrived and Jim and Susan asked their parents if they could take their Christmas money out of savings to go shopping. We'll have to make a list first, said Jim. Do you think we'll have enough to buy something for everybody? asked Susan. I'm not sure, Susie, but if we don't, maybe we could go in together on some of the presents. That's a great idea, Jim! said Susan. Their parents gave them permission to get their money out of savings and drove them to the mall the next Saturday morning. Okay, said Jim. Now that we have our money, where do you want to go first? Well, why don't we try the toy store to take care of the kids on our list. We HAVE to buy for the kids. That's true, said Jim. We'll REALLY be in trouble if we forget any of them! The two kids shopped all day. When their parents picked them up at four o'clock, two very tired youngsters climbed wearily into the car. Well, said Susan, we did it. We got something for everyone on our list. That's fantastic, said Mom. You must be pretty good money-managers to make your money go that far! The whole family is going to be so pleased that you remembered them. Susan thought for a moment. That's true, she said, which probably means that they'll get us something really nice in return. Well, you don't sound very happy about that, observed Dad. But, Dad! cried Jim. Don't you understand? That just means that we'll have to be sure and get them something really nice in return NEXT year!!

PUNCTUATING DIALOGUE: EXERCISE #2

NAME:_____ DATE:_____

DIRECTIONS: *Rewrite the following story, using correct punctuation and paragraphing.*

Good morning, class said Mrs. Finley. Good morning, Mrs. Finley sang the class in chorus. Today we are going to study the correct punctuation of dialogue. Yechhh! said Sean We always study the same old junk said Stacy You NEVER show us any movies said Becky Yeah said Jason Mr. Johnson's class ALWAYS has movies. How come we never see any movies in here? But, dear students cried Mrs. Finley I thought you LOVED my class. You know how much I care! You know I just want you to be happy and have fun all the time! Don't you enjoy learning all this valuable educational material? Not really said Becky. We want to play games and read plays and see movies shouted Chris. Yeah, who wants to be educated anyway? said Tanya. We'd much rather be ignorant and have fun yelled Bryce. Oh, I see said Mrs. Finley. Ignorance is bliss, is that it? You got it, Mrs. Finley! Well, it grieves me deeply to see you so unhappy said Mrs. Finley, but I'd really hate to see you MISERABLE in a few short years when you hit the REAL WORLD and can't handle it!! So let's get started.

ANALYTICAL GRAMMAR (UNIT #25) NOTES-PAGE 53

PUNCTUATING TITLES

I. Use quotation marks to enclose the titles of articles, short stories, essays, poems, songs, chapters, and television and radio programs.

EXAMPLES:

articles:	"The Truth About OPEC"
short stories:	"The Monkey's Paw"
essays:	"A Modest Proposal"
poems:	"The Cremation of Sam McGee"
songs:	"Hello Dolly"
chapters:	Chapter 10, "The Industrial Revolution"
TV or radio shows:	"The Howdy Doody Show"

II. Use underlining (when you are handwriting or typing) or *italics* (when you're using either print or computer) for the titles of books, plays, movies, periodicals, works of art, long musical compositions, ships, aircraft, and spacecraft.

EXAMPLES:

books:	Tom Sawyer	*Tom Sawyer*
plays:	Romeo and Juliet	*Romeo and Juliet*
movies:	The Blob Eats Cleveland	*The Blob Eats Cleveland*
periodicals:	the Anchorage Times	the *Anchorage Times*
works of art:	the Mona Lisa	the *Mona Lisa*
symphonies, etc.:	Beethoven's Erioca	Beethoven's *Erioca*
ships:	the Titanic	the *Titanic*
aircraft:	the Spirit of St. Louis	the *Spirit of St. Louis*
spacecraft:	Columbia	*Columbia*

REMEMBER: If the title is also an appositive phrase, "set it off" with either italics or quotation marks, but DO NOT put commas around it.

EXAMPLE: My favorite book *Anne of Green Gables* is set on Prince Edward Island.
(*Anne of Green Gables* is an appositive, but the italics set it off; you don't need commas)

III. Use underlining or italics for words, letters, and figures referred to AS SUCH and for foreign words and expressions. When words, letters, and figures are referred to "as such," it means that the word, etc. is being discussed in the sentence as a word and not as its meaning.

EXAMPLES:

Does the word *judgement* have one or two *e's*?

I never could write a *5* very nicely.

In chewing gum at the interview, I was guilty of a horrible *faux pas*.

REMEMBER: UNDERLINING IS TO HANDWRITING AND TYPING AS ITALICS IS TO PRINT OR COMPUTER. If you have access to italics, you should use them. If you don't, then underline instead. NEVER do both.

ANALYTICAL GRAMMAR (UNIT #25)　　　　　　　　　　　　　　　　EXERCISE #1

PUNCTUATING TITLES: EXERCISE #1

NAME:_____ DATE:_____

DIRECTIONS: *Punctuate the following sentences correctly.*

1. Is it true your ancestors came over on the Mayflower?

2. The foreign phrase de riguer refers to something which is fashionable and proper.

3. Mother was completely engrossed in an article entitled The New Wonder Diet in this month's issue of Woman's Day.

4. Many jokes have been made about Rodin's magnificent sculpture The Thinker.

5. The quartet sang Sweet Adeline at the close of the program.

6. The Latin terms cum laude, magna cum laude, and summa cum laude usually appear on the diplomas of the best students.

7. The soprano sang the aria One Fine Day from the opera Madame Butterfly.

8. After seeing Shakespeare's Julius Caesar, I wrote an essay entitled The Bard of Avon, but I was embarrassed to see that I had omitted the first e in his name.

9. The teacher read The Adventure of the Speckled Band from her anthology The Complete Sherlock Holmes.

10. I spent my afternoon at the library reading one-hundred-year-old copies of the New York Times.

PUNCTUATING TITLES: EXERCISE #2

NAME:_____DATE:_____

DIRECTIONS: *Punctuate the following sentences correctly.*

1. The senior class play this year is Arsenic and Old Lace.

2. Class, open your books to the chapter entitled A House Divided in your history books said Mrs. Mendez, holding up a copy of The American Story.

3. The sinking of the Andrea Doria in the mid-fifties was a terrible tragedy.

4. Billy walked slowly up to the chalkboard and wrote kat, peepul, and teechur in a childish scrawl.

5. Did you see the final episode of The Winds of War on television last night?

6. I think my favorite piece of music is the Pastoral symphony by Ludwig van Beethoven.

7. Mom do you pronounce the e in calliope?

8. My subscription to Newsweek magazine runs out next month.

9. I'll never forget seeing Julie Andrews in My Fair Lady said Janet my mother took me to see several Broadway plays that year, but it was my favorite.

10. Edgar Allen Poe is probably best remembered for his poem The Raven.

PUNCTUATING TITLES: EXERCISE #3

NAME:_____ DATE:_____

DIRECTIONS: *Punctuate the following sentences correctly.*

1. Nina, did you see Designing Women this week asked Janie it's my favorite show

2. The Long Search was the most exciting chapter in the story about the lion cubs.

3. (Question) In what poem did Longfellow write the thoughts of youth are long, long thoughts asked Jane.

4. (Answer) I think it was in My Lost Youth replied Mother.

5. Have you read Congress's License to Lie in the latest Reader's Digest asked Lee.

6. What did Romeo mean when he said It is the east and Juliet is the sun in the second act of Romeo and Juliet asked Bill.

7. The tour group stood silently gazing at the magnificence of Michelangelo's David.

8. Sometimes when I watch Saturday Night Live I laugh until I cry said Grace.

9. Pulling on the oars, the boys took the Ginger Lee out to the middle of the lake.

10. Why doesn't anybody pronounce the r in February so a person can remember to spell it correctly wailed Sherry.

ANALYTICAL GRAMMAR (UNIT #25)   TEST

TEST: PUNCTUATING TITLES

NAME:_____ DATE:_____

(RAW SCORE: ____/141 GRADE: _____ POINTS: ____/20)

PART I: DIRECTIONS: *Punctuate the following sentences correctly. Don't change punctuation which is already there.*

1. Diana Ross made the song Stop in the Name of Love popular.

2. The Catbird Seat is a funny short story by James Thurber said Tim in his oral report.

3. Did you see Jean's picture in today's Times?

4. Eric had to read the novel My Darling, My Hamburger for a book report.

5. The drama department is presenting The Miracle Worker for their spring play announced Mr. Conklin.

6. Mr. Gates assigned the fifth chapter Lee and His Generals in our history textbook.

7. Norman Lear changed television history with the series All in the Family.

8. Esther used an article called The Persian Gulf: What Next? from Newsweek as the basis for her history report.

9. Hey, Patty asked Jean you didn't happen to read the article Are You a Good Friend? in this month's Young Miss, did you

10. If you're looking for a shocking ending said my English teacher you should read Shirley Jackson's famous short story The Lottery

11. I'll never forget when my teacher read us An Occurrence at Owl Creek Bridge, a famous short story said Kelly.

12. Vincent Van Gogh's famous Sunflowers was the first painting which sold for over a million dollars

13. The plane which dropped the atomic bomb on Hiroshima was called the Enola Gay

14. The Latin term non sequitur refers to a statement which is not logical.

15. Mozart's comic opera The Magic Flute has always been a favorite of mine said Sean

16. I'll never forget how embarrassed I was when I learned I had been mispronouncing epitome. It was a big word I used all the time to try and impress people! laughed Jill.

(over)

Photocopying this product is strictly prohibited by copyright law.   287

ANALYTICAL GRAMMAR (UNIT #25)   TEST - PAGE 2

17. Dr. Gates announced Since you obviously have studied Shakespeare's Othello so thoroughly, I will assign no further reading for the weekend.

18. Lance proudly displayed his diploma on which were the Latin words summa cum laude, meaning "with highest honors."

19. Henry Higgins worked day and night to teach Eliza Doolittle to pronounce rain, Spain, and plain so that the long a was pronounced correctly.

20. Oh look! exclaimed Charles as we leafed through the stack of old magazines. This 1963 issue of Life magazine has an article in it entitled Loch Ness Secret Solved.

PART II: *On a separate sheet of paper, copy the following dialogue, punctuating and paragraphing it correctly. Assume that the punctuation you see written here is correct.*

It was a typical Saturday night at the dorm. All the guys who had dates had already gone out, but a few remained in the lounge Hey said Jim does anybody want to go see a movie tonight Tom, who was dozing in a huge easy chair, opened one eye. I'll go he said I'm just sitting around staring at the walls anyway great said Jim do you want to drive or shall I heaving himself out of the chair, Tom said no I'll drive Why asked Jim. Because I don't want to be seen in that heap of yours I have an image to protect Jim picked up a cushion and heaved it at Tom trust me, pal he laughed just be seen with me and your image is set for life oh yeah? Yeah! okay said (Who is speaking here? Jim or Tom?) you drive

ANALYTICAL GRAMMAR (UNIT #26)	NOTES-PAGE 55

SEMICOLONS & COLONS

I. SEMICOLONS (;)

    A.   Use a semicolon between independent clauses (sentences) if they are NOT joined by a conjunction.

        EXAMPLE: Mary enjoys romantic novels; her brother likes fantasy.

    B.   Use a semicolon between independent clauses joined by such words as *for example, for instance, therefore, that is, besides, accordingly, moreover, nevertheless, furthermore, otherwise, however, consequently, instead, hence.*

        The italicized words above are very useful when a writer is trying to show the relationship between one idea and another. They are often called TRANSITIONAL DEVICES because they help the reader make the transition from one thought to another.

        EXAMPLE: Jane showed me in many ways that she was still my friend. She saved me a seat on the bus. (It's a bit difficult to perceive the relationship between these two ideas.)

                            Jane showed me in many ways that she was still my friend; for example, she saved me a seat on the bus. (Now the relationship between the two ideas is very clear)

    C.   A semicolon (call this a "SUPERCOMMA") may be used to separate the independent clauses of a compound sentence <u>if there are commas within the clauses</u> and there might be some confusion about where the first sentence ends and the second sentence begins.

        EXAMPLE:
        (confusing)   She will invite Elaine, Kim, and Stacey, and Val will ask Molly.

        (clear)   She will invite Elaine, Kim, and Stacey; and Val will ask Molly.

    D.   A semicolon (call this a "SUPERCOMMA") may be used to separate items in a series <u>if there are commas within the items.</u>

        EXAMPLE:
        (confusing)   The dates of the Iowa testing will be Monday, April 4, Tuesday, April 5, and Wednesday, April 6.

        (clear)   The dates of the Iowa testing will be Monday, April 4; Tuesday, April 5; and Wednesday, April 6.

(over)

ANALYTICAL GRAMMAR (UNIT #26)   NOTES - PAGE 56

II. COLONS (:)

    A. Use a colon to mean "note what follows." A colon should be used before a list of items, especially after expression like *as follows* and *the following*.

        EXAMPLES: You will need to take the following things: a heavy jacket, boots, a sleeping bag, a hunting knife, and a backpack.

                          I have three extracurricular activities: reading, skiing, and playing computer games.

        NOTE: If you look carefully at the sentences above, you will notice that THE WORDS IN FRONT OF THE COLON MAKE UP A COMPLETE SENTENCE. A colon should never SPLIT a sentence.

        EXAMPLES: My extracurricular activities are: reading, skiing, and playing computer games. (Note that the colon splits the linking verb and complement. The colon should be LEFT OUT of this sentence.)

                          Mix the sifted flour with: cinnamon, nutmeg, ginger, and sugar.
                          (Note that the colon splits the preposition and its object. The colon should be LEFT OUT of this sentence.)

    B. Use a colon before a quotation when the narrative which introduces the quotation makes up a complete sentence. This is especially true of a long quotation.

        EXAMPLE: Horace Mann had this to say about dealing with those who disagree with you: "Do not think of knocking out another person's brains because he differs in opinion from you. It would be as rational to knock yourself on the head because you differ from yourself ten years ago."

    C. Use a colon in the following situations:

        1. Between the hour and the minute when you write the time. (7:30 etc.)

        2. Between the chapter and verse when referring to passages from the Bible, the Koran, or other books organized in this manner. (Genesis 2:2)

        3. Use a colon after the salutation of a business letter. (Dear Sir:)

ANALYTICAL GRAMMAR (UNIT #26) EXERCISE #1

SEMICOLONS & COLONS: EXERCISE #1

NAME:_____ DATE:_____

DIRECTIONS: *Some of the sentences below require semicolons, some have semicolons that should not be there, some have semicolons that should be commas, and some of the sentences are correct. Put in the missing semicolons, cross out or change the incorrect ones, and leave the sentences which are correct as they are.*

1. Many people feel insecure about punctuation they never know whether they're right or wrong!

2. In ancient times writers didn't use punctuation therefore their writings are difficult to read.

3. As a matter of fact, writers during the days of ancient Greece and Rome didn't even put a space between each word!

4. Life moved at a much slower pace than it does today hence it wasn't that important to be able to read something quickly.

5. The ability to read and write was a rare one consequently few people depended on the written word as we do today.

6. Most people lived their entire lives without ever sending or receiving a letter they didn't need to know how to read and write.

7. Although people honored and respected those who could read; they didn't see the need for it in their own lives.

8. Toward the latter part of the Middle Ages, nations began to trade widely with each other; literacy became a necessity for success in business.

9. A merchant could expect to receive many written messages in a day it became important to be able to read something quickly.

10. Earlier in the Middle Ages, some genius had figured out that, if he left a space between words, his writing could be read more quickly we're all very grateful to this obscure writer!

11. There has to be something to tell us when a sentence ends otherwise we might think that the end of one sentence is the beginning of another.

12. Somewhere along the line a writer decided to put a dot at the end of each sentence this made his writing much clearer.

13. In time other "end marks" of punctuation appeared; one of these is the question mark.

14. When these writers used certain marks, they found it easier to convey their true meaning other people saw the value of it and simply copied what the other guy did!

15. Eventually writers began to use many punctuation marks therefore it became necessary to agree upon some rules.

16. In the early days, punctuation was pretty "free-wheeling" Shakespeare used it pretty much as he pleased!

(over)

17. Commas began to be used in a more orderly way for example commas were used to separate items used in a series.

18. Other situations where a comma became necessary were appositives which are groups of words that restate other nouns nonessential modifiers which are word groups used to modify other nouns and direct address which is a word or words used to refer to the person to whom one is speaking.

19. Everybody needs to know how to punctuate correctly otherwise other people will have a hard time understanding their writing.

20. So next time you get tired of doing these punctuation worksheets, remember what punctuation is really for it helps us all communicate more quickly and clearly!

ANALYTICAL GRAMMAR (UNIT #26)   EXERCISE #2

SEMICOLONS & COLONS: EXERCISE #2

NAME:_____ DATE:_____

DIRECTIONS: *Decide where colons should appear in the following sentences and write them in.*

1. Reading Proverbs 3 13, the minister supported his main point with the following quotation "Happy is the man that findeth wisdom and the man who getteth understanding."

2. In science class we have to learn the meaning of the following words *amphibian*, *chromosome*, *neutron*, *oxidation*, and *vertebrae*.

3. Miss Thomson invited Alden, Richard, and Sammy.

4. The farmer explained the uses of the various parts of the plow landslide, clevis, jointer, and beam.

5. Experts can identify a fingerprint by observing the nature of the following arches, whorls, loops, and composites.

6. At 10 45 the teacher closed the lesson by reading Exodus 20 12 "Honor thy father and thy mother, that thy days may be long upon the land which the Lord thy God giveth thee."

7. At 8 20 the agent told us that the 6 10 train would not arrive before 9 15.

8. Along the midway were several kinds of rides a roller coaster, a ship, two merry-go-rounds, and a Ferris wheel.

9. There were sandwiches, cold drinks, and candy on our trays.

10. At an airport I like to listen to the many noises motors roaring before take-off, loudspeakers announcing departures and arrivals, and telephones ringing at every counter.

ANALYTICAL GRAMMAR (UNIT #26)   EXERCISE #3

SEMICOLONS & COLONS: EXERCISE #3

NAME:_____DATE:_____

DIRECTIONS: Using semicolons and colons, correctly punctuate the following sentences. You may have to change punctuation that is already there into something else.

1. A scrawny, friendly stray dog wandered onto the field, the umpire stopped the game.

2. Because they do not conduct electricity, the following materials can be used as insulators rubber glass cloth and plastics.

3. There are only three primary colors in painting red, blue, and yellow.

4. Other colors are mixtures of primary colors for instance purple is a mixture of red and blue.

5. The ten-gallon hat of the cowboy was used as a protection from the sun, a dipper for water, and a pan for washing his hands, and leather chaps protected him from thorny bushes.

6. The minister began her sermon by quoting these two verses from the Bible Matthew 23 39 and John 16 27.

7. In his speech to the Thespian Society, Mr. Stevenson quoted from several Shakespearean plays *Romeo and Juliet, The Tempest, Macbeth,* and *Julius Caesar.*

8. Captain James Cook explored much of the Pacific Ocean he found the Hawaiian Islands in 1778.

9. From 1851 to 1864, the United States had four Presidents Millard Fillmore, a Whig from New York, Franklin Pierce, a Democrat from New Hampshire, James Buchanan, a Democrat from Pennsylvania, and Abraham Lincoln, a Republican from Illinois.

10. From 1 15 to 1 50 p.m., I was so sleepy that my mind wandered I rested my head on my right palm and let my eyelids sag to half-mast.

Photocopying this product is strictly prohibited by copyright law.

ANALYTICAL GRAMMAR (UNIT #26)   TEST

SEMICOLONS & COLONS: TEST

NAME:_____DATE:_____

(RAW SCORE:_____/120 GRADE:_____POINTS:____/20)

PART I: *Insert semicolons where they are needed. You may need to change some commas to semicolons.*

1. Take Mom's suitcase upstairs you can leave Dad's in the car for now.

2. I wrote to Anne, Beth, and Meghan, and Jean notified Ted and Sue.

3. The Stone of Scone was used in ancient Scottish coronations it lay for years beneath the coronation chair in Westminster Abbey.

4. Alaska is huge and wild, it is also modern and sophisticated.

5. Mother threw the coat away it was worn out.

6. Janet did as she was told, however, she grumbled ungraciously.

7. From 1968 to 1988 the Presidents were Richard Nixon, a Republican from California, Gerald Ford, a Republican from Michigan, Jimmy Carter, a Democrat from Georgia, and Ronald Reagan, a Republican from California.

8. Mr. Baxter, who never raised his voice in the classroom, began to shout obviously he had been pushed beyond his limit.

9. After the fire, the family stood in the smoke-blackened dining room and the house, now a smoking shell, no longer looked like their own.

10. Never be afraid to admit that you don't know something, always be ashamed to admit that you don't care.

PART II: *Some of the sentences below need colons; if so, insert them. Some of them have colons which should not be there; if so, cross them out. Some of them are correct; if so, write C in the space provided.*

_____ 1. A search showed that Jack's pocket contained the following a knife, half an apple, a piece of gum, a dime, and a nickel.

_____ 2. These cookies are made of: flour, brown sugar, butter, eggs, and nuts.

_____ 3. At the drug store I bought a comb, a lipstick, and a box of tissues.

_____ 4. The following students will report to the main office: Anne Brown, Pete Kendall, Mary Jo Derum, and Lane Williams.

(over)

ANALYTICAL GRAMMAR (UNIT #26) — TEST - PAGE 2

_____ 5. The minister opened the service with a reading from John 10 16.

_____ 6. I have always wanted to do three things climb a mountain, ride a race horse, and take a hot-air balloon ride.

_____ 7. We have studied the following kinds of punctuation marks: commas, quotation marks, colons, and semicolons.

_____ 8. To succeed in sports, one should be disciplined, well-coordinated, and motivated.

_____ 9. You need these supplies for this class white lined notebook paper, a blue or black pen, and a pencil.

_____ 10. At exactly 3 15 we will begin our meeting.

PART III: *Punctuate the following sentences correctly, using all the punctuation marks we have studied.*

1. One of my favorite cowboy movies is called The 3 10 to Yuma it's about a law officer who must get his prisoner on the train that leaves for Yuma at ten minutes after three.

2. Lightning has always awed people explained Mrs. Belmont and many of us are still frightened by it

3. Have you read Poe's short story The Pit and the Pendulum? asked Jenna.

4. You'll need the following materials for the art course a brush an easel and some watercolors announced Mr. Greene.

5. Have you seen this month's issue of Seventeen asked Gloria.

6. At 8 15 on March 1 1980 we ate the last of our provisions.

7. We thought we were taking a short cruise however it turned out to be quite a long trip.

8. Robert Burns a Scottish poet wrote the poem Flow Gently, Sweet Afton.

9. In the novel Little Women there are four sisters Meg Jo Beth and Amy.

10. Sally who is my older sister is coming home from college tonight announced Janet.

11. Lenore was a poised self-confident young woman her ambition was to get involved in local politics.

12. The finalists in the Miss Stuffed Artichoke contest were Pearl Button a stunning blonde from West Mudsling Wisconsin Ima Sweathog a dainty brunette from Gnawbone Indiana and Reina Ponderoof a pert redhead from Lower Intestine Nevada.

ANALYTICAL GRAMMAR (UNIT #26) TEST - PAGE 3

13. My brothers and sisters have these characteristics in common kindness unselfishness and loyalty.

14. This morning's sermon said Reverend Jenkins our new minister will be based on Luke 4 18.

15. Opening his copy of the Wall Street Journal Dad settled back in his chair and announced I do not wish to be disturbed I have had a difficult day.

16. Open your books but don't start yet said Miss Ames my math teacher.

17. The members of the senior class who had been working very hard had a great time at the Prom and the Winter Ball which was put on by the juniors was also a big success.

18. Professor Hensley hurrying down the corridor with his nose buried in Steinbeck's great novel The Grapes of Wrath bumped right into Miss Peabody the tall muscular physical education teacher.

19. Since I had planned to stay home and watch Saturday Night Live I decided to make some popcorn that was my first mistake explained Gail.

20. The next morning one of the crew shouted Land ho said Jim.

ANALYTICAL GRAMMAR (UNIT #27)　　　　　　　　　　　NOTES-PAGE 57

FORMING THE POSSESSIVE

When we want to indicate that something belongs to or is owned by somebody or something, we use the POSSESSIVE. We form the possessive by adding either ' or 's to a noun.

I. POSSESSIVE PRONOUNS

These pronouns are already possessive in form. We do not need to add apostrophes to them to make them possessive.

mine	ours	yours	theirs	your
his	hers	its	whose	yours

II. POSSESSIVE NOUNS: To form the possessive you...

   A.   ...take the SINGULAR NOUN and add 's.

   EXAMPLES: lady's dress
   baby's toys
   Marcia's book

   B.   ...take the PLURAL NOUN ENDING IN S and add '.

   EXAMPLES: ladies' room
   four days' delay
   girls' soccer team

   C.   ...take the PLURAL NOUN NOT ENDING IN S and add 's.

   EXAMPLES: children's choir
   men's room
   people's choice

   D.   ...take the NAME ENDING IN S OF MORE THAN ONE SYLLABLE and add '.

   EXAMPLES: Mr. Ellis' house
   Hercules' journey

   When a one-syllable name ends in S, you add 's. (Example: Chris's house)

HERE'S A TRICK: Rather than trying to remember all those rules, learn to "flip the possessive phrase around." For example, suppose you were dealing with

   THE GIRLS BASKETBALL TEAM WON THEIR GAME.

Just "flip the phrase around" like this: "The girls basketball team is the basketball team of the girls." Now "freeze frame" the "word-in-the-box" in your "mind's eye." You have to add to that word to make it possessive, and there are only two possibilities: 's or '. Which one "looks right"? Right! It must be GIRLS' because GIRLS'S "looks wrong." Now go back and put the apostrophe where it belongs in the sentence above.

Photocopying this product is strictly prohibited by copyright law.

ANALYTICAL GRAMMAR (UNIT #27)　　　　　　　　　　　　　　EXERCISE #1

POSSESSIVES: EXERCISE #1

NAME: _____ DATE: _____

PART I: Find and underline the possessives phrase in each sentence below. Then in the space provided, "flip" the phrase and write the "word-in-the-box" in the box provided.

EXAMPLE: The boys basketball team won.   the basketball team of the [boys]

1. Toms team won the game. _____ [   ]

2. The boys soccer tryouts will be next week. _____ [   ]

3. I sell mens clothing in my store. _____ [   ]

4. The store next door sells ladies clothing. _____ [   ]

5. Mr. Gates is in the teachers lounge. _____ [   ]

6. The girls locker room is locked. _____ [   ]

7. Jesus disciples traveled with Him. _____ [   ]

PART II: Using the technique of "flipping the possessive phrase," correctly punctuate the following sentences. Remember to "freeze frame" the word-in-the-box, then add either ' or 's.

1. Bonnies team won the spelling match.

2. Tammys little sister got lost in the store.

3. My two brothers clothes were all over the floor.

4. That girls book fell out of the car.

5. The doctor gently felt the dogs paw.

6. I left my sweater at the dentists office.

7. Richards hobby is collecting ballplayers autographs.

PART III: Rewrite the sentences below. These sentences are already "flipped," so you need to put them back the way they were before they were flipped. Your rewritten sentences must say the same thing as the original sentence, but it must contain a possessive. The first one is done for you as an example.

1. The hat of that fat man blew down the street.
    That fat man's hat blew down the street.

2. There are the coats of two girls in the closet.

3. We found the bike of Ramon in the basement.

4. It was "The Day of Ladies" at Yankee Stadium.

Photocopying this product is strictly prohibited by copyright law.

ANALYTICAL GRAMMAR (UNIT #27) EXERCISE #2

POSSESSIVES: EXERCISE #2

NAME:_____DATE:_____

PART I: *Correctly form the possessives in the sentences below:*

1. The childrens presents are in the hall closet.

2. Anns store sells maps and travel books.

3. Charles golf bag is in my fathers car.

4. That architects designs have won many awards.

5. Many campers tents were destroyed by the forest fire.

6. We used Trish scarf as a bandage.

7. Louis phone number has been changed.

8. The boys basketball team was undefeated.

9. Tess butterfly collection has two dozen specimens.

10. The sailors raincoats protected them from the spray.

PART II: *Rewrite the following sentences so that they say the same thing but contain possessives.*

1. The library for children closes at five o'clock.

2. We found the mittens of George.

3. Which department sells cribs for babies?

4. Where are the tickets of the women?

5. The house of George Jones is on this street.

6. The house of the Joneses is on this street.

7. I will be with you again in the time of two days.

8. I can only take a vacation of one week this year.

9. Please give me the worth of two dollars in quarters.

10. The teachings of Socrates are still studied today.   *(over)*

Photocopying this product is strictly prohibited by copyright law.

PART III: *Write words according to the following directions:*

WORD	POSSESSIVE	PLURAL	PLURAL POSSESSIVE
LADY	_____	_____	_____
CHILD	_____	_____	_____
MAN	_____	_____	_____
GIRL	_____	_____	_____
WOMAN	_____	_____	_____

ANALYTICAL GRAMMAR (UNIT #27)   EXERCISE #3

POSSESSIVES: EXERCISE #3

NAME:_____ DATE:_____

PART I: *Write words according to the following directions:*

WORD	POSSESSIVE	PLURAL	PLURAL POSSESSIVE
BABY	_____	_____	_____
SHEEP	_____	_____	_____
TOM SMITH	_____	THE SMITHS	_____
MOUSE	_____	_____	_____
BOY	_____	_____	_____

PART II: *Place apostrophes in the proper places in the sentences below:*

1. The governors mansion was lit by floodlights.

2. Three policemens uniforms were in the back of the car.

3. My aunts favorite color is magenta; what's yours?

4. We need a stretcher to carry the teams mascot into the locker room.

5. John took three weeks vacation to Tahiti this year.

6. Please give me two dollars worth of change.

7. Let's go to the old swimming hole just for old times sake.

8. Julies skirt was shorter than hers.

9. In college we studied Aristophanes speeches.

10. Coach Gillis daughter is coming to the game this week.

PART III: *Rewrite the following sentences using the possessive.*

1. Tonight we are having dinner at the house of the Finleys.

2. Janie suddenly found herself in the locker room for the boys.

3. I asked for the worth of a dollar in change.

4. I said I would see him in the time of two months.

5. After the study of four years, I considered myself an expert in economics.

PART IV: *On the back compose your own possessive sentences using the following nouns:*

1. Sally   2. Socrates   3. any singular noun   4. Ross   5. any plural noun not ending in S.

Photocopying this product is strictly prohibited by copyright law.

ANALYTICAL GRAMMAR (UNIT #27)   TEST

POSSESSIVES: TEST

NAME:_____DATE:_____

(RAW SCORE:_____ /70 GRADE:_____ POINTS:____/20)

PART I: *Write words according to the following directions:*

	WORD	POSSESSIVE	PLURAL	PLURAL POSSESSIVE
1.	TOOTH	_____	_____	_____
2.	BOX	_____	_____	_____
3.	NURSE	_____	_____	_____
4.	JONES	_____	_____	_____
5.	KISS	_____	_____	_____
6.	WITCH	_____	_____	_____
7.	COUNTRY	_____	_____	_____
8.	PUPPY	_____	_____	_____
9.	MAN	_____	_____	_____
10.	WOMAN	_____	_____	_____

PART II: *Place apostrophes where they are needed in the sentences below:*

1. Dierdre couldn't wait to see her parents reaction.

2. Our school bands original song was quite good.

3. All the horses stalls need to be cleaned out.

4. Are all pigs tails curly?

5. My moms new job begins today.

6. Are you going over to Bob Whites house?

7. The three new students work was best.

8. The two guests gifts were funny.

9. We have to make fifteen other dancers costumes.

10. My dogs left paw is injured.

(over)

ANALYTICAL GRAMMAR (UNIT #27)   TEST - PAGE 2

11. Give me four dollars worth of quarters, please.

12. Those countries main exports are oil and coal.

13. Tonys speech was the best in the class.

14. The ladies room is locked.

15. The womens room is locked.

PART III: *Rewrite the following sentences so that they say the same thing but have possessives.*

1. Hank did the laundry of the whole family last week.

2. The hands of the pianist were long and slender.

3. Glenn likes the symphonies of Beethoven.

4. You should change the water of the goldfish.

5. Bob isn't getting his usual vacation of three weeks this year.

6. The dishes of the cats are empty.

7. Tonight we're going to a party at the house of the Joneses.

8. The house of Ross is on the next street.

9. Someone has borrowed the skates of Lee.

10. The lounge of the teachers is located near the office.

11. The sails of all three boats need fixing.

12. Where is the room of the men?

13. The mother of Curtis is late.

14. We say this prayer in the name of Jesus.

15. There are two kids in the office of the nurse right now.

ANALYTICAL GRAMMAR (UNIT #27)   TEST: PAGE 3

PART IV: *Write original sentences using the words listed below as possessives. BE SURE YOU ARE USING THE WORD AS A POSSESSIVE, NOT A PLURAL.*

    PLURAL: Two girls took the advanced test. (Don't do this!)

    POSSESSIVE: Two girls' coats were hanging in the closet. (Do this!)

1. Hercules

2. boy (singular)

3. boys (plural)

4. lady (singular)

5. lady (plural)

6. Mr. Ellis

7. Chris

8. week (singular)

9. week (plural)

10. Sheila

CAPITALIZATION

I. *Capitalize the names of persons.*
    EXAMPLES: Sandra Wilson   MacDonald (the M and the D are capitalized)
                     Mr. Charles F. Skinner   O'Brien   John McCaffrey, Jr.

Initials & abbreviations after names are capitalized.

II. *Capitalize geographical names*
    EXAMPLES:
       (towns, cities)   Anchorage, Kansas City
       (counties)   Harrison County
       (states)   Alaska, New Hampshire
       (sections)   the East, the Midwest, the South

    NOTE: the words <u>north</u>, <u>west</u>, <u>southeast</u>, etc. are not capitalized when they indicate direction, such as "the south of town" or "traveling northwest."

       (countries)   the United States of America, Brazil
       (continents)   Asia, Antarctica
       (islands)   Prince Edward Island, the Hawaiian Islands
       (mountains)   Mount McKinley, Mount Ararat, the Alps
       (bodies of water)   the Indian Ocean, Lake Hood, Columbia River
       (roads, highways)   Route 10, New Seward Highway, Elm Street
                              Twenty-first Street   *Note that "first" is not capitalized.*
       (parks)   Yellowstone National Park

    NOTE: words like <u>city</u>, <u>park</u>, <u>street</u>, etc. are capitalized if they are part of a name. If they are not part of a name, they are just ordinary common nouns.

III. *Capitalize proper adjectives* (**when you make an adjective out of a proper noun**)
    EXAMPLE: Greek theatre, English literature, Indian maiden, Italian shoes

IV. *Capitalize names of organizations, business firms, institutions, and governmental bodies.*
    EXAMPLES:
       (organizations)   American Red Cross, Boy Scouts of America
       (business firms)   Nordstrom, J.C. Penney, Western Airlines
       (institutions)   Columbia University, Service High School, Providence Hospital

    NOTE: Do NOT capitalize words like <u>hotel, theater, high school</u> unless they are part of a name.

    EXAMPLES: West High School   high school teacher
                      Sheraton Hotel   a hotel in town
                      Fourth Avenue Theatre   a movie theater

       (government bodies)   Congress, Federal Bureau of Investigation

V. *Capitalize the names of historical events and periods, special events, and calendar items.*
    EXAMPLES:
       (historical events)   Boston Tea Party, the Middle Ages, World War I
       (special events)   Fur Rendezvous, Homecoming, Super Bowl
       (calendar items)   Sunday, May, Halloween, Fourth of July

    NOTE: Do not capitalize the names of seasons (summer, spring, etc.) unless they are part of the names of an event. (Winter Carnival)

(over)

VI.   Capitalize the names of nationalities, races, and religions.
       EXAMPLES: (nationalities)   Canadians, an American, a European
                    (races)   Indian, African-American, Asian
                    (religions)   Moslem, Presbyterian, a Christian Scientist

VII. Capitalize the brand names of business products.
       EXAMPLES: Fritos, Cocoa Puffs, Toyota

                    NOTE: Do not capitalize the noun that often follows a brand name (Chevy truck, Guess jeans)

VIII. Capitalize the names of ships, planets, monuments, awards, and any other particular place, thing, or event.
       EXAMPLES: (ships, trains)   the Mayflower, the Silver Streak
                    (aircraft, missiles)   the Enola Gay, the Titan
                    (planets, stars)   the North Star, Jupiter, the Milky Way

                    NOTE: Sun and moon are only capitalized when they are listed with the other bodies in our solar system. Earth is capitalized when it is a name (I will return to Earth.) but not when it's preceded by an article (I will return to the earth.).

                    (monuments, etc.)   Washington Monument, Vietnam Memorial
                    (buildings)   Eiffel Tower, Taj Mahal, World Trade Center
                    (awards)   the Oscar, Congressional Medal of Honor

IX.   Do not capitalize the names of school subjects except languages and the names of particular courses.
       EXAMPLES: Presently I am taking English, science, Geography I, Spanish, and economics.

                    NOTE: Do not capitalize the members of a class (freshman, sophomore, junior, senior) unless it is part of a proper noun (Junior Prom, Senior Picnic)

X.   Capitalize titles
       A.   Capitalize the title of a person when it comes before a name:
             EXAMPLES: President Bush
                          Mrs. Morrison
                          Dr. Jenkins
                          Professor Wright

       B.   Capitalize a title used alone or following a person's name only if it refers to a high official or to someone to whom you wish to show special respect:
             EXAMPLES: Can you name our thirtieth President? (a high official)
                          The General regrets he will be unable to attend.(special respect)
                          The president of our club read the minutes.(not a high official)

             NOTE: When a title is used alone in direct address, it is usually capitalized.
                   EXAMPLES: I'm pleased to see you, Doctor.
                                Tell me, Coach, what are our chances?

       C.   Capitalize words showing family relationship used with or as a person's name but NOT when preceded by an adjective.
             EXAMPLES: Aunt Mabel, Cousin Enid, Mom
                          my mother, your father, Frank's sister

XI. *Capitalize the first word and all words in titles of books, periodicals, etc. EXCEPT ARTICLES, PREPOSITIONS, AND CONJUNCTIONS.*

    EXAMPLES: *Gone with the Wind*
    "The Adventure of the Speckled Band"
    "Just Tell Me That You Love Me"
    Pride and Prejudice

The Bible and the books of the Bible are always capitalized.

XII. *Capitalize words referring to the Diety; do not capitalize the word "god" when referring to a polytheistic pantheon of gods.*

    EXAMPLES: God and His universe.
    The people came to Jesus and they worshipped Him.
    The God of Islam is Allah.
    The Aztec god in the form of a feathered serpent was Quetzalcoatl.

ANALYTICAL GRAMMAR (UNIT #28)   EXERCISE #1

CAPITALIZATION: EXERCISE #1

NAME:_____DATE:_____

DIRECTIONS: *In each of the following items, you are to choose the correct one of the two forms. Circle the letter of the correct item and be prepared to tell me why the other one is wrong.*

1. a. His store is on Front Street in Burlington.
   b. His store is on front street in Burlington.
2. a. We crossed the Snake river.
   b. We crossed the Snake River.
3. a. He now lives in california.
   b. He now lives in California.
4. a. Did you fly over South America?
   b. Did you fly over south America?
5. a. He took a picture of Pike's Peak.
   b. He took a picture of Pike's peak.
6. a. City streets in the West are often wide.
   b. City streets in the west are often wide.
7. a. Yellowstone National Park has many geysers.
   b. Yellowstone national park has many geysers.
8. a. The city of Columbus is the capital of Ohio.
   b. The City of Columbus is the capital of Ohio.
9. a. The hurricane swept over the gulf of Mexico.
   b. The hurricane swept over the Gulf of Mexico.
10. a. Drive east on U.S. Highway 35.
    b. Drive East on U.S.Highway 35.
11. a. We are proud of our State parks.
    b. We are proud of our state parks.
12. a. I live on Forty-Fifth Street.
    b. I live on Forty-fifth Street.
13. a. The headquarters is in Travis County.
    b. The headquarters is in Travis county.
14. a. The Vikings called the atlantic ocean the sea of darkness.
    b. The Vikings called the Atlantic Ocean the Sea of Darkness.
15. a. The states of the Midwest are referred to as the nation's breadbasket.
    b. The states of the midwest are referred to as the nation's breadbasket.
16. a. A three-lane Highway is dangerous.
    b. A three-lane highway is dangerous.
17. a. I have a map of the Virgin Islands.
    b. I have a map of the Virgin islands.
18. a. New York city is the largest city in the east.
    b. New York City is the largest city in the East.
19. a. The Great Salt Lake is near the Nevada border.
    b. The Great Salt lake is near the Nevada Border.
20. a. His address is 2009 Bell Avenue.
    b. His address is 2009 Bell avenue.

Photocopying this product is strictly prohibited by copyright law.

ANALYTICAL GRAMMAR (UNIT #28)   EXERCISE #2

CAPITALIZATION: EXERCISE #2

NAME:_____DATE:_____

DIRECTIONS: *Circle the letters which should be capitalized in the sentences below.*

1. mr. ronson mentioned the fact that mercury and venus are closer to earth than jupiter.

2. every freshman at jefferson high school knows he will take at least three years of english and two years of mathematics.

3. while in the city of washington, we saw the ford theater where lincoln was shot.

4. a methodist, a moslem, and a roman catholic conducted an interesting panel discussion.

5. since I plan to study medicine at northwestern university, I'm taking latin and biology I.

6. after I had gone to the grocery store at the corner of thirty-first street and stonewall avenue, I stopped at the twin oaks lumber company, which is two blocks south of cooper avenue.

7. vacationing in the west, we saw electric peak, which is on the northern boundary of yellowstone national park; we also saw the devil's tower, which is in northeastern wyoming.

8. later we drove along riverside drive and saw the lincoln memorial, which is the site of dr. martin luther king, jr.'s famous "I have a dream" speech.

9. in the spring, usually the first saturday after easter, the women's missionary society, a baptist organization, gives a picnic for our class.

10. leaving ecuador in south america on a banana boat named *bonanza*, they went through the panama canal and sailed through the caribbean sea to nassau in the bahamas.

CAPITALIZATION: EXERCISE #3

NAME:_____ DATE:_____

DIRECTIONS: *Circle the letters which should be capitalized in the sentences below.*

1. speaking to the seniors of westfield high school, mr. carter praised *the tragedy of american compassion*, a book by marvin olasky.

2. on the sunday before labor day, we drove as far as the murphy motel, a mile west of salem, virginia; the manager, mr. kelly, proudly announced that he was a member of the virginia tourist court association.

3. waiting for a city bus at the corner of twenty-first street and hampton drive, we admired the anne klein clothes in dillard's window display.

4. father and his brother, my uncle julian, told me about rockefeller center and about the shops on fifth avenue in new york city.

5. professor massey studied at the library of congress and the folger shakespeare library during july and august.

6. althea gibson's autobiography *I always wanted to be somebody* was published by harper & row.

7. I especially like the photograph - made by alaska airlines - of mt. mckinley in alaska.

8. in his junior year at sheridan high school, uncle rufus studied latin, french, english, geometry, and art.

9. the reverend walker said that the gods of the ancient greeks did not offer the promise of immortality that our god does.

10. after the texans so bravely fought against the forces of general santa anna in 1836, the alamo became famous as a memorial to texas liberty, a symbol of american freedom like the statue of liberty.

ANALYTICAL GRAMMAR (UNIT #28)   TEST

CAPITALIZATION: TEST

NAME:_____ DATE:_____

(RAW SCORE:_____ /89 GRADE:_____ POINTS:_____ /20)

PART I: DIRECTIONS: *Some of the following sentences are correct and some need capitalization. If the sentence is correct, write a C in the space provided; if it is not correct, circle the letters to be capitalized.*

1. In the fall everyone looks forward to the football season. _____

2. Football fans can see their favorite high school or college team play on saturday and their favorite professional teams on sunday. _____

3. Last weekend I saw ohio state play michigan. _____

4. Kay's aunt introduced her to the captain of one of the world's largest passenger ships, the *queen elizabeth II*. _____

5. The greeks believed that their various dieties met on mount olympus to listen to zeus, the king of the gods. _____

6. Ann likes geography and history, but she does the best in english and french. _____

7. The chief justice explained the ruling of the supreme court. _____

8. On July 4 the Bayshore Mall puts on a spectacular fireworks display. _____

9. The *titanic* sank after hitting an iceberg off the coast of newfoundland. _____

10. My aunt went to amsterdam to see rembrandt's *the night watch*. _____

PART II: DIRECTIONS: *Circle any letter that should be capitalized in the sentences below.*

1. Mail the letter to the union of south africa and the package to genoa, italy.

2. This year palm sunday is the last sunday in march.

3. Among the early settlers were roman catholics and congregationalists.

4. like other north american indians, the ancient iriquois believed in many gods.

5. The department of agriculture publishes many pamphlets that are useful to the home gardener.

6. Did aunt josie send you that mexican straw hat?

7. The *windy jane* is a small white sailboat.

8. Last winter Carrie had an iceboat on greenwood lake.

(over)

ANALYTICAL GRAMMAR (UNIT #28)   TEST - PAGE 2

9. In history and in spanish, we are studying the same european renaissance.

10. One woman is an armenian; the other is a greek.

PART III: DIRECTIONS: *If a sentence is correct, write C in the space. If it needs capitalization, circle the letter that should be capitalized.*

1. nan and I are spending the summer at camp medomak in washington, maine. _____

2. Tommy has a new English bicycle, a gift from his aunt. _____

3. Suddenly I saw the boeing 747 darting across the sky. _____

4. Here is a new series of Norwegian airmail stamps. _____

5. The waters of the Mediterranean are very blue. _____

6. The table is made of asian teakwood. _____

7. The Acme Tractor Company is looking for a qualified computer analyst. _____

8. Have you ever seen a Mexican jumping bean? _____

9. We heard the performance of Verdi's *aida*. _____

10. My sister is taking english, math II, social studies, biology, and french. _____

11. Just then I noticed her new persian rug. _____

12. Is the goldstar bus company still on strike? _____

13. Silk is an important Japanese export. _____

14. Jerry lives on the west side of oak street. _____

15. Sometimes the boys go fishing on Lake Oswego. _____

16. At Aspen, Colorado, I learned to ride a horse. _____

17. She is traveling by northwest airlines. _____

18. My favorite program is sponsored by cocoa crispies cereal. _____

19. Colgate has introduced a new kind of toothpaste. _____

20. Octopuses lurk in the mediterranean sea. _____

ANALYTICAL GRAMMAR (REVIEW)   EXERCISE #1

PUNCTUATION REVIEW: EXERCISE #1

NAME:_____ DATE:_____

DIRECTIONS: *Punctuate the following sentences correctly, using everything you have been taught about punctuation and capitalization.*

1. Our national heroes people like abraham lincoln martin luther king jr and cesar chavez fought for these rights life liberty and equality.

2. Rod evans sailing over the last hurdle won the race easily roger evans his brother came in a slow second.

3. I knew you'd make it rod shouted winston when are you headed for the olympics your father said last night my son rod is going to be all-american this year

4. Rosemary is knitting her first sweater a soft cuddly wool one with no sleeves. She is making it according to directions in the may issue of seventeen magazine.

5. John does I believe still live at 268 fairway lane fairbanks alaska.

6. Fathers day comes on the third sunday in june mothers day comes on the second sunday in may.

7. Jim dreams of doing research at the rockefeller national laboratory in albany new york.

8. I've carefully chapter 23 punctuating quotations in our textbook adventures in punctuation therefore I feel prepared for the test tomorrow.

9. Wisteria a lovely purple flower was named after caspar wistar an 18th century anatomist and jimson weed was named after jamestown virginia .

10. A computer can be used for making lists of things to do keeping track of household accounts and doing your homework and term papers done on a computer always look nicer.

ANALYTICAL GRAMMAR (REVIEW)   EXERCISE #2

PUNCTUATION REVIEW: EXERCISE #2

NAME:_____DATE:_____

DIRECTIONS: *Add all the necessary punctuation and capitalization you have been taught to the sentences below.*

1. The race was over the jockey leaped from her horse and smilingly accepted the glittering shimmering gold cup.

2. Mr. cameron our shop teacher announced bring the following supplies wood nails and glue.

3. The girls mittens are missing said mother they said they left them in the pockets of their new gap jackets.

4. Have you seen kevin costners movie dances with wolves cara asked

5. Caseys story the night they burned the outhouse will appear in this months issue of sanitation gazette.

6. I think I should point out said mr. henries the store manager that michaels dog isn't welcome here.

7. watch out for shaving cream yelled mike it's halloween you know

8. Did mrs. finley say in my opinion tom selleck is a dweeb asked john or am i hearing things

9. First I read the sports section of todays washington post said jim and then I did the crossword puzzle.

10. The judge staring with a ferocious scowl at the skinny terrified prisoner asked do you plead guilty or not guilty

Photocopying this product is strictly prohibited by copyright law.   **327**

PUNCTUATION REVIEW: EXERCISE #3

NAME:_____ DATE:_____

DIRECTIONS: Add all the necessary punctuation and capitalization you have been taught to the sentences below.

1. can you lend me five dollars for a week or so old buddy asked mr. gardner fathers best friend.

2. Jim the cleaning woman is here but she says she doesn't do windows yelled mom.

3. His program which we watch regularly is on sunday afternoons.

4. People who live in glass houses shouldn't throw stones said miss phillips.

5. why even you can work this gadget mary cried elaine.

6. it was jean as a matter of fact who memorized the poem stopping by woods on a snowy evening from our poetry anthology americas major poets said robert.

7. The test was long and difficult however everyone finished.

8. His grades are as follows english his favorite class an A history a really tough class a B science his least favorite a C and math a B

9. The sermon opened with a reading of deuteronomy 3 24 from the king james version of the holy bible.

10. how richard asked mopping his brow listlessly do you people stand this climate

ANALYTICAL GRAMMAR (PUNCTUATION FINAL)   TEST

PUNCTUATION/CAPITALIZATION REVIEW:TEST

NAME:_____DATE:_____

(RAW SCORE:_____ /342 GRADE:_____POINTS:_____ /100)

PART I: Add the necessary **punctuation and capitalization** to the sentences below.

1. the teacher said I will assign no homework tonight she yelled jubilantly

2. over the drinking fountain at school said bob there is a sign that says old faceful

3. as the president of the united states entered the band played hail to the chief

4. john adams and thomas jefferson old rivals died on the same day the fourth of july

5. most of the engineers were pleased with the new design but helen had doubts about it

6. to eat the little old man from china used chopsticks

7. mrs. curtis shoes hurt her feet but she wore them anyway

8. the parents are invited to the teachers meeting said mrs. haynes

9. the new high school has many excellent features however it needs more equipment in the gymnasium

10. this traffic control system will be introduced in the following cities buffalo new york st. louis missouri dallas texas and los angeles california

11. we'll soon catch this culprit he has left several fingerprints on this glass said detective grogan

12. the following were thomas ambitions to go to harvard to graduate summa cum laude and to get a job in a prestigious new york law firm

13. I did not read this weeks newsweek said frank but I heard there was an article called life on other planets

14. the waitresses names appear on their checks said the manager please let us know if there is any problem

15. we were so thirsty after our run that milk or water or even ink would have tasted good

16. the happy tired victorious crew staggered over the rocks and fell on the sand

17. roy shouted in anger you heard my dad say I won't allow you boys to go out tonight

18. we can now hope said dr. peters chief of surgery at harbor general hospital for a complete recovery

19. the call of the wild jack londons great novel is a popular favorite with alaskans

20. the man or woman who enjoys reading is never lonely said my english teacher

(over)

ANALYTICAL GRAMMAR (PUNCTUATION FINAL)

PART II: *Punctuate the following **possessive** situations correctly.*

1. The three contestants entries were all good.

2. The judges work could be observed by visiting their courtrooms.

3. One judges choice was different from the rest.

4. That is one of this years best new television series.

5. The storys ending leaves many readers puzzled.

6. The four ships cargoes are on the pier.

7. The drill team girls jackets are at the cleaners.

8. Three womens cars were left in the parking lot.

9. That customers complaints did not impress the manager.

10. Have you read the exciting tales of Ulysses adventures?

PART III: *Put **colons** where they are needed in the sentences below.*

1. The book has photographs of some of the most beautiful mountain ranges in the world the Himalayas, the Andes, the Alps, and the Rockies.

2. Here is a list of the possible times for our meeting 12 30, 2 00, or 5 30.

3. I arrived at the station at 3 30 in the morning.

4. You will need to find the following a fishing rod, some night crawlers, a few hooks, and a bag to take home any fish we catch.

5. If I wake up after 7 30, I can't get to school before 9 00.

6. Whenever I see a poster of Italy, I think of all the wonderful food I ate there delicious cream sauces, ripe black olives, succulent meats, and golden cheeses.

7. The train will depart from Anchorage at 7 15 and arrive in Fairbanks at 4 30.

8. Please give this message to all the following people Sandy Pressman, Judy Pruitt, Mike Scott, and Alex Wolfson.

9. If you want to be in Fresno before 4 00, you should leave here by 10 30.

10. Tell me which of these presents you would prefer a bicycle, a canoe, a radio, or a dog.

ANALYTICAL GRAMMAR (PUNCTUATION FINAL) — TEST - PAGE 3

PART IV: *Insert **semicolons** where they are needed in the sentences below.*

1. The team members are on the field they are ready to play.

2. Mr. Short ordered several new model kits: Skyblaster, a delta-winged aircraft, Killer Diller, a new chopper bike, Conquerer, an interplanetary cruiser, and Conestoga, a replica of a covered wagon.

3. Traveling was Mary's hobby she planned a trip to Paris last year.

4. The test, a review of all the rules of punctuation and capitalization, was a tough one I think I did well on it.

5. The math problem was solved by Tom, Andrea, and James, and Brandon did it in two minutes.

6. Sylvia is still looking for the solution she has tried almost everything.

7. My favorite books as a child were *Anne of Green Gables*, the story of a red-haired orphan, *Daddy-Long-Legs*, the story of an orphan who was sent to college, and *Elsie Dinsmore*, the story of a rich little orphan whose relatives are trying to get her money I guess I was fascinated by orphans!

8. A storm is coming black clouds are forming.

9. Frank picked beans, cauliflower, and broccoli, and Mary hoed the other end of the garden.

10. Something is wrong with my computer it keeps making mistakes!

PART V: *Insert **commas** where they are needed.*

1. We first heard this story in Sydney Australia during our vacation.

2. On December 31 1977 a stranger arrived in Nestor North Dakota.

3. Between January 31 1978 and February 23 1978 he worked in the garage of his house.

4. On November 22 1978 the stranger went to Grand Rapids Michigan.

5. He returned on December 1 1978 with a large box.

6. On December 10 1978 young Tim Hartley peeked into the garage.

7. From that day until the Hartleys moved to Kingsport Tennessee Tim told wild tales of what he had seen in that garage.

8. Between February 24 1979 and March 15 1979 neighbors heard strange noises coming from the garage.

9. The neighbors met on March 16 1979 and decided to complain to the police.

10. The police visited the house on March 16 1979 and on March 17 1979 but no one seemed to be at home.

(over)

ANALYTICAL GRAMMAR (PUNCTUATION FINAL)   TEST - PAGE 4

11.   The police obtained a search warrant on March 18 1979.

12.   Half the people of Nestor North Dakota were watching as the police entered the garage.

13.   All they found was an empty box and a newspaper dated February 28 2089.

PART VI: DIRECTIONS: *In each sentence below there is a comma splice. In the spaces below each sentence are the numbers of all the commas in the sentence. Find the comma splice and write its number in the space at the left. Write what it is splicing beside that comma's number below the sentence. By the other numbers, write the "buzzwords" of the correct commas.*

_____ 1.   In the business world of the future, machines designed for specific functions, will do a lot of the
                                             1   2
work which we now do ourselves, but I don't believe the human mind can ever be completely
                              3
replaced.

#1 _____

#2 _____

#3 _____

_____ 2.   Yes, we have machines which can do math functions, keep track of data, and check our spelling,
            1   2   3   4
but only a human being can perform, certain types of work.
                           5

#1 _____

#2 _____

#3 _____

#4 _____

#5 _____

_____ 3.   If we wish to communicate ideas to other people, we often use jokes, examples, and analogies as
                                       1   2   3
a means of explaining complex, detailed, concepts.
                        4   5

#1 _____

#2 _____

#3 _____

#4 _____

#5 _____

ANALYTICAL GRAMMAR (PUNCTUATION FINAL)   TEST - PAGE 5

_____ 4. Even a machine which has been programmed to write, could not come up with jokes or plays
                                                         1
           on words, those little extras that even an average, well educated person would use.
                      2   3
           #1 _____

           #2 _____

           #3 _____

_____ 5. Whenever our future employment is looking more and more, doubtful because machines are
                                                                 1
           taking over, remember that an educated human being, using all his or her creative talents to the
                    2   3
           utmost, can never be completely replaced by a machine.
                   4
           #1 _____

           #2 _____

           #3 _____

           #4 _____

PART VII: *On a piece of lined notebook paper, write the following dialogue, using correct* **paragraphing, capitalization, and punctuation.**

Sean and Jason walked slowly into Mrs. Finley's classroom Sean sat down, put his books under his desk, and leaned over to Jason hey he said are you as worried about this test as I am are you kidding said Jason I worked until midnight you mean you studied asked Sean, beginning to chew his fingernails I kind of thought I'd try to fake it are you out of your mind Jason hissed I studied for two hours I looked over all my notes and went over the review worksheets Sean smiled weakly at Jason wow he said looking over your notes and going over the review sheets what a great idea wish I'd thought of it Jason stared at Sean in disgust it's a little late now, pal

PRONOUN-ANTECEDENT AGREEMENT

I. When we learned about pronouns, we learned that an antecedent is the noun that the pronoun stands for. A pronoun must agree with its antecedent in NUMBER, GENDER, and PERSON.

    A. NUMBER refers to whether a pronoun is singular or plural.

        1. The following pronouns are SINGULAR:

each	one	everybody	someone
either	anybody	everyone	nobody
neither	anyone	somebody	no one

        EXAMPLES: EACH of the men had HIS rifle ready for inspection.
                       EVERYONE has a right to HIS own opinion.
                       SOMEONE had left HIS OR HER books under a tree.

        2. The following pronouns are either singular or plural depending on the antecedent.

all	any	some	none

        EXAMPLES: SOME of the STUDENTS looked tired when THEY were finished.
                       SOME of the SYRUP looks funny when IT is poured.

        3. Two or more singular antecedents joined by <u>or</u> or <u>nor</u> are treated as singular.

        EXAMPLES: Either Jack OR Hal will bring HIS tape recorder.
                       Neither the teacher NOR his aide would repeat what HE had said.

    B. GENDER refers to whether the pronoun is MASCULINE, FEMININE, or NEUTER.

        EXAMPLES: The whale was fighting for ITS life. (neuter gender)
                       The postman said HE was tired. (masculine gender)
                       The waitress took HER time. (feminine gender)

When an antecedent is meant to indicate both masculine and feminine, it is correct to use masculine pronouns. However, to be "politically correct," it is often advisable to use the phrase "his or her."

(over)

C. PERSON refers to the following:

    I, me are in the FIRST PERSON

    you, your, yours are in the SECOND PERSON

    he, she, him, her, his, hers are in the THIRD PERSON

EXAMPLES: (WRONG) ONE should never let YOUR disappointment show.

This sentence starts off in 3rd person and switches to 2nd!

(RIGHT) ONE should never let HIS (OR ONE'S) disappointment show.

(WRONG) I find that night driving is hard on YOUR eyes.

This sentence starts off in 1st person and ends up in 2nd!

(RIGHT) I find that night driving is hard on MY eyes.

ANALYTICAL GRAMMAR (UNIT #29)　　　　　　　　　　　　　　EXERCISE #1

PRONOUN-ANTECEDENT AGREEMENT: EX. #1

NAME:_____DATE:_____

DIRECTIONS: *Change whatever you have to change in the sentences below to correct any errors in agreement.*

1. Neither the buyer nor the seller had made up their mind.

2. Everyone has a right to their own opinion.

3. Each of the winning essays had their good points.

4. Will each student please turn in their schedule tomorrow?

5. One should always write ahead for their hotel reservations.

6. Each of us needs to start thinking about their career now.

7. If one tries hard enough, you can usually finish the reports in an hour.

8. Everyone applying for the scholarship must bring their birth certificate.

9. Neither Lynn nor Sue has written their thank-you notes.

10. Everybody in the office has made their vacation plans.

DIRECTIONS: *In each blank write a pronoun that will agree with its antecedent.*

1. A person should not expect too much from _____ friends.

2. The postman brought Jack and Ray the books that _____ had ordered.

3. Either Norma or Jill will stay after school so that _____ can help decorate.

4. Several of the convicts refused to eat _____ food.

5. Each of the seals caught the fish that were thrown to _____.

Photocopying this product is strictly prohibited by copyright law. 　339

PRONOUN-ANTECEDENT AGREEMENT: EX. #2

NAME:_____ DATE:_____

DIRECTIONS: *Some of the sentences below contain errors in agreement. If so, cross out the incorrect pronoun and write in the correct form.*

1. One of my aunts takes a great deal of pride in her furniture.

2. Knowing this, nobody in our family puts their feet on chairs or sits on beds at her house.

3. One of her brothers used to think they could be an exception to the rule.

4. Uncle Charlie would come home late at night, undress in the dark, and dive into his bed, nearly knocking every slat out of their place.

5. Each of these plunges left their mark on the rickety bed.

6. At first, both Aunt Mary and my mother offered their advice and asked him to be careful.

7. Anybody else would have mended their ways, but not Charlie; he needed discipline!

8. Late one night there was a loud crash, and everyone ran out of their room to investigate.

9. No one could believe their eyes! Lying on the floor was Charlie, groaning loudly.

10. If anybody asks you why Charlie suddenly reformed, tell them that one day Aunt Mary merely decided to rearrange her furniture.

DIRECTIONS: *In each blank write a pronoun that will agree with its antecedent.*

1. Both of the boys forgot _____ promises.

2. Everyone needs _____ own pen.

3. Neither apologized for _____ blunder.

4. Each of the players felt that _____ had failed the coach.

5. When Susan sees one of her girlfriends, she always stops and talks to _____.

SUBJECT-VERB AGREEMENT

Verbs have number too. In other words, a singular subject (boy) takes a singular verb (runs). BOY RUNS. A plural subject (boys) takes a plural verb (run). BOYS RUN. This is usually not a problem except in these cases:

I. When there are modifiers between the subject and verb.

   EXAMPLE: A **GROUP** of demonstrators **WAS** starting a sit-in.

II. When the subject is an indefinite pronoun. In the last unit you learned which of these pronouns is singular and which is plural. Refer to that list again.

   EXAMPLE: **EACH** of the girls **IS** an excellent student.

   BOTH of the girls **ARE** excellent students.

III. When singular subjects are joined by OR or NOR - they need a singular verb.

   EXAMPLE: **NEITHER** the customer **NOR** the clerk **IS** always right.

   BOTH the customer **AND** the clerk **ARE** right.

IV. When the sentence begins with HERE, THERE, WHERE, WHEN, WHY, or HOW, be sure that the verb agrees with the subject. In these sentences the subject is usually located after or to the right of the verb.

   EXAMPLE: There **ARE** two **ATHLETES** in this race.

   When **IS** the **CURTAIN GOING** up?

V. When a sentence has a compound subject joined by "or" or "nor" - and one subject is singular and the other one is plural - then the verb agrees with the subject closest to it.

   EXAMPLE: Either my uncle or my **COUSINS ARE** coming for a visit.

   Neither the drill team girls nor the marching **BAND IS** participating in the parade.

SUBJECT-VERB AGREEMENT: EX. #1

NAME:_____ DATE:_____

DIRECTIONS: *Underline the correct verb in the sentences below.*

1. Cells in your brain (needs, need) oxygen.

2. Our boys, in position at the line of scrimmage, (was, were) awaiting the snap.

3. Broadway, with its flashing lights and bright colors, (impress, impresses) a visitor.

4. A change in the rules often (confuse, confuses) the spectators.

5. The silence inside the Carlsbad Caverns (is, are) awe-inspiring.

6. There (is, are) many vacation destinations to choose from.

7. Where (was, were) your ancestors from?

8. The flowers in the garden at the back of my house (is, are) excellent for cutting.

9. The crowd at the Homecoming Game (was, were) in excellent spirits.

10. These exercises on the proper way to speak English (is, are) not what I call great fun!

DIRECTIONS: *Rewrite the following sentences, changing the conjunction from AND to OR or vice versa. Change the verb to agree with the new situation.*

1. Ned and Larry have gone to the science fair.

    EXAMPLE: EITHER Ned OR Larry HAS gone to the science fair.

2. Either rain or snow has been predicted for tomorrow.

3. Either Jane or Mary has prepared the lunch.

4. The car in front of us and the car on the other side of the street are to blame.

5. The house on the hill and the cottage in the valley are for sale.

ANALYTICAL GRAMMAR (UNIT #30) EXERCISE #2

SUBJECT-VERB AGREEMENT: EX. #2

NAME:_____DATE:_____

DIRECTIONS: *Underline the correct verb in the sentences below.*

1. Many of us (like, likes) long books.

2. There (is, are) many reasons why I can't go.

3. Somebody among the spectators (was, were) snoring.

4. (Has, Have) all of the senators returned?

5. Nobody in my family (is, are) able to remember phone numbers.

6. (Have, Has) either of you been to Mexico before?

7. Where (is, are) the ingredients for this recipe?

8. Each of the girls (was, were) eligible for the award.

9. People in the position in which you find yourself often (try, tries) to find new jobs.

10. The author who had written all those books (don't, doesn't) like to sign autographs.

DIRECTIONS: *Rewrite the following sentences, changing the conjunction from AND to OR or vice versa. Change the verb to agree with the new situation.*

1. Venus and Mars do not seem far away when you consider the vast distances of outer space.

2. Each week a poem and an essay appear in the school newspaper.

3. Both the boy in the third row and the girl at the door have been called to the office.

4. Either my uncle or my father-in-law was present when Kennedy was shot.

5. Both my brother and my sister have graduated *magna cum laude*.

WHICH PRONOUN?

I. When using the personal pronouns I or ME along with another noun, always **PUT THE OTHER GUY FIRST.**

   EXAMPLE: (wrong) He told me and Jim to return after lunch.
   (right)   He told Jim and me to return after lunch.

II. When listing multiple subjects, place them in the appropriate "social" order. In other words, **LADIES BEFORE GENTLEMEN AND OLDER FOLKS BEFORE YOUNGER.**

   EXAMPLE: (wrong) My dad, my mom, my grandma, and I went out for brunch on Sunday.
   (right) My grandma, my mom, my dad, and I went out for brunch on Sunday.

III. Does one say, "Give this book to either Bob or I," or "Give this book to either Bob or me"? Does one say, "We girls had a great time," or "Us girls had a great time"?

   TAKE THE OTHER GUY OUT: In most instances, there is a simple, easy-to-use trick which is helpful in solving this problem. The trick is called "**TAKE THE OTHER GUY OUT.**" In the first example above, take "either Bob or" out. Would you ever say, "Give this book to I"? Of course not. So, you wouldn't say, "Give this book to either Bob or I" either. You would say, "Give this book to either Bob or me."

   In the second example above, just take the "girls" out and you immediately know which pronoun to use.

   In some cases, however, the above "TAKE THE OTHER GUY OUT" trick won't work. In these cases, you have to know your grammar to solve the problem. You already know enough about the structure of the sentence. The only other thing you need to know is that pronouns come in two CASES: the NOMINATIVE (sometimes called the SUBJECTIVE) case and the OBJECTIVE case.

   The nominative case is used for the job of SUBJECT or PREDICATE NOMINATIVE.

   The objective case is used for the job of DIRECT OBJECT, INDIRECT OBJECT, or OBJECT OF THE PREPOSITION.

   NOMINATIVE PRONOUNS: I, we, you, he, she, it, they, who, whoever

   OBJECTIVE PRONOUNS: me, us, you, him, her, it, them, whom, whomever

   Notice how this works: look at the sentence, "Give this book to either Bob or me." What job is *me* doing? Correct; it's being the **object** of the preposition. That's why you need the **object**ive pronoun *me*.

   IN ANY CASE, IT'S A TOTAL "COP-OUT" TO USE THE WORD "MYSELF" INSTEAD OF "I" AND "ME"!!

   In the sentence, "We girls had a great time," *we* is the subject of the sentence (*girls* is an appositive); therefore, you need the nominative pronoun *we*.

IV. PRONOUN AS PREDICATE NOMINATIVE: Is it correct to say, "It was me whom they wanted," or "It was I whom they wanted"?

   In informal speech, we would usually say, "It was me," and - even though technically this is incorrect - it is now acceptable. However, in formal written work (and in grammar tests), we need to know that, since *I* is the predicate nominative in the above sentence, the nominative form is correct.

   EXAMPLE: The documents proved that it was he who committed the crime.

ANALYTICAL GRAMMAR (UNIT #31)   EXERCISE #1

WHICH PRONOUN: EX. #1

NAME:_____DATE:_____

DIRECTIONS: *Circle the right pronoun in parentheses. If the pronouns are in the wrong ORDER, rewrite the sentence.*

1. Next Saturday (I, me) and Tom will make all the arrangements.

2. Ted invited (I, me) and (she, her) to the party.

3. The guests of honor were (I, me) and Harry.

4. How many goals did (he, him) and Chuck make?

5. Tell Betty and (she, her) the whole story.

6. (I, me) and (she, her) volunteered to help in the Red Cross blood drive.

7. (They, Them) and the Clark boys were to blame.

8. Dad gave Chuck and (I, me) a ride to town.

9. Was it (he, him) who called the fire department?

10. (She, Her) and (he, him) were on the bus.

DIRECTIONS: *Rewrite the sentences below to make them correct.*

1. Me and Janie went to the Mall yesterday.

2. Either Jason, Wendy, or myself will be there to be sure the doors are open.

3. Please give your tickets to either Julie, Crystal, or I.

4. Me, my mom, my dad, and my grandma went to Gallo's for dinner.

5. Mrs. Phillips gave Bob and I a makeup test.

Photocopying this product is strictly prohibited by copyright law.

ANALYTICAL GRAMMAR (UNIT #31) EXERCISE #2

WHICH PRONOUN: EX. #2

NAME:_____DATE:_____

DIRECTIONS: *Circle the correct pronoun in parentheses. Rewrite the sentence if the people are in the wrong order.*

1. (Me, I) and John are going to the mall this afternoon.

2. My grandpa loves to read stories to (I, me) and my brother.

3. Mom said (I, me) and (she, her) were not going to need more money.

4. We distributed the money amongst Sally, Diane, and (I, me).

5. (We, Us) Alaskans are an independent bunch!

6. Dad packed a lunch for (he, him) and (she, her).

7. Will you help (I, me) and Bev clean the recreation room?

8. Jerome wrote a poem to (we, us) girls in the senior class.

9. (She, Her) and (I, me) will join you later for lunch.

10. Mr. Wilson gave (he, him) and (I, me) a few pointers about football.

DIRECTIONS: *Rewrite the sentences below to make them correct.*

1. Mr. Bates gave a copy of the Winners' List to Mrs. Sampson and myself.

2. Either Erin or myself will see you later.

3. Me, my uncle, and my aunt went to Disney World last summer.

4. Him and John were the ones who had their notes typed.

5. John, my grandpa, me, and my dad all went to the baseball game last night.

Photocopying this product is strictly prohibited by copyright law.

ANALYTICAL GRAMMAR (UNIT #31)   TEST

USAGE FINAL #1

NAME:_____DATE:_____

(RAW SCORE:_____/67 GRADE:_____POINTS:_____/20)

PART I: PRONOUN-ANTECEDENT AGREEMENT: *Circle the correct pronoun.*

1. Neither Bill nor Mark had told me what (he, they) wanted.

2. I had to read each of the essays carefully before I could grade (it, them).

3. Jim and Mike will lend us (his, their) history notes.

4. If one makes the effort, (he, they, you) can usually accomplish a goal.

5. I feel that cleaning (my, your, one's) room is my least favorite chore.

PART II: *Write the correct pronoun in the blank space.*

1. Angelo and Mario will attend with _____parents.

2. Either Tim or Tyler will sponsor _____ own team this year.

3. Neither Ray nor Brad will do _____ homework alone.

4. Is either Beth or Betsy going to read _____ essay aloud?

5. Neither this dish nor that plate is in _____ regular place on the shelf.

6. Either Mr. Marley or Mr. Engels parked _____ car in the driveway.

7. Did either Earl or Dave turn in _____ book report early?

8. Both Wes and Paul came to run _____ laps on the track.

9. Should either Al or Jane call _____ parents before we begin?

10. Neither Sarah nor Marian wants _____ name called.

PART III: SUBJECT-VERB AGREEMENT: *Circle the correct verb in parentheses.*

1. John, as well as some of the other club members, (plans, plan) to ask questions.

2. As each one of you students (know, knows), your reports will be due on Friday.

3. There (is, are) some leftover sandwiches in the refrigerator.

4. Nobody in my family (is, are) any good at video games.

5. (Has, Have) all of the team members suited up?

(over)

ANALYTICAL GRAMMAR (UNIT #31)   TEST - PAGE 2

PART IV: *Read the sentences below carefully. If the verb agrees with its subject, write Y in the space; if it does not agree, write N in the space.*

_____ 1. One of the cabinets contains the club's banner and membership rolls.

_____ 2. Each of the hostesses are standing in the doorway.

_____ 3. The numbers on the license plate was covered with mud.

_____ 4. Every one of the clerks have to punch the time clock.

_____ 5. The bridges on Highway 34 are extremely narrow.

_____ 6. One of the assistants answer the telephone.

_____ 7. Our assignment for the next two days cover events during the French Revolution.

_____ 8. A bag of golf clubs, as well as two tennis rackets, stand in the corner of the closet.

_____ 9. Each of the farmers uses modern machines.

_____ 10. Does either of the girls play the piano?

PART V: *Rewrite these sentences, following the directions in parentheses. You will have to change the verb accordingly.*

EXAMPLE: The boys have finished delivering the papers. (Change BOYS to EACH OF THE BOYS)

   Each of the boys has finished delivering the papers.

1. My sister is planning to attend summer school. (Change SISTER to SISTERS)

2. Nobody in our town intends to participate in the ceremony. (Change NOBODY to MANY)

3. Most of the money was contributed by children. (Change MONEY to QUARTERS)

4. Neither the students nor the teacher has found the missing book. (Remove NEITHER and change NOR to AND)

5. Some of the workers spend too much time in the snack bar. (Change SOME to ONE)

ANALYTICAL GRAMMAR (UNIT #31)   TEST - PAGE 3

PART VI: *The sentences below contain unnecessary changes in VERB TENSE. Change either verb so that it matches the other in tense.*

EXAMPLE: Patty spoke so quickly that no one understands her.

Patty speaks so quickly that no one understands her. or
Patty spoke so quickly that no one understood her.

1. Paul walks into the room and we all looked up.

2. There was a great movie on TV, but Leah has to work.

3. Time is running out and we were still three points behind.

4. Rick played Romeo and Keith plays Tybalt.

5. Toni didn't understand the question, so she raises her hand.

PART VII: *Circle the correct pronoun in parentheses. If the pronoun is in the wrong place, rewrite the sentence and put the words in the correct order.*

1. The accident taught (I, me) and (he, him) a lesson.

2. The waiter asked (I, me) and (she, her) what we wanted.

3. Have you been avoiding (I, me) and Jack?

4. Have you and (her, she) had an argument?

5. It was (he, him) who notified the police.

6. Is it (she, her) whom you are marrying?

7. Sam helped (I, me) and Ben paint the garage.

8. I haven't heard a word from either Judy or (her, she).

9. The letters are for you, Paula, and (I, me).

10. Please give (I, me) and Frank another chance.

11. He rode his bike between (I, me) and Clara.

12. The job of buying refreshments was assigned to (I, me) and Jerry.

13. You have to choose between (I, me) and (she, her).

14. (We, Us) three have to sing the solo parts.

15 (Me, I), Mom, and Grandma all went on the ferris wheel.

Photocopying this product is strictly prohibited by copyright law.

WHO AND WHOM

In the previous unit, you were taught a trick to help you decide which pronoun to use called TAKE THE OTHER GUY OUT. When deciding when to use WHO and when to use WHOM, however, there is no nifty little trick. People who know when to use WHO and when to use WHOM show that they are well educated because they understand the structure of the sentences they are using. To solve this problem, you must analyze the sentence grammatically and figure out what job that pronoun is doing In time, the correct pronoun choice will "sound right" to you.

WHO is used when the pronoun is being a <u>subject</u> or a <u>predicate nominative</u>. That's why it's called the SUBJECTIVE or NOMINATIVE CASE.

WHOM is used when the pronoun is being an <u>object</u> (direct object, indirect object, or object of the preposition). That's why it's called the OBJECTIVE case.

Look at these example sentences. In each one the word *WHO* or *WHOM* is doing a specific job. If that job is subject or predicate nominative, *WHO* is used. If it's some kind of object, *WHOM* is used.

EXAMPLES: To WHOM are you speaking? (WHOM is the <u>object</u> of the preposition *to*)

WHO are those men? (*WHO* is the <u>subject</u> of *are*)

WHOM was the speaker attacking? (*WHOM* is the direct <u>object</u> of *attacking*)

We did not know WHOM the man wanted. (*WHOM* is the direct <u>object</u> of *wanted*)

John is the boy WHO needs your help. (*WHO* is the <u>subject</u> of *needs*)

Do not be mislead by interrupting expressions such as "do you think," "shall I say," or do you suppose."

EXAMPLES: WHO do you suppose will be elected? (*WHO* is the <u>subject</u> of *will be elected*)

WHOM do you think he meant? (*WHOM* is the direct <u>object</u> of *meant*)

WHO shall I say is calling? (*WHO* is the <u>subject</u> of *is calling*)

NIFTY TRICK DEPARTMENT: One quick way to find out what job the pronoun is doing is to **"match up" all the subjects and verbs** in the sentence. Find all the verbs and look for their subjects. If you find a verb without a subject, your pronoun *WHO* is probably it. Also, watch out for those linking verbs - because *WHO* could be a predicate nominative. If it's not a subject, it's probably an object - so it should be *WHOM*.

Sometimes it helps if you think of *WHO* as *HE* and *WHOM* as *HIM*

ANALYTICAL GRAMMAR (UNIT #32)　　　　　　　　　EXERCISE #1

WHO AND WHOM: EX. #1

NAME:_____DATE:_____

DIRECTIONS: *Circle the correct pronoun in parentheses. In the space provided below each sentence, write what job it's doing. If it's a subject, write the word that it's the subject of, etc.*

1. (Who, (Whom)) did you see at the station?
   __WHOM is the direct object of "did see"__

2. He is the one (who, whom) we least suspected.

3. To (who, whom) did you apply for a job?

4. Please support (whoever, whomever) is elected.

5. I shall support (whoever, whomever) the class chooses.

6. (Whom, Who) do you think will win the election?

7. We nominated candidates (who, whom) we thought would win.

8. From (who, whom) did you get that information?

9. Sam says "hello" to (whoever, whomever) he sees.

10. The door is open to (whoever, whomever) wants to come.

Photocopying this product is strictly prohibited by copyright law.

ANALYTICAL GRAMMAR (UNIT #32)   EXERCISE #2

WHO AND WHOM: EX. #2

NAME:_____DATE:_____

DIRECTIONS: *Circle the correct pronoun in parentheses. In the space provided below each sentence, write what job it's doing. If it's a subject, write the word that it's the subject of, etc.*

1. Most of the people (who, whom) are hired are under thirty.
   _____

2. Most of the people (who, whom) they hire are under thirty.
   _____

3. Give this report to (whoever, whomever) is in the office.
   _____

4. (Who, Whom) do you need to see, Mr. Jones?
   _____

5. (Who, Whom) do you suppose is the winner of the contest?
   _____

6. I don't remember (who, whom) you want to invite.
   _____

7. (Who, Whom) do you think called the police?
   _____

8. Do you know (who, whom) the police suspect?
   _____

9. (Who, Whom) do you want to speak to?
   _____

10. She is the one (who, whom) we must stop.
    _____

Photocopying this product is strictly prohibited by copyright law.

ADJECTIVE OR ADVERB?

I. Another common usage problem is when people use an <u>adjective</u> when they should use an <u>adverb</u>.

    EXAMPLE: (substandard)   That dress fits perfect.
                    (standard)   That dress fits perfectly.

The word *perfect* is an adjective and modifies a noun, as in "a perfect fit." *Perfectly*, however, is an adverb. In the sentence above, the adverb *perfectly* is there to describe HOW the dress "fits."

NOTE: Remember that when your sentence (or clause) contains a linking verb, the complement may be a predicate adjective. In this case you don't want an adverb.

    EXAMPLE: (wrong)   That dress looks well on her.
                    (right)   That dress looks good on her.

II. People seem to have the most trouble choosing between the adjectives *GOOD* and *BAD* and the adverbs *WELL* and *BADLY*.

    A.   *GOOD* and *BAD* are adjectives that either modify nouns or complete linking verbs.

        EXAMPLE: It was a GOOD (or BAD) day for a picnic.

    B.   *WELL* and *BADLY* are adverbs that modify verbs or other modifiers.

        EXAMPLE: He did WELL (or BADLY) on the test.

    C.   *WELL* is used as an adjective only when it means "in good health."

        EXAMPLE: Mrs. Thatcher does not look well today.

                        I haven't felt well for several days.

III. When using comparatives and superlatives, be sure you are using the correct form for either an adjective or an adverb. Look at the following examples:

<u>ADJECTIVE</u>	<u>COMPARATIVE</u>	<u>SUPERLATIVE</u>	<u>ADVERB</u>	<u>COMPARATIVE</u>	<u>SUPERLATIVE</u>
quiet	quieter	quietest	**quietly**	more quietly	most quietly

(wrong) This engine will run quieter than that one.

(right) This engine will run more quietly than that one.

ANALYTICAL GRAMMAR (UNIT #33)   EXERCISE #1

ADJECTIVE OR ADVERB: EXERCISE #1

NAME:_____ DATE:_____

DIRECTIONS: *Underline the correct word in parentheses. In the space provided below each sentence, write either ADJECTIVE or ADVERB and what it modifies. If it's a predicate adjective following a linking verb, write PREDICATE ADJECTIVE and the verb it completes.*

1. You can finish the job (easy, <u>easily</u>) in an hour.
       ADVERB modifying "can finish"

2. The sky remained (clear, clearly) all day long.

3. The mechanic stayed (steady, steadily) on the job until it was finished.

4. The rancher acted (uneasy, uneasily) about the weather bureau's storm warning.

5. Mary felt (unhappy, unhappily) about her report card.

DIRECTIONS: *If the capitalized word is incorrect in the sentence below, substitute the correct form.*

1. Harry sounded ANGRILY over the phone.

2. The repair job was done CAREFUL.

3. The left shoe now seemed to fit PERFECT.

4. Football is played DIFFERENTLY in Canada.

5. Jane gazed UNHAPPY at her ruined dress.

Photocopying this product is strictly prohibited by copyright law.

ANALYTICAL GRAMMAR (UNIT #33) EXERCISE #2

ADJECTIVE OR ADVERB: EXERCISE #2

NAME:_____DATE:_____

DIRECTIONS: *Underline the correct word in parentheses. In the space provided below each sentence, write either ADJECTIVE or ADVERB and what it modifies. If it's a predicate adjective following a linking verb, write PREDICATE ADJECTIVE and the verb it completes.*

1. Doris picked up her purse (quick, quickly), threw on a coat, and ran out the door.
   _____

2. You can run a small car more (economical, economically) than a large one.
   _____

3. The poem sounds (different, differently) in French.
   _____

4. Mark's knee was hurt (bad, badly) during the first game.
   _____

5. Students should talk (quieter, more quietly) in the halls during classes.
   _____

DIRECTIONS: *If the capitalized word is incorrect in the sentence below, substitute the correct form.*

1. Stir the mixture GOOD before adding the milk.

2. Caroline did BAD on the exam.

3. Be sure and mix the sand and cement GOOD.

4. You can see just as WELL from the balcony.

5. Harriet feels BADLY about losing your earring.

TRANSITIVE/INTRANSITIVE VERBS & ASSORTED ERRORS

I. Transitive verbs are verbs which can take a direct object; in other words, they "transport" the action of the subject to the direct object.

Try using the verb *have* in a sentence that doesn't have a direct object. Can't be done, can it? That's because you must **have** something; you can't just **have.**

II. Intrasitive verbs are verbs which do not take a direct object.

Try using the verb *arrive* in a sentence which has a direct object. Can't do it, can you? That's because you don't ever **arrive** anything; you just **arrive**.

III. Many verbs can be transitive in some sentences and intransitive in others.

In the sentence, "He eats lunch with me," the verb is transitive because it takes the direct object *lunch*. In the sentence, "He eats with me," the verb is intransitive because it has no direct object.

IV: There is a relatively small group of verbs with which people have difficulty. Three of the most common will be discussed in this unit. They are *lie/lay, sit/set*, and *rise/raise*.

PRESENT	**PAST**	**PAST PARTICIPLE**
lay	laid	laid
lie	lay	lain

To lay is a transitive verb which can take a direct object; *to lie* is intransitive and cannot take a direct object.

| I am laying the cup on the table | I laid the book down. | The hen has laid an egg. |
| She lies on the sofa. | We lay in the sun. | He has lain in bed for a month. |

| raise | raised | raised |
| rise | rose | risen |

To raise is a transitive verb which can take a direct object; *to rise* is intransitive and cannot take a direct object.

| Vern is raising alfalfa this year. | He raised his eyebrows. | We have raised greyhounds for years. |
| The sun rises in the east. | Al rose to make a speech. | The temperature has risen since noon. |

| sit | sat | sat |
| set | set | set |

To sit is an intransitive verb which cannot take a direct object; *to set* is transitive and must take a direct object.

| We always sit on the porch. | Joe sat in the third row. | You have sat in front of that TV all day. |
| Renee set a record today. | I set the cup on the table. | Have you two se |

ANALYTICAL GRAMMAR (UNIT #34)

I. THIS, THAT, THESE, and THOSE:

THIS and *THAT* are singular modifiers; *THESE* and *THOSE* are plural modifiers.

EXAMPLES:
(wrong) These kind are my favorites.
(right) This kind is my favorite. (Notice that everything agrees: modifier, subject, verb)

(wrong) These sort of shoes hurt my feet.
(right) This sort of shoe hurts my feet. (Notice, everything agrees)

II. FEWER and LESS

FEWER is a plural modifier; *LESS* is a singular modifier. (*FEWER* modifies things that can be counted; *LESS* modifies things which cannot be counted.)

EXAMPLES:
Jack had FEWER colds this year. (Can you count "colds"?)
There is LESS snow this year than last. (Can you count "snow"?)
This product contains LESS fat. (Can you count "fat"?)
This cheese has FEWER calories. (Can you count "calories"?)

III. The following is a list of serious usage errors to avoid:

AIN'T	Once acceptable, but no longer so. Now replaced by *AM NOT, IS NOT,* or *ARE NOT.*
IT, HE, SHE DON'T	Misused for "it, he, or she doesn't"
SEEN for SAW	I seen that movie" is incorrect. *SEEN* can only be used with *HAVE*: "I have seen that movie." In this context, the correct usage is "I saw that movie."
DOUBLE SUBJECT	Tracy she got an A on the test. (Just take out the *SHE*)
THEM	Misused for *THOSE*, as in "Give me them gloves," instead of "Give me those gloves." *THEM* is a pronoun in the objective case, never a modifier.
GOT	Misused for *HAVE*. "Do you got your homework?" is incorrect. "Do you have your homework?" is correct. *GOT* means RECEIVED, as in "I got an A on the test."
SHOULD OF	There is no such construction. It sounds like *SHOULD OF* when you say *SHOULD'VE*, but what you are really saying is *SHOULD HAVE*.
DOUBLE NEGATIVE	As in "I didn't do nothing." Should be "I did nothing," or "I didn't do anything."

HARDLY, BARELY, or *SCARCELY* are negative words that should not be used with another negative. "There wasn't hardly anyone on the tennis court," is incorrect. It should be "There was hardly anyone on the tennis court."

TRANSITIVE/INTRANSITIVE VERBS & ASSORTED ERRORS: EXERCISE #1

NAME:_____ DATE:_____

DIRECTIONS: *Correct the following sentences by rewriting them in the space provided below each sentence.*

1. That there is my new jacket.

2. It really don't matter if you come or not.

3. We don't want no trouble here.

4. You should of seen that movie!

5. We don't got no assignment in math tonight.

DIRECTIONS: *Circle the correct form of the verb in the sentences below.*

1. The mother goose (lay, laid) her eggs in the tall grass.
2. The moon (raises, rises) in the night sky like a white balloon.
3. We (sat, set) in the rocking chairs on the front porch last evening.
4. Sally had (laid, lain) down to take a nap.
5. Winston always (raises, rises) to the occasion.

DIRECTIONS: *Circle the correct word in parentheses.*

1. The advertisers say there are (fewer, less) types of tar in these cigarettes.
2. He certainly ate enough of (that, those) (kind, kinds) of cookies.
3. Ted had (fewer, less) first-place votes than George.
4. You will have (fewer, less) interruptions in the library.
5. I have never seen (these, this) (types, type) of notebook before.
6. We have never eaten (these, this) kind before.
7. We have had (fewer, less) tourism in Alaska this year.

ANALYTICAL GRAMMAR (UNIT #34)　　　　　　　　　　　　　　　　　　EXERCISE #2

TRANSITIVE/INTRANSITIVE VERBS & ASSORTED ERRORS: EXERCISE #2

NAME:_____DATE:_____

DIRECTIONS: *Circle the correct word in parentheses.*

1. The store does not sell (this, these) (type, types) of stoves any more.

2. Next time you bake a cake, use (fewer, less) eggs.

3. Next time you bake a cake, use (fewer, less) vanilla.

4. This beverage is less filling because it has (fewer, less) calories.

5. (That, Those) (sort, sorts) of candies upset my stomach.

DIRECTIONS: *Correct the following sentences by rewriting them in the space provided below each sentence.*

1. Do you got any homework in math tonight?

2. We didn't have barely any candy left after the kids finished

3. There wasn't hardly no people left on the beach.

4. You should of gone to the party.

5. It's really important to speak and write English good, ain't it?

DIRECTIONS: *Circle the correct form of the verb in the sentences below.*

1. The little girl (lay, laid) her toy gently on the shelf.

2. Sarah has (lain, laid) out in the sun too long without sunscreen!

3. The temperature has (raised, risen) by at least twenty degrees.

4.. We (set, sat) the statue carefully on its platform.

5. Josephine (rose, raised) teacup poodles.

A transitive verb _____.

ANALYTICAL GRAMMAR (UNIT #34)   TEST

USAGE FINAL #2

NAME:_____ DATE:_____

(RAW SCORE: __/76__ GRADE:_____ POINTS:____/20__)

PART I: *If necessary, correct the double negative in the sentence below.*

1. We couldn't hardly hear the speaker.

2. The car didn't stop for no stoplights.

3. Connie hadn't never flown in an airplane.

4. The injured horse couldn't barely walk.

5. Seniors don't have nothing to complain about.

PART II: *If necessary, correct the usage errors in the sentence below.*

1. We could of gone to see the Beach Boys, but we couldn't get tickets.

2. Do you got your homework for math class today?

3. Jack he said he seen the car speeding southbound on Main Street.

4. Has anybody seen my math book?

5. When we got to the house, there wasn't nobody there.

PART III: *If necessary, correct the following sentences in any way that's needed.*

1. With algebra you can solve this problem easy.

2. Football is played differently in Canada.

3. The driver turned quick at the corner and sped away.

4. Run quick and see if the mail is here.

5. Lynn's feelings were hurt bad when Sherry laughed at her.

6. I think she did very bad last night.

7. Does she always sing so good?

8. Mrs. Hoffman argued her point well.

9. Mike plays basketball almost as good as his brother.

10. I slept so well last night!

(over)

Photocopying this product is strictly prohibited by copyright law.   377

ANALYTICAL GRAMMAR (UNIT #34) — TEST - PAGE 2

PART IV: *Rewrite the sentences in the space provided. If it is correct, leave it alone.*

1. Me and him went to the mall.

2. Her and her best friend are having a fight.

3. The test was retaken by John, Brandon, and me.

4. Give that book to me and him.

5. Them and us have to leave early.

PART V: *In the space provided, write what job the capitalized pronoun is doing. (SUBJECT, PREDICATE NOMINATIVE, DIRECT OBJECT, INDIRECT OBJECT, OBJECT OF THE PREPOSITION)*

1. Mr. Doyle is a man WHO likes young people. _____

2. Mr. Doyle is a man WHOM young people like. _____

3. The girl WHO spoke to me has just won a prize. _____

4. The girl WHOM I spoke to has just won a prize. _____

5. Can you tell me WHO that player is? _____

PART VI: *Circle the correct words in parentheses.*

1. Our gym class does (that, those) (kind, kinds) of exercises.

2. (This, These) (brand, brands) of tape (have, has) inferior sound quality.

3. Nurses wear (this, these) type of (shoe, shoes.)

4. Campers use (this, these) (sort, sorts) of tents.

5. Lola can perform (that, those) (sort, sorts) of back dive.

PART VII: *Circle the correct modifier in parentheses.*

1. We have (less, fewer) school holidays this year.

2. Unfortunately, there seems to be (less, fewer) volunteerism on my committee.

3. The commercials say there are (less, fewer) problems with this model.

4. This frozen dinner has (less, fewer) calories than the other.

5. We have had (less, fewer) inches of snow this year.

ANALYTICAL GRAMMAR (UNIT #34)   TEST - PAGE 3

PART VIII: *Choose which pronoun is correct. Then in the space provided, write what job that pronoun is doing.*

1. Ladies (who, whom) lived during the fifteenth century painted their teeth instead of their nails.
   _____

2. Her older sister, to (who, whom) she sent the article, has moved to Santa Fe.
   _____

3. It was Napoleon (who, whom) invaded Spain in 1808. _____

4. Maureen finally guessed (who, whom) it was. _____

5. I visited with Mr. Winslow, (who, whom) was mowing his lawn. _____

6. Mr. Ross, (who, whom) I work for, owns two wheat farms. _____

7. Is there anyone (who, whom) plans to leave early? _____

8. He is a teacher (who, whom) I respect. _____

9. There is the man (who, whom) you were asking about. _____

10. Francis Drake, (who, whom) Queen Elizabeth I knighted, defeated the Spanish Armada.
    _____

PART IX: *Circle the correct word in parentheses.*

1. Each of the boys finished (his, their) hotdogs.

2. Both of my uncles went to (his, their) college reunion.

3. Either Janie or Tracy got an A on (her, their) exam.

4. Several of the players renegotiated (his, their) contracts.

5. A person should know what (he wants, they want) in life.

PART X *Circle the correct word in parentheses.*

1. George has (risen, raised) the flag every morning for ten years.

2.. My grandparents love to (set, sit) on their front porch in the cool of the evening.

3. Try not to kill the goose that (lies, lays) the golden egg!

4. Has Penelope (raised, risen) from her "bed of pain" yet?

5. He (lay, laid) a bet on Knuckleduster to win the third race.

ANALYTICAL GRAMMAR (UNIT #35)   NOTES- PAGE 75

ACTIVE & PASSIVE VOICE

Active and passive voice are terms you will hear a LOT when you write. It's important to know what active and passive voice is, when each is appropriate, and how to fix a passive sentence (because in writing the active voice is usually preferred).

I. ACTIVE VOICE: In general you'll hear that **active voice is better than passive**. What does it mean when a sentence is in **active voice**?

A sentence in active voice means that the **subject is performing the action of the verb**. Here are some examples:

The boy threw the ball.
My mother sings beautifully.
Watch your step. (This subject is the understood "you" but still performs the action.)

Use of the active voice generally makes your writing more vivid and clear.

II. PASSIVE VOICE: A sentence in passive voice has the **object of an action acting as the subject.** Many times this results in the subject not being in the sentence at all. Here are passive versions of the above sentences:

The ball was thrown by the boy. OR *The ball was thrown.*
A song was beautifully sung by my mother.
Steps should be taken carefully.

III. SPOTTING THE PASSIVE VOICE: Passive voice can be spotted (WAIT! That's passive! Let's try again …)

You can spot passive voice by looking for this verb construction:

form of "to be" + past participle

("To be" forms can include *are, am, is, was, were, has been, had been, will be, will have been, being*, etc.)

Also, does the sentence end with a preposition phrase using the preposition *by*? Many passive voice sentences put the do-er of the action at the end of the sentence as the object of the prepositional phrase. Here's an example:

The exercise was written by the teacher. or *The test was taken by the student.*

IV. IS PASSIVE VOICE ALWAYS INCORRECT? Not always. It should be avoided in general, but there are times when it is necessary or appropriate. Sometimes you need to put the emphasis on the object rather than the subject. Let's say that you were writng a murder mystery, the murder having taken place in a hotel room. The forensics teams is there, looking for clues. The following sentence -

The room had been cleaned an hour prior to the murder.

is preferable to

The maid had cleaned the room an hour prior to the murder.

because you don't want to bring attention to the maid as a character in your story.

Or let's say you're writing an obituary. You might use the sentence -

The body was interred at Forest Lawn Cemetery.

rather than -

The gravediggers interred the body at Forest Lawn Cemetery.

I expect the reasons for the choice of the passive voice would be obvious in this case!

V. WHY DO PEOPLE USE THE PASSIVE VOICE? You need to become aware of how people use language to shape the way the sentence is perceived. Because it's easy to leave the doer of the action out of a passive sentence, some people use the passive voice to avoid mentioning who is responsible for certain actions. Here are some examples:

Mistakes were made.
Tthe Acme Oil Company stipulates that a few gallons of crude might have been spilled.

ANALYTICAL GRAMMAR (UNIT #35)   EXERCISE #1

ACTIVE & PASSIVE VOICE: EX. #1

NAME:_____ DATE:_____

DIRECTIONS: *Identify whether each sentence is active or passive by wring A (active) or P (passive" in the space provided next to each sentence.*

_____1. The man painted the room a bright shade of blue.

_____2. The book was put on the shelf.

_____3. Cars were made on the factory line by the workmen.

_____4. I bought a brand new car this weekend.

_____5. We've all made mistakes.

_____6. Errors were made along the way.

_____7. The results are being tabulated as we speak.

_____8. I'm writing a new book about my trials and tribulations in college.

_____9. The refrigerator was plugged into the wrong socket.

_____10. I am going to write my paper after lunch.

DIRECTIONS: *In the space provided, re-write the above sentences. If they're passive, re-write them in the active voice; if the active, re-write them in the passive voice. Try to include all the elements in the original sentence, although when you re-write into passive voice, the subject frequently disappears. Because passive voice sentences are often unclear, a subject has to be inserted.*

1. _____

_____

2. _____

_____

3. _____

_____

(over)

Photocopying this product is strictly prohibited by copyright law.

4.

5.

6.

7.

8.

9.

10.

ANALYTICAL GRAMMAR (UNIT #35)　　　　　　　　　　EXERCISE #2

ACTIVE & PASSIVE VOICE: EX. #2

NAME:_____DATE:_____

DIRECTIONS: *Identify whether each sentence is active or passive by wring A (active) or P (passive" in the space provided next to each sentence. Then re-write the sentence in the opposite voice on the lines provided.*

_____1. At this evening's concert selected famous arias will be sung by our star soprano.

_____2. Beginning tomorrow morning, workmen will begin the removal of the windows.

_____3. Although Melissa took great care in washing the dishes, a treasured wine glass was broken.

_____4 Using Brad's telephone touchpad, all his spring semester classes were chosen in one hour.

_____5. The packages were wrapped and taken to the post office by our shipping clerk yesteerday.

_____6. Using their state-of-the-art 3D glasses, the audience saw the new action thriller.

(over)

ANALYTICAL GRAMMAR (UNIT #35)   EXERCISE #2 - PAGE 2

_____7. The CEO and the Vice-President of Operations planned all the next year's conventions.

_____8. The crumpled party dress was washed and ironed by the maid before the next evening.

_____9. While the fascinated science class watched, the secret ingredient was stirred into the mixture.

_____10. By ten a.m. of the third day of their camping trip, the tents had been packed neatly away.

ANALYTICAL GRAMMAR (UNIT #35)   EXERCISE #3

ACTIVE & PASSIVE VOICE: EXERCISE #3

NAME:_____ DATE:_____

DIRECTIONS: *In the space provided, re-write the sentences below. If they're passive, re-write them in the active voice; if the active, re-write them in the passive voice. Try to include all the elements in the original sentence, although when you re-write into passive voice, the subject frequently disappears. Because passive voice sentences are often unclear, a subject has to be inserted.*

_____1. Despite the massive public protests, the bill was passed by the Senate and the House.

_____2. Even though the pitcher was trying to pitch a fair game, the batter was hit by a fast ball.

_____3. Why did the chicken cross the road?

_____4. Even though Meg, Jo, Beth, and Amy didn't let on, they surprised Marmee with gifts.

_____5. At the expense of the federal taxpayers, a fence has been built across our southern border.

(over)

ANALYTICAL GRAMMAR (UNIT #35)   EXERCISE #3 - PAGE 2

_____6 The outside "prejudice reduction" consultant damaged many relationships in our office.

_____7. A huge new marketing plan has been put into place in our company.

_____8. Some of today's champions on Civil Rights voted against the Civil Rights Act of 1964.

_____9. Prior to 1920 women in the United States were denied the right to vote.

_____10. While they were on the raft, Tom and Huck shielded each other from the evils of civilization.

ANALYTICAL GRAMMAR (UNIT #35)   TEST

ACTIVE & PASSIVE VOICE: TEST

NAME:_____ DATE:_____

RAW SCORE: _____ /120 = GRADE:_____ PERCENTAGE:_____

DIRECTIONS: *In the space provided, re-write the sentences below. If they're passive, re-write them in the active voice; if the active, re-write them in the passive voice. Try to include all the elements in the original sentence, although when you re-write into passive voice, the subject frequently disappears. Because passive voice sentences are often unclear, a subject has to be inserted.*

_____1. Two key findings are indicated by the results of this test.

_____2. Researchers have found that heart disease is the leading cause of death in the USA.

_____3. Why did you pack my stuff and leave it on the front lawn?

_____4. Dr. Huang delivered the twins at 5:30 a.m. on May 5, 2010.

_____5. Before he left the theater the rock star was beseiged by screaming fans.

_____6. A souvenir of her trip to give to her nephew was purchased by Nikki

Photocopying this product is strictly prohibited by copyright law.

ANALYTICAL GRAMMAR (UNIT #35) — TEST - PAGE 2

_____7. Before the test began, the students read the directions very carefully.

_____8. The U.S. Constitution was signed on September 17, 1787.

_____9. Witnesses saw a man wearing a hooded sweatshirt and jeans leaving the scene of the crime.

_____10. As a result of our baseball game, Mrs. Hawkins' window was broken.

_____11. The girl sitting next to me was asked to share her notes from the prior lecture.

_____12. When the bell rang, the teacher told the class that they could leave.

_____13. When were you planning to tell me about the broken vase?

_____14. The man carrying the marked $100 bills finally admitted that he had stolen them.

ANALYTICAL GRAMMAR (UNIT #35) TEST - PAGE 3

_____15. The college athletic department has awarded James a full-ride scholarship for soccer.

_____16. The Christmas money had been saved by the children all year long.

_____17. Mrs. Dragonbottom's sarcasm had been patiently endured by the students for a month.

_____18. The drama class presented their spring play The Crucible for the student body.

_____19. My senior class trip began with a tour of D.C. which was taken by everybody in the group.

_____20. In ancient times punctuation wasn't used, which makes their writing hard for us to read.

You did it! You made it through Analytical Grammar! After all that hard work we don't want you to forget everything you've learned. Make sure you follow up with our High School Reinforcements to keep practicing throughout high school.

Photocopying this product is strictly prohibited by copyright law.

INDEX

Action Verb; defined, 7
Active Voice; defined 75
Adjective; defined, 1
    after linking verb, 15
    predicate adjective, diagramed, 25
    proper, capitalization of, 59
Adjective phrase, 6
    diagramed, 6
Adverb; defined, 9
    diagramed, 9
Adjective or Adverb?, 71
Adverb phrase, 6
    diagramed, 6
Agreement of subject & verb, 65
Ain't, 73
Apostrophe
    for showing possession, 57
    with plural possessives, 57
    with singular possessives, 57
Article, defined, 1
    diagramed, 8
Assorted Usage Errors, 73

Base line, 7
Be
    as helping verb, 17
    as linking verb, 15

Calendar Items
    capitalization of, 59
    punctuation of, 47
Capitalization, 59-61
Case
    nominative, 3, 67 (see also subjective)
    objective, 3, 67
    possessive, 3
Clause
    adjective, 31
    adverb, 33
    noun, 35
Closing
    in business letter, 47
    in friendly letter, 47
Colon
    after salutation in bus. letter, 47, 56
    between hour and minute, 56
    in Biblical citations, 56
    introducing list of items, 55

Comma, 37-47
    splices, 37
    splits, 37 - 47
Commands
    subject of, 8
Comparative, 71
Complement
    direct object; defined, 11
    indirect object, defined; 13
    predicate adjective; defined, 15
    predicate nominative; defined, 15
Compound direct object, 20
Compound predicate, 20
Compound sentence
    comma in, 40
    diagramed, 21
    semicolon in, 55
Compound situations; diagramed, 20-22
Compound subject; diagramed, 20
Compound Verb; defined, 19
    diagramed, 20
Conjunction; defined, 19
    diagramed, 20-22

Dates & Addresses; commas with, 47
Deity, capitalization of, 61
Diagraming
    adjective, 8; adjective phrase, 8
    adverb, 9; adverb phrase, 9
    compound sentence, 21
    compound adjective, 8
    predicate adjective, 15
    predicate nominative, 15
    prepositional phrase, 6-9
    subject:, 7
    verb, 7
Dialogue; punctuation of, 51
Direct Address; commas with, 45
    capitalization of titles in, 60
Direct Object, 11
    diagramed, 11
Direct quotation; capital letter with, 49
    commas with, 49
    quotation marks with, 49
Double Negative, 73
Double Subject, 73

Fewer and Less, 73

ANALYTICAL GRAMMAR — INDEX

Friendly letter; closing, 47
    salutation, 47

Gender; defined, 63
"Got" for "Have", 73
Government Bodies; capitalization of, 59

Helping Verbs; list of, 17

Indefinite Pronouns, 3
Indirect Object, 13
    diagramed, 13
Infinitive clause, 28
Infinitive phrase, 27
Institutions; capitalization of, 59
Intransitive verbs; 73
Interrupters; set off by commas, 45
Italics; for titles, 53
Items in a series; commas with, 39

Languages, capitalization of, 60
Less and Fewer, 73
Linking Verbs, 15

Main Verb, 17

Names; proper; capitalization of, 59
Nationalities; capitalization of, 60
Noun, 1
Number; in pronouns, 63
    in verbs, 65

Object; direct, 11; indirect, 13
Object of Preposition, 5
    diagramed, 6
Objective Case; list of pronouns in, 3
    object of preposition in, 69
    object of verb in, 69
Organizations; capitalization of, 59

Parallelism, 39
Participle; present & past, 23
Passive Voice; defined, 75
Person; defined, 63
Phrase; adverb, 6
    adjective, 8
    appositive, 29
    gerund, 35
    infinitive, 27
    participial, 23
    prepositional, 5

Possessives, 57
Predicate Adjective, 15
    diagramed, 15
Predicate Nominative, 15
    diagramed, 15
Preposition, 5
Prepositional Phrase, 5
    diagramed, 6
Pronoun, 3
    agreement w/ antecedent, 63
    choice of, 67
    demonstrative, list of, 3
    indefinite, list of, 3
    interrogative, list of, 3
    personal, list of, 3
    relative, list of, 31
Proper Adjective; capitalization of, 59
Proper Names; capitalization of, 59
Proper Nouns; capitalization of, 1
Punctuation; colon, 56
    comma, 37-47
    in dialogue, 51
    italics, 53
    quotation marks, 49
    semicolon, 55
    underlining, 53

Question Mark; with quotation marks, 49
Questions; position of subject in, 18
Quotation Marks; with direct quotes, 49
    with indirect quotes, 49
    within quotation, 50
    with titles, 53

Races; capitalization of, 60
Religions; capitalization of, 60

Salutation; in business letter, 47
    in friendly letter, 47
School Subjects; capitalization of, 60
Seasons; not capitalized, 59
"Seen" for "Saw", 73
Semicolon, 55
Sentence; beginning with there, here, 8
    compound, diagramed, 21
    imperative, 8
    patterns, 11-15
Sentence Base, 7
Series; comma with, 39
Single Quotation; use of, 50
"Should of" for Should Have", 73

Subject; Order of Compound, 67
Subject-Verb Agreement, 65
Subject-Verb; diagramed, 7
Superlative, 71

Titles; punctuation of, 61
    articles, 61
    movies, 61
    poems, 61
    publications, 61
    ships, 60
    short stories, 61
    television programs, 61
    works of art, 61
This, That, These, Those, 73
Transitive verbs, 73
Usage; 63-73
Voice, Active & Passive, 75